Last Of A Dying Breed

A Novel By

Leon "Buckshot" Anderson

ISBN: 1-4033-4443-4 (e-book)
ISBN: 1-4033-4444-2 (Paperback)
ISBN: 1-4033-4445-0 (RocketBook)

This book is printed on acid free paper.

1st Books - rev. 07/23/02

Dedication

This work of fiction is dedicated to the thousands of individuals, past and present, who have chosen to endure hardships and often loneliness in remote or far away places.

Their reasons for doing so usually stem from a desire for the lure of adventure, plus a burning inner need to live close to, and in harmony with, Mother Nature.

And often,....... simply to escape the insanity of the so called civilized world, with it's hoards of humans.

Table of Contents

Thank you!

To "Uncle Bud", who spent all of his seventy years living in and enjoying the great out of doors. He, who so lovingly and patiently taught me so much about the delicate balance between man and nature. He, the inspiration for the story herein.

Prolog

"The Beginning"

Kerosene lamps were still burning brightly throughout the Larson homestead, although the time was well beyond the hour which usually found Ole and Martha sound asleep. A brilliant yellow full moon illuminated the late winter landscape as the mercury in the thermometer, nailed to an ancient red oak, nudged minus thirty below zero. Countless millions of snowflakes sparkled and danced in the dazzling moonlight, and equal numbers of stars twinkled overhead. Below the Larson's home, a narrow sliver of ice-free water in the mighty Tahquamenon River, mirrored the nighttime sky, as it silently meandered east, towards the Great Lake the Indians called "Gitche Gumee".

The outside world was locked in frozen muted silence. But from the Larson's home came muffled groans and an occasional scream of labor induced pain. The ordeal of child birth had been dragging on for nearly eleven hours.

Dr. Herb Christensen had been ushered to the scene some eight hours earlier, transported to the Larson home with a horse drawn buckboard. The unusual and unexpected bitter cold wave had rendered nearly all automobiles in a hundred-mile radius useless.

At precisely eleven forty five pm, on the twenty fourth of February, the blessed event finally took place. The Larson's first child, a healthy baby boy, became the third child born in the Newberry, Michigan area since New Year's Day, 1932.

Besides the good news that Dr. Christensen delivered to Ole, and congratulations on the birth of his son, there was also some bad news. Ole's wife, Martha, would probably not be able to bear any more children. But Eric Sever Larson had arrived safely and was vocally announcing to the world that he was here to stay.

The years, as always, tumbled by much too quickly. The baby soon became a child, the child expanded into adolescence, which in turn blended into the teen age years.

The Larson Boy's genes were a mixture of Scandinavian and English, with a tad of Laplander thrown in. The resulting ethnic mixture produced a bright mind, blessed with a great sense of subtle humor and a nearly total optimistic outlook on life. But above and beyond these mental characteristics shone a fierce sense of personal independence.

His early years of physical and mental growth were accented by the bitter and ruthless tough times The Great Depression created for rural Americans. The depths of which went totally un-noticed by those who also struggled to survive in the urban centers scattered throughout the world beyond Michigan's Upper Peninsula.

However, the wild, desolate expanse of forests, swamps, lakes and rivers, which make up the U.P., became the salvation to those hearty individuals who lived there. For in its sheltered wilderness lived an abundance of fish, fur and game, which sustained its citizens, and provided hope for their futures.

Eric Sever Larson, like nearly all the children who lived in rural households, was trained in the methods of harvesting this wild bounty. And was likewise expected to help gather the necessary raw materials to help sustain his family. The act of harvesting fish and game for sustenance became as natural as today's journey to the local super market for supplies.

But in Eric's case, the act of wrestling from Mother Nature, what she had to offer to survive, became more than an act of necessity. It became a way of life!

(Chapter one)

"NOR'EASTER"

Part One: "The Letter"

The wind, or perhaps breeze would be a better term, had been blowing from the southeast for the past three days. "Strange," thought Hap "should have had some nasty weather move in by now." But the skies had remained hazy and temperatures had risen into the teens, making the two-week cold snap that had just ended almost a distant memory.

Winter had come quickly and hard to northern Quebec this year. Hap predicted the early, harsh winter by the earlier than normal migrating caribou herds. Even some wolves had been caught off guard by the early caribou migration and missed out on some easy kills to fatten themselves up for the long sub-arctic winter.

But the early winter had produced at least one blessing for Hap; he had been able to string out his trap line almost three weeks sooner than normal. Fur had primed out early with the colder fall weather and Hap had put a nice stash of pelts in his root cellar by mid March. And with fur prices on the down side, more trapping time meant more fur and more fur meant a tad more trading power in the spring when the Hudson Bay buyer came calling in Nitchequon.

Hap continued to ponder the current weather pattern as he split some firewood and paused often to look at the sky and puff on his corncob pipe. His five sled dogs stirred restlessly on their chains as if they too noted the fine weather and wondered why Hap had not hooked up the sled and ran his trap line for three days. Hap scooped

1

up an armload of freshly split spruce and kicked open his cabin door. "Dang it", he muttered to himself, "should have run my line instead of worrin' about that dern east wind. Any fur in my traps now has probably been chewed ta pieces by some fisher or ornery wolverine."

Hap Larson was no rookie to the North Country. Hap had grown up in the wilds of Michigan's Upper Peninsula and had taken to running a trap line to help "keep the wolf away from the door', as his Pa, Ole Larson had said many times. His Pa and Uncle Lars, both expert trappers in their own right, had nurtured Hap and provided a comprehensive education about living and surviving in the bush. And, as with most boys who grow up in the north woods, his schooling had included expert instruction in hunting, fishing, camping and surviving in the out of doors.

Hap was not really Hap's name. He had been christened Erik Sever Larson. As a youngster, his disposition had always been happy, so he was dubbed "Hap" by Grandpa Larson at the tender age of five.

Hap's trap line had indeed helped keep the wolf away from the family's door, and had even created a small bit of spending money for important things like a deer rifle, a shotgun, several fishing poles and assorted camping equipment. All of which he learned to use well.

Although a bright boy, Hap and school never really got along together very well. Oh, he did o.k. Did just enough to make Ma and Pa Larson accept his report cards. But while Mr. Capalinni drolled on and on about some boring ancient history epic, Hap would be miles away in day dream land tending his trap line, or trailing a wily whitetail, or netting a scrappy brook trout. Hap was the classic example of the woods getting into the boy and the boy not being able to get out of the woods.

Hap graduated from Newberry High School in the spring of 1949. Work was a hard thing to find in the U.P., and Hap, like most young men and women just out of high school, spent the summer at a few part time jobs and wondering about what the future had in store for him.

A letter from an uncle on Hap's mother's side of the family, who lived in Canada, arrived in late July. Hap had only met Uncle Edwin Baldwin twice. Edwin had paid a visit to the Larson homestead north of Newberry when Hap was still in grade school. And during his sophomore year in high school, Ma and Pa Larson had taken Hap to visit his Uncle Edwin and Aunt Bertha. Hap also remembered Edwin and Bertha's only child, a son named Charles, who like Hap, was really into the out of doors. The two boys had hit it off from the start, but time and distance had prevented them from really striking up a true friendship.

The letter would change all that!

Part Two: "The Cabin"

The letter was postmarked "Chibauqamau, Quebec", and dated almost two weeks earlier than it had arrived in Newberry. It was addressed to "Ole Larson & Family". Ole remarked, prior to opening the letter, that the Canadian and U.S. Postal Services must both still be using dog sleds, even in the summer. The letter was short, and to the point.

Dear Ole & All,

As you all probably guessed, Charles graduated from high school this past spring. He hasn't been able to find any steady work, so has begged us to let him head north in late August to Grandpa Oscar's old trapping cabin and spend the winter trapping. We told him we'd only allow such a fool thing if he had someone else to go with him. We thought right away about Hap, and are wondering if he'd like such an adventure, if it's ok with you folks. Let us know as soon as possible, as things need to get done if Hap wants to tag along with Charles for the winter trapping season.

our best regards,

Edwin and Bertha

After a great deal of begging and pleading, the Larson's reluctantly agreed to let Hap pack his duffle bag and head for Chibaugamau. He arrived at the Baldwin home on the 26th of August. Charles was packed and ready to head north.

Eighty-five of their hard-earned dollars were spent to hire a bush pilot to fly the two young adventurers nearly 300 kilometers northeast to the little trading outpost of Nitchequon. A few curious onlookers watched the two lanky lads unload their gear, and untie a 17 foot Old Town canoe from the plane's floats. A few additional supplies were purchased from the Nitchequon General Store and the final leg of their journey was begun on August 30th.

The journey from Nitchequon to Grandpa Oscar's cabin took four days. The route included lots of paddling an overloaded canoe upstream, coupled with three long and tough portages. Charles had taken this trip with his father several times and once with his Uncle Oscar, so he knew the route fairly well. Hap had spent most of his young life in the out of doors, but never had he seen such raw, wild unspoiled beauty as he passed through on the way to the cabin.

The cabin was located about 60 kilometers, by water, north and west of Nitchequon on a small tributary, named Otter Creek, which drained into the Canioapiscau River system. This in turn, flowed northward into Unganda Bay, which is part of the Davis Strait. It was situated on the north bank of the stream, nestled in a thick grove of black spruce trees. The location offered maximum protection from the cold north winds of winter, yet was positioned to catch the greatest amount of sunlight during the daylight hours. And daylight hours were rather brief during the long winter months!

Grandpa Baldwin had built the cabin in 1917, using black spruce and tamarack logs for the walls and roof. Sheets of corrugated, galvanized tin had been used to cover the roof, making for one snug cabin. No lumber was available for flooring, so the floor was simply composed of dirt. Two small windows on the south and west walls were added in 1922. The exterior dimensions measured a scant 16 x 20 feet, which made the cabin easy to heat with the small cast iron wood burner and an equally small wood burning kitchen range. A double bunk bed, also made out of black spruce poles, occupied the northeast corner. A rough plank table, with two crude stools, served as a work bench and dining location under the south window. Spikes had been driven into the walls at random, which served as clothes hangers, gun racks, fishing rod holder or whatever. Several strands of stovepipe wire criss crossed the cabin on which wet clothes or pelts could be dried. The cabin was marvelous!

Although a few pounds lighter in weight by spring, Charles and Hap survived that first winter and returned to trap and enjoy the peace and quiet of the remote forest for another seven seasons between 1950 and 1956. Charles finally gave up the adventurous life to marry his high school sweetheart and settled down in Sept Iles, a coastal community near the mouth of the St. Lawrence River.

Hap too married a sweetheart from Newberry, but the marriage only lasted four years. Hap just couldn't adjust to living in a town and hungered to return to the life of a trapper. Hap just sort of inherited the cabin without anyone really saying so or objecting. In 1962 Hap returned to living in the wilds, enjoying the life he had learned to love. So, by early September of that year Hap had moved all his meager belongings to the cabin, and before he knew it more than a quarter of a century had slipped away and he was celebrating his 60th birthday!

Part Three: "The Mistake"

Although still uneasy about the strange weather pattern, Hap decided to run his trap line. If he delayed yet a fourth day, surely much of the fur in his traps could be ruined, or the carcasses would be frozen so hard it'd take another three days to thaw them out so he could skin them.

Hap was up an hour before dawn, packing his backpack with the usual items, which he toted along, on a trap line run. Some dried moose jerky, a few slices of sour dough bread, a canteen of water, waterproof catches, a few extra shell for his .30-06 rifle and .44 magnum revolver, wool blanket, candle, extra wool socks and mittens, hatchet, compass and map, a "D" cell flashlight and two spare batteries, and a hand full of tea bags. In a second plastic bag he packed some scraps from the last moose he had shot, which would be used to bait some of his traps and snacks for his dogs.

The southeastern horizon was just beginning to show signs of daylight as Hap began to harness his team of dogs. They barked and squirmed and howled with sheer delight with the knowledge they at last would get a chance to run the trap line circuit again. With nearly four days of rest, they were wild with anticipation. Hap took turns cursing each dog, as he struggled to get the harness in place. But the cursing was not in anger. Hap cared for and loved each dog as much as any man could love anything. These dogs were his only friends and companions, and the bond which had been welded between man and dog was as strong and as old as time itself.

Besides the two bags of supplies Hap had packed so carefully earlier, the sled contained a number of additional items which were permanently stored in the sled. A propane gas lantern with an extra tank of fuel and extra mantles. A coil of stovepipe wire and some rope. An ice spud, to chop open beaver and muskrat sets. Or sometimes to chop a hole and do a little ice fishing for brook trout in a frozen beaver pond. A short ice fishing jig pole and a small box of assorted ice fishing jigs. A pair of long, pickerel style snowshoes and a heavy plastic tarp.

Even as Hap finalized the packing of his sled and hitched his yelping dogs in proper sequence, his senses were computing the continuing strange weather pattern. The smoke from the cabin's stovepipe was drifting northwest, with a bit more intensity than it had the previous three days. The breeze, although still from the southeast, had a slight rawness to it. The sky, which had brightened considerably in the last twenty minutes, was still hazy, but the haze was noticeably thicker than it had been at sunset yesterday.

Hap paused briefly to reconsider his decision to run the trap line, pulled down his wool Kromer tightly to his head, released the brake on the sled, and yelled, "mush".

Part Four: "Trouble"

Hap's trap line consisted of forty-two sets. This encompassed a circuit of nearly twenty miles. If everything went smoothly, Hap could run this circuit in about twelve to fourteen hours. Even by leaving his cabin at daybreak, it would be well into full dark by the time the circuit was completed. Generally, the final eight or ten traps had to be checked by the light of his lantern or flashlight.

The first trap was a fisher or pine marten set. An ancient spruce tree that had been uprooted by a storm provided the perfect place for a set under the protected overhanging roots. A bit of bait tucked securely in the tangle of roots would cause any self-respecting predator, like a fisher or pine marten to make an inspection. Hap smiled broadly as he removed a mature male fisher from his first set. It appeared that this animal had probably been caught the previous night, as it as yet had not frozen solid. "Mighty good start!", Hap told his team, as he allowed each dog a sniff of the carcass. With renewed yelping, the party set out for set number two.

The next four sets yielded nothing, although a wise fox had confiscated the bait in one set. Sets five through nine were located on the first of three beaver ponds Hap had selected for beaver and muskrat sets.

Two number four long spring traps had been set near the beaver lodge attached to long spruce poles shoved under the ice at a rather acute angle. A bundle of tender young alder branches were wired to the pole just above the trap. A beaver, trying to reach this succulent snack would theoretically get caught in the trap and drown. Hap had already taken three young beavers from this pond, leaving perhaps only a couple of crafty adults. Both baits were missing and neither trap had been sprung. "Dang the luck, that ole beaver must be the Albert Einstein of the beaver world.", muttered Hap to himself as he attached a new bundle of twigs to the pole sets with extra stovepipe wire.

The remaining three sets, which had been placed near the beaver dam that controlled the depth of the pond, each contained the body of a muskrat. "Warm weather musta brung 'um out of their dens ta look for some fresh food.", observed Hap, again to himself. After resetting the last set, Hap and his team were again on the trail. It was already ten forty five.

Sets ten through nineteen produced a pine marten, one fox and two more fishers. Hap's earlier fears that fur in his traps might be damaged by other predators were not founded. His spirits were high, and he was thankful that the warmer weather had made the furbearers more active. It was now nearly noon. Only four good hours of daylight remained and he was slightly behind schedule. But at least the weather was holding!

At set number twenty, which was unmolested, Hap paused for twenty minutes to grab a quick bite to eat and give each dog a small chunk of frozen moose meat. It was here Hap detected the first hint of impending trouble!

His course had basically been north to northeast during this first leg of the circuit. The breeze, which had picked up a tad since sunrise, had been blowing mostly on his back. But then, with a suddenness rarely experienced, Hap felt the wind switch from southeast to northeast! And Hap knew deep down in his gut, although he didn't want to admit it, he was in trouble!

Part Five: "The Storm"

As Hap readied his team to move on, several options quickly filtered through his mind. The sudden wind shift was bad enough, but now other ominous signs troubled Hap. The hazy sky had thickened throughout the day, but not rapidly enough to draw Hap's attention to it. The faint light spot in the clouds that pinpointed the sun's position was circled by a brilliant "sundog", a rainbow type weather situation that was a sure indicator of an impending weather change. And sundogs never indicated an improving weather condition! The raw wind that Hap noticed earlier in the day had not been an icy, cutting wind as it was now, which was beginning to gust with increasing velocity. But most of all, Hap knew and feared the quarter from which the wind was now blowing. The northeast!

Hap continued to sift through his options. Option one would be to turn the sled around and head back to his cabin as quickly as possible. Hap estimated he could make that run in less than three hours. Even if the expected storm moved in quickly, he'd have daylight to spare in returning home. Option two would be to construct a make shift emergency shelter and ride out the storm. This he had done many times before over the years he had spent trapping during the sub-arctic winters. Option three would be to continue on the circuit and check as many more sets as he could before making an emergency camp. Or, possibly, the impending storm might hold off long enough for him to complete the circuit.

"Really should check these traps today. A good storm might cover my sets ta the point a man may not even find some of the buggers till spring.", Hap mumbled to himself. "Need all the fur I kin get with the price the way it is.", he added. Hap took one more quick look at the sky and headed his team northwest by west on the homeward bound leg of the circuit.

The twenty first set yielded the torn up body of a pine martin. Hap's jaw was set grimly in displeasure as he tossed the worthless, mangled martin aside and reset his trap. "Yep, I knowed it," Hap sputtered, "dang wolverine in the area. He'll probably hang around the rest of the dang winter knowin' there's free chow fer the takin', and easy pickin's too."

Shortly after leaving set number twenty one the first snow flake hit Hap on his forehead. And within a half-hour the full fury of the nor'easter struck!

Despite the intensity of the storm, Hap checked four more sets. Nothing. Even though his watch indicated he should have at least an hour and a half of reasonable daylight left, the forest was growing dark. Visibility was rapidly dwindling as the snow intensified, driven earthward by an ever-increasing wind. Hap realized it was time to make a shelter.

Turning his team off the well-packed trail, he directed the dogs into a small, but dense, stand of black spruce and tamarack. Each of the five dogs were unhitched from the sled and tethered to separate trees with a short steel cable. Next, Hap used one of his snowshoes to scoop the snow out from beneath the thick, overhanging branches of a stout spruce tree. Then he fashioned the plastic tarp in a teepee fashion around the trunk and secured it with rope. This would give him maximum protection from the biting wind and blowing snow. Next, he fired up his propane lantern and placed his backpack containing his personal gear in the shelter. And last but not least, Hap gave each dog a reasonable portion of moose scraps. Hap watched as each of his companions gulped the frozen meat as if they hadn't eaten in a week. Then each dog curled up in the snow, with its back facing the wind, covered its nose with its tail, and settled down to wait out the storm. Hap knew his dogs would be totally covered by an insulating blanket of snow in a matter of minutes. His dogs would be just fine, and so would he.

Before Hap returned to his make shift shelter, he used his hatchet to chop a large armload of spruce boughs from several nearby trees. The boughs were carried to his shelter and after removing the last of the snow from the base of the tree, the boughs were spread out on the ground to offer comfort and insulation. With the heat generated by the propane lantern, the shelter was quite cozy.

Hap placed one of his tea bags in a tin cup of water and heated it over his lantern. After the tea had warmed he sipped it as he nibbled on some jerky and a slice of bread, and listened to the storm further intensify. Wrapping up in his wool blanket, he dozed on and off during the late afternoon and early night as the nor'easter raged on and on. The wind caused the tarp to rattle and flap, filling the interior of his shelter with enough noise to make sound sleep all but impossible. Hap had spent nights like this before, but never had he felt so much fury from any other storm!

It was nearing midnight, as he emerged from a short dozing session, to discover his lantern had exhausted its supply of fuel. With the aid of his flashlight, he removed the spare cylinder of propane from his sled and relit the mantle. Conditions outside his shelter could definitely be called a blizzard. Hap was well aware that a full tank of fuel, even on the lowest setting, would only last about seven hours. But seven hours would be plenty. Hap expected the storm would blow itself out by daybreak.

But it didn't!

Part Six: "Disaster!"

The blizzard was still full blown at 7:15 a.m. when the last tank of propane, which had been fueling the lantern, ran out. The spruce tree that supported Hap's make shift shelter was creaking and groaning with each gust of arctic wind. Being unable to withhold a basic nature call any longer, Hap opened the flap of his tarp shelter and stepped out into the dim first light of morning.

Over two feet of new snow had fallen during the night and it was still being pelted earthward by a raging northeast wind. Hap suspected the temperature had already fallen from yesterday's balmy mid teens into the below zero range. Five faint lumps in the fresh snow indicated his dogs were still curled up, waiting for the storm to subside. Having taken care of his immediate problem, Hap slipped back into his shelter.

Hap lit his candle and warmed up another cup of tea. The tea really never got warm, but the candle had enough energy to take the chill out of it. Hap sipped the tea and consumed his last two sticks of moose jerky between the last slice of his sourdough bread. Slowly he savored the salty flavor of the jerky and washed it down with tepid tea, as he silently evaluated his situation.

Really, there were no sensible options to consider but to stay where he was until the storm finally eased. Hap knew from his vast experience with sub-arctic storms that temperatures would drop like a rock once the snow ended and the skies began to clear. At best, the cabin was at least four hours distance, considering the depth of the new snow. The hard packed trail that he and his dogs had been running all winter would be of little value, even if he could somehow follow it. As soon as the storm gave any indication of letting up, Hap and his team would make a break for his cabin. "If this dang storm ever quits!", Hap snarled under his breath.

It was nearly noon when Hap knew the bulk of the storm was over. The wind had begun to swing towards the northwest and the quantity of wind driven snow had greatly diminished. Hap changed his damp socks for two pairs of dry wool ones, pulled on his last pair of dry gloves and dismantled his shelter. One by one the five lumps of snow shook themselves and were once again transformed into dogs. They, at least, were well-rested and ready to pull. Hap divided up the last of his moose scraps and gave each dog an equal portion. Within fifteen minutes Hap and his team were heading south.

No consideration was given to trying to find or check anymore of the remaining sets. Most of them were no doubt so drifted over with fresh snow that they probably wouldn't be found until the spring meltdown. At the moment, checking traps was a very low priority item. Hap knew he and his dogs had a long, hard trip ahead of them. And time was their enemy!

Within an hour, Hap could detect his dogs were already beginning to tire. The heavy load of animal carcasses, plus the deep powdery snow was taking its toll. The temperature had continued its downward plunge. Hap could tell by the sting in his lungs and the icicles forming on his moustache and beard. Stopping to rest his team, Hap decided to leave his precious cargo of fur behind. He'd run his trap line again in a couple of days anyway, and he could pick up the discarded fur then. The reduced weight of the sled would greatly increase his chances of making the cabin before dark. And the bitter northwest wind that whistled around his body left little doubt that tonight would not be a good time to attempt survival under a plastic tarp, with no heat!

Half way into the second hour on the homeward leg, Hap put on his snowshoes and began breaking trail for his team. He sensed his dogs would drop of exhaustion if he kept pushing them in these severe conditions. Besides, Hap's body was beginning to absorb the cold, due to his lack of physical activity on the back of the sled.

Within minutes of breaking trail with his snowshoes, he was beginning to sweat.

The normal route back to the cabin included a westward bulge in the circuit, which added some five or six kilometers to the length of the trip. This meandering westward bulge had been programmed into Hap's circuit to include two large beaver ponds. They were both prime beaver and muskrat habitat. Hap had mentally charted a new route, which would bypass this westward bulge and put him on a straight heading back to the cabin. This would cut nearly an hour and a half off the trip. That was the good news. The bad news was that the river on which the beaver ponds were located ran between Hap and his cabin. And unlike the solidly frozen surfaces of the placid beaver ponds, this river ran swift.

It was nearly three in the afternoon when Hap and his tired team reached the river. His cabin was now just a little over an hour away. Although both Hap and his dogs were tired, he knew they had enough energy left for the final leg of the journey. But the river worried Hap. The banks were steep, and finding a level spot to cross would not be easy. Hap had crossed this river several times during late fall while hunting moose and looking for signs of fur bearers. This he had done by wading across a shallow area. But he had never tried to cross in winter with his dogs.

Hap halted his team at the crest of the riverbank. There was nearly an eight-foot vertical drop from where he stood to the level of the ice-covered river. He would have to scout for a more gradual slope in order to get the sled in position to cross. Hap set the brake on the sled and headed upstream in hope of locating a satisfactory crossing point. Less than a hundred yards from his team and sled he found what looked like a descending slope that would permit his team a running start when crossing.

Even though the river was frozen, Hap knew a treacherous current swirled under that ice. And there was no way of knowing just how thick the ice really was. Hap was well aware that the recent warm spell might have allowed the swift moving water beneath the ice to eat away at its thickness. Hap returned to the sleigh to get his hatchet and ice spud. Hap considered bringing his team and sled to where he would be checking the thickness of the ice and then packing a trail with his snowshoes across the river. But his tired dogs were all sprawled out in he snow taking a well-deserved rest. Hap patted their heads and let them rest. "You'll need all the spunk you kin muster when we hit that river crossin'. Rest up pups!" The dogs looked at Hap and wagged their tails, as if they understood every word.

Hap returned to his selected crossing point and prepared to check the ice depth. If the ice proved thick enough, he would put on his snowshoes and pack a trail, making it easier and quicker for his dogs to cross. First he cut a sapling about ten feet long and trimmed all the branches from its trunk. This pole would be held cross ways in front of him as he gingerly worked his way out onto the ice-covered river. If by ill fate the ice should give way, the pole would bridge the hole in the ice and prevent Hap from being sucked under the ice. At least that was the theory. "Hope I don't need this dang pole, but better safe than sorry, I always say.", Hap grumbled.

Hap put one foot on the ice and shifted all his weigh forward. The ice creaked slightly, but felt firm. Next he gave the ice a sharp jab with his spud. The ice withheld the force of the blow. The other foot now stepped forward and the process was repeated. Again the ice held firm. It took Hap nearly fifteen minutes to cross the scant twenty yards of river. Reaching the other side, he breathed a sigh of relief and turned just in time to see a disaster in the making!

Part Seven: "The Ordeal"

Hap had no way of knowing, in advance of crossing the ice, that the spruce thicket on the south bank of the river was the very location a wolverine had selected to seek shelter from the nor'easter. Hap's presence had unnerved the animal, causing it to suddenly, but quietly, bolt from the thicket. The wolverine had naturally selected an escape route along the brushy bank of the river, which caused it to pass directly opposite Hap's team of dogs, who were resting on the north bank of the river.

Hap's first inkling that something was wrong was the alarmed barking of his dogs. The swirling wind had carried the wolverine's scent across the river, alerting the dogs that one of their archenemies was nearby. The unsuspecting wolverine was so intent on keeping track of where Hap was located that it never realized the dog team was present. Until they began barking.

A horrible chain of events unfolded before Hap's eyes! A chain of events that later seemed to have taken place in slow motion. A chain of events that would forever be recorded in Hap's memory! A chain of events that Hap was helpless to prevent!

Instinctively, all five dogs lunged towards the fleeing wolverine. Their combined power dislodged the drag brake on the sled that Hap had carelessly used, rather than tie the team to a tree. The drag ripped loose from the snow and allowed the team and sled to lurch forward......, and over the nearly vertical drop towards the river. The sled rolled over several times, spewing its cargo of valuable equipment into the soft snow. A sizable tamarack tree near the riverbank stopped the sled, but in doing so the brittle cedar frame burst into a shower of broken splinters! Now freed from the weight of the sled, the dogs sped across the ice-covered river in hot pursuit of the departing wolverine.

As the barking dogs neared the south bank of the river, a sharp crunching sound preceded a cave in of a sizable chunk of thin river ice. The entire team of dogs plunged headlong into the icy, swirling water. Hap stood mesmerized in utter horror as he watched his beloved team of dogs struggle against the deadly current, which was trying to drag them under the ice. But being harnessed together, they never had a chance. Hap helplessly watched as all five of his companions were sucked under the ice......,to their deaths!

Dazed, Hap stumbled back across the river and reached the remains of his sled. He stood mute; looking out into the swirling black water that had taken the lives of his beloved dogs. He whispered their names, as though somehow they might reappear and make all of what had just happened simply a nightmare. Hap stood in the deep snow for several minutes, just staring at the empty river, anger swelling up inside of him like a balloon ready to burst. Hap cursed the river. He cursed the storm. He cursed the wolverine. He cursed the loneliness he felt. But most of all he cursed himself for leaving his team unattended and unsecured. How could he, a man with nearly forty years of experience surviving in the sub-arctic, make such a stupid mistake? Dogs were what often stood between keeping a man alive and death. And he had allowed the threat of death to take a giant step towards claiming him!

Hap had made it through many a tight scrape during his lifetime in the out of doors, but the situation in which he now found himself would test his ability to survive as never before. And he would be tested beyond the limits of what any human being could expect to endure!

Part Eight: "Stranded"

The late afternoon light was already beginning to rapidly fade before Hap regained his composure. He had crouched in the snow and cried the first tears he had shed in many a year. Tears of sadness. Tears of anger. Tears of depression. Tears of frustration. And for the first time in his life he shed tears of fear!

But Hap was a fighter. He wouldn't give up without a dang good fight. As his instinct for survival quickly returned, his mind began to form a plan. "Man's got ta have a plan!", he told himself over and over. And in his mind a plan rapidly developed.

Hap kicked around in the snow to recover the equipment he would need in order to have a fighting chance to survive the bone chilling night that was rapidly falling. And have enough strength to make it back to his cabin tomorrow! His snowshoes were easy to locate, as they rested on top of the snow. But the left snowshoe had a broken inside frame from its impact with the tamarack tree. The snowshoe frame could be mended. Like the snowshoes, his backpack was easily visible, only partly buried in the snow. It held most of the major items Hap needed most. Likewise, the plastic tarp was in plain sight, blown up against the vertical riverbank. His rifle was a bit harder to find, but it too was located in a few minutes of digging with the good snowshoe.

The undamaged snowshoe became the first tool Hap would use to aid in creating a shelter which would allow him to have a chance surviving a second night in severe sub-zero temperatures. Tonight, a tee-pee constructed by wrapping a plastic tarp around a spruce tree and warmed by a candle would not prevent a sweat soaked man from freezing to death. Tonight, Hap needed to build a snow cave.

Deep, hard packed snow was found all along the vertical riverbank. Throughout the winter north winds had blown tons of snow over the nearly vertical bank, packing it ever more densely. The fresh snow from yesterday's nor'easter had added several feet of powder. Hap quickly removed the layer of fresh powder with his unbroken snowshoe. Next, he began chopping an opening for a small tunnel into the hard packed snow with his hatchet. Once he had an opening just large enough for his body to crawl into, he began enlarging the size of the tunnel as it angled deeper into the snowdrift. When finished, the snow cave was nearly six feet long. by three feet wide and about two and a half feet high. Spruce boughs were once again used to cover the floor of the cave for insulation. Finally, the tarp was placed on top of the branches to keep Hap's clothing from soaking up any moisture that might be formed by melting snow.

By the time the cave was finished it should have been full dark, but a nearly full moon was cresting the eastern horizon, lighting up the snow shrouded forest with unbelievable intensity. Hap estimated the temperature was now more than minus twenty and still dropping. Before entering his snow hut to spend a second night in an emergency shelter, Hap selected two sections of very straight spruce branches about two feet long and slightly larger than his thumb. He would need these to mend his broken snowshoe. Hap crawled into his snow cave, blocked the entrance with several chunks of hard packed snow, lit his candle, and prepared to settle in for the night.

The flame from Hap's candle illuminated the interior of his snug snow cave quite well. And that same tiny flame, coupled with the heat generated by his body, would keep the interior of the snow cave near thirty-two degrees. It mattered not how cold it might became outside! Hap had spent nights in snow caves before and marveled at their superb insulating quality.

The first order of business was to maintain as much body heat and strength as possible. The strenuous

21

activity of breaking trail and building the snow cave had left Hap's inner clothing soaked with sweat. He knew all too well that moisture close to his skin would soon allow the cold to be transferred through his garments and into his body. Hap wrapped the wool blanket around him to save as much body heat as possible. But due to a lack of activity during the night, he knew he would be chilled to the bone by morning!

Next Hap melted a cup of snow over the candle in his tin cup, and added one of his two remaining tea bags. This time he allowed the candle to warm the tea to a luke warm state. Sipping the tea added a slight warming to his insides, but did nothing to improve his spirits. Knowing the tea was the only semblance of food he had left, he savored every drop. Next he tackled the job of repairing his damaged snowshoe.

Using his knife, Hap removed all the bark from the two sections of spruce branches. Then he placed the peeled blanches on either side of the broken snowshoe frame and secured them in place with pieces of stovepipe wire. It was just like splinting a broken leg. The snowshoe would support him on his attempt to reach his cabin tomorrow. But he silently wondered if his body would be able to make it. The cold, lack of sleep and food, plus the mental anguish over the loss of his dogs had taken their toll. Much of his energy reserves had already been exhausted. And a man of sixty has lost much of his ability to quickly rebuild lost energy reserves.

The night lasted longer than any other Hap had ever experienced. He tried to sleep, but sound restful sleep was impossible. Little probing fingers of cold kept him shivering and awake much of the night, and every time he closed his eyes he saw his team being sucked to their deaths by the icy, black, swirling river!

Part Nine: "Encounters"

The candle burned out somewhere around four in the morning. Hap emerged from a fitful doze to find himself in total darkness. For several moments he was seized by the panic which results from awakening and not really knowing where one is. Once recovered from his mild panic, Hap brought all his senses to bear on the present. The snow cave was as quiet as a tomb. So quiet he could hear his own breathing. As he lay curled up in his blanket he became aware that his shivering was becoming more and more violent. Now a new fear was added to his already precarious predicament. Hypothermia!

Hap fumbled in the darkness for his flashlight. He played its beam upon his watch and illuminated its hands, which were nudging five o'clock. "Still almost two hours till full daylight.", Hap mumbled to himself. "Might as well drag my freezin' body autta of this cave and get movin'. A man might as well freeze ta death tryin' ta get someplace rather than layin' 'round in some stupid snow cave and turn ta ice."

By the feeble light of his dying flashlight, Hap sorted out which items he would carry along with him and which ones would be left behind. He carefully folded his tarp and blanket, placing them in the bottom of his backpack. The compass stayed, as well as his last tea bag and tin cup. He considered leaving the extra shells for his .30-06 and .44 magnum, but put them back in the pack.

"Them shells are jist too dang 'spensive ta leave layin' 'round in the woods." Satisfied with his choices, Hap rolled aside the chunks of snow that had sealed the entrance to his snow cave and crawled out into the stabbing pre-dawn cold.

The moon was now but a faint glow below the tree line on the western horizon. Hap guessed the temperature to be over forty below zero! Not unusual for a post nor'easter morning. But what was very unusual was the fact that Hap Larson was still five miles from his cabin without a dog team and without food or dry clothing.

The leather harnesses on Hap's snowshoes were so stiff from the cold that he had difficulty getting them buckled tightly to his boots. Hefting the lightened backpack to his shoulders and slinging his .30-06 rifle, Hap took one last look at the freshly frozen black spot in the river that marked the location where his faithful companions had perished. Two large tears froze to his cheeks as he whispered their names one final time. "Good-bye Aurora, good-bye Duke, good-bye Pepper, good-bye Timid, good-bye Silver. Rest well where ever you are!" With anger once more boiling up within his body, Hap turned towards the southeast and began what he hoped and prayed would be his last day fighting the aftermath of the nor'easters......and, his blunder.

Despite the forty below temperature, Hap's body warmed rapidly as he trudged ever so slowly through the deep, fresh snow. Even with his long pickerel style snowshoes, which usually allowed his one hundred and forty five-pound body to almost float over the surface, each step sunk nearly a foot into the powdery snow. Within the first hour Hap needed to stop and rest three times. He was well aware of the signal his body was giving him. Fatigue was already setting in!

It had been over twenty-four hours since Hap had ingested any food. Pangs of hunger began to stab at his stomach with increasing regularity and intensity. Hap filled his corncob pipe and took his first puff of tobacco in three days. "At least it'll take my mind off my achin' gut fer awhile.", Hap thought as he rested under a hemlock tree. He took a quick glance at his watch; mentally figuring the time and distance he had spent on the trail. He had been traveling for just a little over an hour. "Ain't even made a mile yet!", Hap sputtered, disgusted with his slow progress. With his pipe still spewing blue smoke, he once again headed southeast,

Hap was now fighting a double battle. He needed to conserve his rapidly dwindling supply of energy, if indeed he had enough left to reach his cabin. But yet, he must reach the cabin before nightfall, as he surely would not have enough body heat nor energy left in him to survive a third night in an emergency shelter. Fifteen minutes later Hap's luck took a major turn for the better!

Years of outdoor experience had taught Hap many valuable lessons. One such lesson involved how an outdoorsman approaches a small clearing in the forest. Hunters and hunted alike gravitate towards small clearings. Hap could detect such an opening in the forest ahead, as he continued his ever so slow pace in the direction of his cabin. A "sixth sense", so often developed by those who spend much of their time in the out of doors, commanded Hap to ease to the edge of the clearing rather than plunge headlong into it. It was a break that possibly saved his life!

Using a bushy spruce to shield his approach, Hap silently snow shoed to a position of concealment behind the spruce. He stood motionless, with a nagging feeling that something else beside himself was near the clearing. Several minutes passed. Then, out of the corner of his left eye, Hap detected a slight motion of something very large and very dark. Slowly turning his head the silhouette of a moose took shape. The animal was partly concealed behind a spruce tree feeding on the branches of some small saplings, totally unaware of Hap's presence. The wind was in Hap's favor. The cold northwest breeze of early morning had gradually swung towards the west and then southwest, blowing Hap's scent away from the unsuspecting animal. Hap knew this moose might very well spell the difference between making it to his cabin, or dying on the trail.

With a smooth, but yet unhurried motion, Hap unslung the .30-06 from his shoulder. lined up the sights low and behind the moose's left shoulder, and squeezed the trigger. The young bull hunched as the two hundred and twenty grain bullet struck it's heart and lungs with over three thousand foot pounds of energy, delivered at over twenty nine hundred feet per second. The bull took two teetering steps, and fell dead in the snow.

Within a half-hour, Hap had removed the moose's internal organs. He cut the heart and liver into thin strips and covered them with snow to draw out the blood. Next, Hap built a small fire under the protection of the overhanging branches of a large bushy spruce tree. When the intensity of the fire was perfect, a generous portion of the heart and liver were impaled on long, sharp sticks and propped up over the fire to roast. Hap filled his tin cup with snow and placed it beside the fire. The snow rapidly melted, making it possible to use his last tea bag to make hot tea. Hap's spirits had risen considerably!

As Hap waited for his meal to reach perfection, he scrapped the snow from the base of the tree, unfolded his blanket and tarp and relaxed with his back resting against the tree trunk. As he sipped his tea and puffed on his corncob pipe, his face contained just a hint of a grin. He had taken a giant step forward in beating the Grim Reaper!

Hap resisted the temptation to gorge on the first real meal he had consumed in over three days. But he did ingest nearly two pounds of succulent fresh liver and heart. The remaining uncooked strips of meat were wrapped in his tarp and packed in his backpack. Next he covered the moose carcass with snow. This, he hoped, would decrease the chance of some wandering wolves or a miserable wolverine from smelling the fresh kill and tearing up what Hap expected would be enough meat to last out the remainder of the winter. Satisfied with his work, and feeling much better with a full stomach, he once again headed southeast. His cabin was now less than two miles distance, and Hap was confident he would reach it well before dark.

It was nearing twelve thirty when Hap saw his first familiar landmark. A large granite outcropping jutted defiantly skyward. This outcropping was on Hap's normal circuit and he had passed it many times over the many winters he had spent running his trap line. At the base of the nearly vertical granite monolith was a tiny cave. A cave just large enough for a perfect set. Over the years Hap had taken dozens of pelts from this single location.

The hard packed trail that Hap and his team had been traveling on all winter passed the tiny cave where one of Hap's well-placed traps was set. Hap was certain it would contain the frozen body of some type of furbearer. And Hap just had to check his trap.

No matter how long one lives and learns in the out of doors, there will be times when just plain carelessness gets one into trouble. Sometimes serious trouble. This was one of those times!

Hap rounded the granite outcropping with high expectations of finding another profitable pelt in his trap. There was indeed a furbearer in Hap's trap, but there was also an uninvited guest feeding on the body of a frozen fisher!

Neither Hap nor the wolverine expected to come face to face with each other, and in such close quarters! Hap knelt down with one knee on his snowshoe to peer into the tiny cave. The darkness of the shadowed cave did not allow Hap's eyes to see the danger in time. The wolverine, on the other hand, had a perfect view of what the wolverine thought was some human who was attempting to challenge his right to a meal of frozen fisher. And instinctively, the wolverine attacked!

Part Ten: "Revenge"

The wolverine was on Hap before he even had a chance to defend himself. The vicious jaws clamped down on Hap's right arm and the slashing claws dug themselves into his wool jacket. The sudden impact of the wolverine's charge, coupled with the unexpected nature of the situation, caused Hap to be hurtled backward and sprawling in the snow.

But the old woodsmen's reactions were swift, after recovering from his initial shock. Hap rolled over, pushing the snarling wolverine under the fluffy snow. This defensive maneuver caused the attacker to release its grip on Hap's arm and scurry for the surface. Hap's movement was greatly hindered, due to the fact he still had his snowshoes firmly strapped to his boots. Plus, the cumbersome backpack and rifle were still in place on his back and shoulders.

Hap jerked his right arm free of the rifle sling and shoulder strap on the backpack. He then rolled another quarter turn and freed his left arm from the pack. As he struggled to regain his feet, the wolverine struck again!

This time the tearing fangs grabbed the back of Hap's neck. Indescribable rivers of pain shot to all parts of his body. Hap tore open his coat, fumbling to release the holster strap, which held his .44 magnum revolver securely in place. His right arm was still numb from the wolverine's initial attack. Hap could feel warm blood running down his back, as the stubborn animal continued tearing at his neck.

A rush of adrenaline gave Hap the strength he needed to free the revolver from its holster. Twisting the weapon around his body, Hap cocked the hammer and fired point blank into the wolverine's side.

The deafening roar of the .44 echoed through the forest as the impact of two hundred and fifty grains of hollow point bullet sent the wolverine hurtling through the air, crashing against the side of the granite outcropping. As Hap slumped forward to his knees in the snow, he was able to glimpse the wolverine gasp it's last dying breath. The world then turned black, as Hap fell into unconsciousness face down in the snow!

For nearly twenty minutes Hap's still form remained where he had fallen. Consciousness slowly returned, leaving Hap gasping for breath and brushing the icy snow from his nearly frozen face. It was at though he was awaking from yet another nightmare! But like his memory of his team being dragged beneath the ice, Hap knew this nightmare was real!

Waves of nausea swept through his body. He gagged several times and then vomited up his recent meal of liver and heart. Slowly the sick feeling in his stomach subsided. Once again he felt tired and weak. Hap unstrapped his snowshoes and sat upon them, his back resting against the face of the granite outcropping. Only inches away lay the still form of his attacker, who had once again placed Hap in a most serious situation. Hap sat starring at the dead wolverine, his sides heaving as he sucked in great quantities of fresh air. "Hope you're the same son of a gun who drove my dogs ta their deaths." His words were barely whispered, but they dripped with hatred and contempt.

Wolverines had long been the enemy of those who lived and trapped in the far north and sub-arctic regions of North America. Besides stealing fur from the trapper's traps, they often broke into vacant cabins and literally trashed them. Many a trapper had returned from running his trap line or visiting a distant village, to find his cabin in ruins and his stash of food supplies missing or torn to shreds. The wolverine's bad reputation was well deserved.

Hap's thoughts drifted back to the present and he began to evaluate his current situation. He was still losing blood from the deep wounds in his neck and arm. That loss had to be stopped, and quickly, as every drop of lost blood would continue to weaken his already stressed body.

Hap retrieved his backpack and removed the wool blanket. Using his skinning knife, he cut several wide strips to be used as bandages. Hap placed a large lump of snow in his homemade bandage and wrapped it as tight as he dared around his bleeding neck. The wounds to his arm were not nearly as bad. His heavy wool jacket and shirt had done a good job in protecting him from those slashing teeth. Satisfied his makeshift bandages would stop, or greatly slow his loss of blood, Hap began to ready himself to continue the journey to his cabin. The body of the wolverine was unceremoniously tossed into the tiny cave to join the shredded carcass of the fisher. "I'll be back fer yer dang hide later, Or what's left a it!", Hap sneered.

Once again, Hap strapped on his snowshoes, shouldered the backpack and rifle, and headed eastward towards his cabin. The cabin, which was now only a mile in distance. Just one mile. But to Hap, that one-mile would seem like a thousand miles and a thousand years!

Part Eleven: "The Trek"

Hap's encounter with the wolverine had cost Hap more than blood and pain. It has also cost him nearly two hours of precious daylight. It was closing in on three o'clock by the time he was able to resume his trek towards his cabin. Less than two hours of good daylight remained, and Hap knew the temperature would once again drop quickly as soon as the sun disappeared. And seeing as the daytime high had only peaked in the minus teens, any drop in temperature would cause Hap's already drained energy supply to be diminished even more rapidly. But he knew his goal was attainable, if he kept a steady, but sensible pace. And,.....if no additional hardships befell him!

Within the next half-hour, Hap was forced to rest four times. His physical condition was worse than he had imagined. Each leg felt like a chunk of lifeless flesh. Each step caused throbbing pain to shoot from his neck into his back, arms and legs. Several times he again tried to vomit, but nothing was left in his stomach. His throat felt parched and burned as if it was on fire. And even though he knew it was wrong to do so, he began eating handfuls of snow.

Several times Hap thought he was about to pass out again. After just a few minutes of travel time his head would begin to spin, he saw spots before his eyes and that feeling of nausea would sweep through his internal organs. He wanted so much to lie down and rest. Oh, just a few minutes of sleep would be so nice. But Hap knew that if he were to lie down, he would never get up again. He had to keep going!

His stops to rest became more and more frequent. All he could do was trudge on a few steps and then lean against a tree to rest until a small amount of energy returned to his aching body. And then he would force himself to repeat the sequence. Never had Hap experienced so much agony! But still he kept pushing himself eastward, towards his cabin.

By four thirty daylight began to fade. Total darkness would soon engulf the land until the moon crested the eastern horizon once again. And the moonrise was getting later and later each night. Hap felt he must be getting close to his destination, but even though he knew he was passing through familiar territory, he recognized nothing! He constantly kept checking his compass to make sure he was staying on course. It seemed like he had entered a dream world, a world of changing shapes and shades that made no sense. The constant pain in his body was keeping his brain from shutting down completely, and still he kept forcing himself to keep putting one snowshoe ahead of the other.

The last visible signs of light were nearly gone by five fifteen when Hap nearly stumbled into the side of his cabin! It leaped at him out of the dark forest like some yet undiscovered monster. His startled reaction quickly melted away into sheer joy! Joy like he had not felt in many years! He had weathered the storm! He was safe! He was still alive! He was home! At last!

With what was probably his last tiny bit of energy reserves, Hap removed his snowshoes and entered his cabin. It seemed to him as though he had been away for months! He dropped his backpack on the floor and leaned his rifle in a corner. Groping in the darkness, he located his kerosene lantern and matches on the table. Light flickered to every corner of his small cabin for the first time in three days. Gathering up a small bundle of kindling, with quivering hand he was able to ignite a fire in the cast iron stove. Within minutes the tiny flame had spread enough for Hap to pile on a heaping quantity of dry black spruce logs. Turning down the draft and giving the damper a quarter turn set the stove for maximum length of burning time. Hap pulled off his sweat soaked clothes and fell into bed like a dead man. He slept for nearly sixteen hours!

When Hap awoke from his long slumber, the cabin was once again ice cold. The fire had died out some eight hours earlier. He stayed under his thick blankets for nearly a half-hour, going over and over in his mind the events of the past three days. He kept hoping he was still asleep, just having a very bad dream. But he was well aware the events he had been re-living in his mind were all too real!

Keeping one blanket snuggled around him, Hap relit the now cold stove. Within a few minutes the radiating hear encouraged him to put on a fresh set of clothing and begin seriously treating his wounds. The throbbing pain in his neck told him that an infection had probably already set in. Hap unwrapped the strips of wool blanket from his neck that had served so well as a bandage. It was caked with dry blood and evidence of puss. Several areas of fresh blood indicated some of the wounds were still open and draining. Using a small mirror to examine his wounds, he discovered they looked worse than they felt. And they felt plenty painful. Hap applied liberal applications of hydrogen peroxide to the punctures and grimaced as the chemical bubbled and seeped into the raw flesh wounds. Next he started a fire in his cook stove and fried up another giant portion of moose liver and moose heart. He ate until he thought his insides would burst. Two cups of hot tea were consumed to settle everything into place in his stomach. And then he slept for another seven hours.

Part Twelve: "The Note"

The weeks dragged by. Hap slowly regained his strength. The ugly wounds on his neck and arms healed, but the scars would remain with him for the rest of his life. Scars to remind him of how fragile ones life can become when Mother Nature goes on a rampage. And,.....when a man makes mistakes. Stupid mistakes that only a rookie should have made. But that is what makes us human. Everybody makes mistake. And if you're lucky, your mistakes won't kill you!

As the sub-arctic winter slowly gave way to spring, Hap made five trips back to the body of the moose that had given its life so that Hap might survive. The meat was smoked and stored in jars and plastic bags. He was also able to recover most of his traps and retrieved the pelts of the fur bearers he had discarded during his attempt to reach his cabin before his dogs had been lost. These were important tasks, as they kept Hap busy and helped to bolster his sagging spirits.

But his nights were filled with loneliness,..... and thinking. Hap still had nightmares about his team being sucked to their deaths in a black hole of swirling water. And his waking moments were spent considering his future. If indeed he had much of a future.

Many options were sorted out in his mind. He considered retiring from his life as a trapper in the wilderness and return to civilization. After all, he was over sixty years old, and he had lived a tough life. But then if he did retire from his chosen life style, where would he go? And what would he do? He certainly wouldn't finish out his life living in some home for old folks. And he was dang sure he didn't want to move in with any of his relatives! Or even live close to them! Why, shoot fire, they had disowned him years ago. Some of them even accused him of being crazy! Living alone way out in the middle of nowhere, why you'd have to be nuts, some of them had said.

Hap even seriously considered one unspeakable alternative. He had nothing but time to make up his mind. And by early May, just as the ice began breaking up in the river, his mind was made up.

Sergeant Bill Osborne of the Northwest Mounted Police was several weeks late making his spring tour in the most remote area of his assigned district. His schedule included visiting the five old trappers, who were the last of a dying breed, still trapping in the sub-arctic region of Sergeant Osborne's territory. The sergeant usually made three visits each year, spring, fall and winter. But Sergeant Osborne had missed his winter visit, due to a very long and tough bout with the flu bug. It had been late September since he had last toured the northern most area of his vast district, for which he was the only law enforcement officer.

Bill Osborne was a nineteen-year veteran of the Mountie force. He had met Hap Larson on his very first tour of duty. Over the years he had bonded a fine friendship with the old trapper, and always looked forward to spending some time with Hap on each and every visit. Though it was against department rules, Bill spent many nights in the comfort of Hap's cozy cabin; sharing stories with old his friend and simply enjoying each other's company. Bill also loved Hap's cooking. He always seemed to have some special dish ready to share, such as baked beaver, or moose tenderloins, fresh brook trout, caribou steaks, or fried breast of spruce grouse.

Bill arrived at Hap's cabin on the thirteenth of May. It was a Friday. Even before the sergeant's canoe reached shore, Bill knew something was wrong! Everything was quiet. By now the dogs should have scented him or heard the splashing of his canoe paddle. They should have been yowling up a storm.

As he stepped ashore, he noted no smoke drifted from the cabin's stovepipe. The chains that usually held Hap's sled dogs were vacant. Bill felt a pang of uneasiness sweep through his body as he slowly made his way to the cabin door.

Once before, Sergeant Osborne had encountered a situation like this. Old Ned Wilson had probably died in his sleep sometime around late January or early February, and Bill had found his remains about mid May. It was not a pleasant memory. Cold sweat was popping out on his forehead as he lifted the latch and slowly pushed open the cabin door.

Sunlight spewed into the interior of the dark cabin as the door creaked open. It took several seconds for Bill's eyes to adjust to the dim interior. He was slightly startled at what first caught his eye!

In the middle of the cabin's dirt floor stood a brand new sled. It was slightly smaller than the one he had remembered Hap using. The frame was made of finely split cedar rails and the runners were hewn from tamarack. Strips of moose hide had been used to bind all the parts together. It was truly a thing of beauty. Bill looked around the remainder of the small cabin, and it was then he saw the note lying on the crude table. It was short, and to the point.

> Dear Bill,
> Was going to wait for you a few more days to see if you'd show. But maybe you won't, as you didn't show up all winter. Hope you're ok. Had some bad luck during that last big nor'easter in March. Lost my team in the river. Also had a bad run in with a wolverine. But he came out on the short end of the stick. Decided to run my fur to Nitchequon while the river's still running good. If you show up, make your self to home. Got a little tea left in the tin container on the table and a couple chunks of smoked moose hanging in the rafters. Should be back by the end of the month.
>
> Hap

P.S. Got to buy five new pups and get them trained by fall. Trapping season will be here before you know it.

(Chapter Two)

THE PUPS OF NITCHEQUON

Part One: "Nitchequon"

Hap made his final decision by May 8th. The weather suddenly had taken a turn towards summer type conditions. The sun shone brightly from a cloudless royal blue sky, driving the thermometer past the 70 degree mark. Flock after flock of migrating Canada Geese passed overhead, pushing northward towards their spring and summer breeding grounds by a warm and friendly southwest breeze. It was one of those days that made a person feel so very lucky to be alive.

Despite his tragic experiences during the Nor'easter in March, Hap's winter take of fur was the most he had harvested in many seasons. In fact, Hap had so much fur that he would be unable to haul the entire load to Nitchequon in one trip! He packed his ancient 17 foot Old Town canoe with as many prime pelts as he could squeeze into the narrow craft without overloading it. The furs were tied in bundles and held securely in place with a plastic tarp. Hap left for Nitchequon early the following morning.

The rivers were running high, filled to capacity with the spring snow melt, and Hap expected he would make it to his destination in three days, rather than the usual four. This would require spending ten hours a day on the water, but all his traveling would be downstream, except for the final three kilometers. It would be an easy trip, despite several long portages.

Because of his large cargo of fur, Hap traveled light. A change of clothing, rain suit, wool blanket, plastic tarp, some tea, smoked moose, a loaf of sourdough bread, small frying pan, a little salt and pepper, flour, and his tin cup. He also bought along a small spinning rod and reel, some trout spinners, an extra canoe paddle, ax, and his .44 magnum. Anticipation about the upcoming trip prevented Hap from sound sleep. It was nearly an hour before full daylight when he wrote a note for Sergeant Osborne, just in case he showed up, and shoved off for Nitchequon.

The warm summer type weather held. Hap indeed did have an easy trip. He caught enough brook trout and small lake trout to eat well. The weather remained so warm and dry that Hap did not even erect his tarp over his sleeping areas during the two nights he had to sleep in the out of doors. By three thirty on the afternoon of May twelfth he stepped ashore in Nitchequon.

The village of Nitchequon is situated on the north bank of the Grande Riviere, not far from where this westward flowing stream exits Lac Nichicum. The river eventually deposits it's waters into James Bay, a distance of nearly seven hundred kilometers from it's headwaters.

As usual, the tiny village was quiet. Several wandering dogs gave him a few barks and sniffs, then wandered away to investigate something more exciting. Hap began unloading his cargo of furs. He would have to make many trips from the river bank to the Nitchequon General Store, where the Hudson Bay fur buyer would be housed. But fortunately, help was close at hand.

A half dozen children, who had been at play in the dusty street, had seen Hap arrive. They, like the wandering dogs, were curious as to who had arrived in their village. Hap looked up from his labors to see six grinning faces peering at him.

"Well, hello there!", Hap greeted his onlookers. "What's ya youngins up ta?

"Nuttin much.", mumbled the largest boy. "What you up to?"

"Gotta haul all these furs up ta the store.", replied Hap. "Think I could git some help?"

"I da know, we were right in the middle of playin' a game.", responded the stocky leader of the group.

"How's about if I buy ya all a treat if ya'll help?", Hap inquired.

"What kinda treat?", asked the leader, with a bit more enthusiasm.

"I'll let ya all pick out a big bag of your favorite candy at the store. Jist as long as it ain't gonna cost me a fortune.", added Hap.

"Deal!", shouted the leader, as all six shouldered a bundle of furs and followed Hap towards the Nitchequon General Store.

Part Two: The Deal

Hap Larson was no stranger to the citizens of Nitchequon. Though never spending much time here, he had been coming and going from this small trading community for over a quarter century. And the friendly citizens of the village always made him feel welcome.

The Nitchequon General Store was owned and operated by Jacque LePage, a fourth generation of LePages, who built and had been running the town's only store for nearly a century. Over the years, Hap and Jacque had become good friends.

Jacque was busy with some routine bookkeeping when Hap and his band of little bearers entered the store. A warm smile spread quickly across Jacque's face and his dark eyes flashed a warm greeting even before he spoke.

"Hap, my old friend! Looks like you made it through another long winter! Good to see you!

And it looks like you have found some willing helpers!".

As Hap put down his bundle of furs and extended his right hand in greeting, he responded, "Yep, survived another one. But as ta my helpers, they wasn't so willin' till I offered 'um a little bribe.", chuckled Hap.

Hap turned towards his assistants and said, "O.K., now hustle back ta the river and fetch the rest a my furs, and then I'll get down ta payin' ya off." In a flash the six were running towards the river.

While Hap and Jacque waited for the helpers to haul the remaining bundles of furs to the trading post, they swapped gossip as to what had happened in their lives during the nearly eight months since they had last seen each other. Jacque was genuinely shaken when Hap told his tragic story of how his dogs had been lost in the river, plus his battle to survive the wolverine attack and it's aftermath. Other than that, not much of interest had taken place in Nitchequon, nor in Hap's life. By the time the two friends had completed sharing stories, all the fur was piled on the floor of the store and the workers were awaiting their reward.

"Gimme six a them two liter paper bags, Jacque.", Hap instructed the store owner. Then, after each helper had a bag, Hap said, "O.K., now fill them bags ta the brim with whatever kind a candy and gum ya like. The treat's on me, and a mighty big thanks fer yer help!" Within two minutes the children had the bags bulging with their favorite candies and chewing gum. Grinning at Hap and waving good-bye, the six were out the door and headed somewhere to enjoy the fruits of their labors. Jacque and Hap smiled as they watched them disappear down the village's only street.

"Right nice bunch a kids.", Hap added.

"Yes, and they'll be watching for you again next May, my friend!", Jacque predicted. "I think you've just made six new friends."

"They ain't gonna have ta wait till next May, I gotta make another trip ta bring in the rest a my furs. Couldn't haul 'um all in one load."

"Hey, by the way, has Pete showed up here yet?", asked Hap, finally getting to one of the three main reasons he had come to Nitchequon.

"Yep.", replied Jacque, "Got here Wednesday of last week, and will probably stick around for another couple of weeks. Quite a bit of fur has come in already. Looks like it might be one of the best trapping seasons in some time. Pete's out in the shed where he usually sets up shop. Here, I'll give you a hand carrying your furs out back."

Peter Mackenzie had been employed by the Hudson Bay Company for over thirty years. His great, great, great grandfather was Alexander Mackenzie, who had explored the great northern river that now bears the Mackenzie name. The Mackenzie River flows northwestward from Great Slave Lake into the Beaufort Sea, which is part of the Arctic Ocean. And it rivals the

Yukon River as northern Canada's largest and most historic river.

Pete was organizing his piles of furs and packing them in shipping cartons as Hap and Jacque entered the storage building that served as the fur buyer's office. At the sight of Hap, Pete offered his personal greeting at once again seeing an old friend.

"Well, well, well. Look what the cat dragged in. Good to see you, Hap!"

"Good ta see you too, Pete. And if you don't have anything else ta do at the moment, you kin help me and Jacque tote the rest a my furs from his store ta here."

The two warmly shook hands, and in a few minutes all of Hap's pelts had been transferred to Pete's office. Pete was impressed by the quantity and quality of Hap's harvest.

"Tell ya what, let's go back in the store and I'll buy coffee so the three of us can chat and catch up on all the wilderness gossip. Unless you're in a hurry Hap.", suggested Pete.

"Best offer I've had in months!", replied Hap.

For the next half hour the three friends chatted about old times, old acquaintances, and in general, things that old friends talk about when they have not seen each other for months. Renewing old friendships was one of Hap's favorite pastimes during his brief visits to civilization. It was a half hour well spent.

As their conversations wore down, Hap made his usual suggestion. One that Jacque and Pete had heard many times over the many years that Hap had been bringing his winter catch of furs to Nitchequon.

"Well Pete, What'd ya think about this deal? I'll jist leave my furs in yer good hands. Give ya a day or two ta look 'um over and give me an offer. In the mean time I'm a gonna head over ta Edna's Boardin' House and order the biggest dang steak in the place. Then I'll git myself a room, take a good hot bath and sleep between some genuine clean sheets. That o.k. with you Pete?"

"Best offer I've had in weeks, Hap. But, I was going to mention the fact you needed a bath." All three laughed at Pete's good natured jab at Hap. "Enjoy yourself at Edna's.", added Pete.

Hap shook hands with his two old friends, hitched up his pants and headed out the door towards Edna's.

Part Three: "Edna's"

Edna's Boarding House was at the far end of Nitchequon's main, and only street, which stretched a scant four blocks, running north from the river. Most of the buildings that bordered the street were small homes, largely occupied by families of Indians and mixed bloods, most of whom were related to the Crees. Besides LePage's General Store, Edna's Boarding House was the only other business establishment in Nitchequon.

Edna Sullivan and her husband Michael had moved to Nitchequon in the late 50's. Mike had been employed as a dock worker in Montreal, but had gotten laid off from work fairly often during the winter months when much of the shipping on the Great Lakes came to a halt. Generally the shipping ended when the lakes iced up, and that period of time usually lasted about three months. Edna, on the other hand had nearly completed a course of study in a school of medicine. One more year of study would have made her a licensed nurse. But the O'Sullivan's had become disenchanted with city life and decided to resettle in a more rural area.

Tired of Mike's on and off again work schedule, plus the hustle and bustle of a growing Montreal, the couple opted to head north into the vast wilderness of Quebec to seek a new life. They heard about an old abandoned boarding house in a remote village named Nitchequon, and sight unseen they had purchased it.

After putting the run down building back in shape, Edna took over operating the business while Mike worked at several different jobs. He logged pulp wood during much of the winter months for a Canadian lumber company. Throughout the spring and summer he guided a few trout fishermen who ventured into the area after trophy brook trout and lake trout. Fall found him doing a bit of trapping. There never had been much money coming in, but then again, it didn't take much money to live comfortably in Nitchequon.

Edna had born two children. A girl, who they named Colleen, and a boy, Shawn. Both had been home schooled and eventually moved from Nitchequon to a more civilized area. Colleen graduated with a teaching degree from a college in Quebec, married a minister, and produced three children of her own. Shawn decided on a life of adventure. He graduated from a school of navigation in Ottawa and eventually became a first mate on a Great Lakes ore freighter. Shawn had remained a bachelor.

And then in 1978 there had been an accident. Mike was killed when a log slipped from the grasp of a fork lift as a logging truck was being loaded. Edna was left to fend for herself. But she had survived!

As usual, Edna was at the her desk, fussing with papers and waving a dust cloth. Her red hair, slightly streaked with gray, hung in loose whips to her shoulders. Even now, at age 62,one could tell she had been a very beautiful Irish lass. In fact, she still was! Edna had somehow managed to keep a slender figure and Hap generally took more than one look at her shapely and generous bosom which always filled out her blouse or sweater quite nicely. Hap considered her very attractive, and felt she looked at least fifteen years younger than she really was. Her blue eyes still snapped with vigor and energy. Yes indeed, Edna O'Sullivan was no ordinary senior citizen!

Edna looked up as the front door opened and at once gave a wide smile of greeting. She, like all the adult citizens of Nitchequon, knew and admired Hap Larson.

"Well land sakes, if it isn't that old Hap Larson coming again for some decent food and a clean bed!", chirped Edna. "Look's like the world has been treating you o.k. I only see a couple of more wrinkles in that ugly old face of yours." But then warmly added, "Good to see you Hap. How have you been?"

"Can't complain, and it never does no good if I do.", Hap retaliated. But I gotta tell ya Edna, those new wrinkles came from spendin' a few days at your place last September! Dang good ta see you too Edna!"

Once again, Hap was prompted to give an accounting about his adventures since his last visit to Nichequon. Edna dabbed away a couple of tears when Hap detailed the living nightmare of watching his dogs being dragged under the ice, and his harrowing scrape with the wolverine. Within twenty minutes Hap and Edna had caught each other up on all the news from the past eight months. It was time for Hap to get down to business.

"Well Edna," Hap began, "I dropped my catch a furs off at Pete's office, and I won't be getting any cash fer a day or two. Is it o.k. with you if I run a tab till I get paid?"

"Hap Larson, what a silly question. You've been doing this now for how many years? If I can't trust you to pay your bill, who in the world could I trust?"

"Thanks Edna. I'll be hangin' around fer two or three days. Depends on how my schedule works out. I'll know better by tomorra afternoon. In the meantime, rustle me up the biggest beef steak ya kin find, with all the trimmin's, and give me a room next ta the bathroom with the big tub."

"Hap, you know dang well I only got that one bathroom and one tub. Or are you getting forgetful in your old age? You can go on up and take any room you please. Ain't another soul staying here at the moment. Your steak will be ready in about a half hour."

Hap carried his small bag of personal items up the flight of stairs and entered the same sleeping room he had rented on most of his twice a year visits to Nitchequon. It was a simple sleeping room, but Hap was used to a simple life and thought the accommodations to be just fine. A double bed fit snuggly in one corner. Beside it was a small three drawer clothes chest. The top drawer held a bible. On top of the chest was a porcelain wash bowl and a matching water pitcher. Two towels and a wash cloth were neatly folded over a towel bar attached to the wall above the wash bowl. The final piece of furniture in the room was a straight back chair next to the single window, that allowed one to view the length of Nitchequon's main street. Hap took one towel and the wash cloth, plus a change of clothing, and headed for the bathroom and that hot bath he had so much looked forward to.

By a bit after ten o'clock Hap was laying in his bed, trying to relax enough to fall asleep. He had taken his time eating a sixteen ounce t-bone steak along with a giant baked potato, plus a generous portion of creamed corn and three slices of Edna's homemade rye bread. He indulged by washing it all down with two bottles of imported German beer. After chatting a bit with Edna, he had taken a leisurely stroll down main street to the bank of the river and smoked a bowl of tobacco. Several residents of the village stopped and conversed with Hap about this and that, making him feel very welcome. But still, Hap found sleep difficult to find. He was just too keyed up thinking about what he was going to do tomorrow. Something he had been anticipating for nearly two months!

Part Four: "New Arrivals"

Hap had been watching the window in his small sleeping room for over an hour before he detected a softening of the night's darkness. A few early rising song birds began chirping and a "cock a doodle do" from somebody's rooster confirmed Hap's assumption that dawn was about to crack. Still he lay in the soft bed, planning his day's activities. Hap had long since realized that much of the satisfaction one gets out of life is planning new and exciting ventures. Often the planning is more rewarding than achieving the goal. His mind was jerked back to the present when he heard Edna banging around in her kitchen, and smelled the aroma of fresh coffee brewing.

Rising from his resting place, Hap filled the porcelain wash bowl with water from the matching porcelain pitcher. A quick clean up of his face, hands, and several other body parts made him feel better and somewhat more presentable. He pulled on a clean change of clothing, brushed his teeth and combed his shaggy hair. He even gave his mustache and beard a brief brushing. Then grabbing his coat and whistling a lively tune, he headed downstairs to see what Edna was preparing for his breakfast.

After consuming two fresh eggs, fried sunny side up, a half pound of crisp bacon, three slices of home made toast covered with blueberry jam and a mound of hash brown potatoes, all washed down with two cups of coffee and a giant glass of orange juice, Hap was ready to face the day. A day he had long been waiting for!

Shafts of early morning sunlight were just beginning to poke their earth warming beams through the branches of the trees as Hap left Edna's. He sat for a few minutes on one of her steps and loaded his corncob pipe with Bond Street, his favorite pipe tobacco. Striking a kitchen match

49

on the step, he ignited the mixture and took a deep draw. The first puff in the morning was always the best tasting.

The town was quite. Not unusual for Nitchequon at almost any time of the day or night. The only evidence of life consisted of the same roaming dogs that had greeted his arrival yesterday. A flock of geese honked from the river. Song birds of various shapes and sizes vocalized a warm welcome to a new day. How beautiful the world was. Hap gave thanks to be a part of it.

Not a breath of wind stirred as Hap slowly ambled his way down Nichequon's only street, heading towards the river. A check of his watch indicated it was only a few minutes past seven o'clock. Jacque and Pete would not be open for business for another hour. If they opened on schedule. That would be Hap's first stop of the day. He needed to collect some of the money he had coming from the sale of his pelts. Money he would need for the purchase of five important items later. Meanwhile he'd sit by the river and watch the rest of the world wake up.

Hap had a favorite place at the river's edge where he had spent many hours in the past. Moving water always had a soothing effect on his mind and body. And the therapy didn't cost a penny! Someone had placed a rusty metal folding chair under an old spruce tree, just a few feet from the river. It was a place where some of the towns people often relaxed in the late afternoon or evening. Hap preferred early morning. The chair was always empty in the morning. Today was no different.

For over a half hour Hap gazed out over the river, watching it's water slowly gurgle by. He wondered how long it took for each drop of water to reach James Bay. Small areas of early morning mist floated upward from it's surface, only to be vaporized by the warming sun. It was times like this, listening to Mother Nature and watching her every changing show, that make Hap realize why he loved the early morning hours.

It was a few minutes before eight when Hap heard a foreign sound. Around the bend of the river came the distinct "clunk" of a canoe paddle on the metal gunwhale of a canoe. Seconds later a canoe carrying two passengers hove into view. Hap could tell immediately the two paddlers were certainly not experts. They were doing everything all wrong. They splashed water each time the paddles were inserted for another stroke. They switched sides seemingly without reason. Sometimes they both paddled on the same side. The canoe zig zagged, rather than cutting a straight course. Hap thought it looked like an accident about to happen. And the two occupants seemed to be in a big hurry.

Within five minutes the canoe reached the landing area. It was an old thirteen foot Alumacraft, which had seen much hard use. Strange, Hap thought, not many aluminum canoes were used by the locals in this area. Most opted for kevlar or fiber glass canoes. And rarely did you see a canoe shorter than fifteen feet.

Something else seemed strange. Besides the two human paddlers, there appeared to be little or no additional cargo. No furs. No fishing equipment, no coolers, tents, cooking gear or camping equipment. No visible weapons. Just one small canvas bag. Hap supposed they lived close by and had come to Nitchequon on business of some kind.

The man seated in the front leaped from the canoe, nearly capsizing it. The man in the rear swore at his partner and grumbled something else that Hap couldn't hear. They quickly dragged the canoe up on the beach and headed for the general store. Both men appeared to be in their late thirties or early forties, but were not dressed as one would expect from local inhabitants. The shorter of the two men wore a dirty baseball cap and the larger man was bare headed. Their hair was long and looked dirty and un-kept. Both wore woolen jackets, although the fabric looked rather thin and threadbare . Faded blue jeans with holes in the knees revealed they wore no long underwear, despite the chilly spring morning. At this time of year, most men still wore their wool pants or at least a wind breaker while canoeing even short distances. And most puzzling of all, both men wore tennis shoes rather than insulated leather or rubber boots.

Neither of the two new arrivals noticed Hap sitting quietly under the old spruce tree. As Hap watched them walk away, he had but one thought. "Them two are a couple of tough looking customers!"

Part Five: "Transactions"

Hap watched as the two new arrivals tried the front door of the general store. It was still locked. But Jacque must have been nearly ready to open for business, as only a few seconds passed before the door swung open and Jacque greeted his first customers of the morning. Hap pounded out the ashes of his pipe and headed for the store.

Jacque was putting change in his cash register when Hap sauntered up to the counter. "This is a stick up!", he joked. Jacque looked up and grinned.

"You look pretty harmless to me, you old coot!", countered Jacque. "What can I do for you this fine morning, Hap?"

"Nuthin' yet. I'm here ta see Pete. Is he up yet?"

"Ya, he's out back in the shed. Go on through the back room. I'm sure you'll find him sipping a cup of coffee and tryin' to look busy."

Hap nodded in reply and walked around the end of the counter. Out of the corner of his eye he saw the two unsavory characters, that had recently landed their canoe, selecting canned goods from a shelve and putting them in a shopping basket.

As Jacque suspected, Pete was savoring a cup of steaming coffee and munching on a sweet roll that looked to be at least two days old. It crunched.

"Well, Hap my friend. You're up bright and early.", greeted Pete.

"Ya call this early. Heck I got a half days work done already.", grinned Hap.

"I suppose you're here to collect that hundred dollars your fur is worth?", teased Pete.

"That much hey! What'd ya do, double your prices. That's way more than I usually git otta ya!", retorted Hap.

"Really Hap, you have one fine catch of prime furs. And you say there's still more to bring in?", asked Pete, seriously this time.

"Yep, got about another third a what I brung this trip." But if ya ain't paying what they're worth, maybe I'll just fling 'um in the river." Hap was still joking.

Pete produced an offer form from a small stack of papers on his desk and handed it to Hap. "Here's my offer. I think you'll be pleased!", smiled Pete.

Hap silently studied the numbers for nearly a minute. Then he let out a soft whistle and looked at Pete saying "I'll take it!"

The value of Hap's pelts had added up to four thousand, six hundred and seventy five dollars!

Nearly a thousand dollars more than he usually received, and he still had at least a thousand dollars worth back in the root cellar of his cabin! Hap indeed had had a productive trapping season.

"Well," Hap began, "Kin ya give me about a thousand in cash and transfer the balance ta my savings account at my bank in Val-d'Or?"

"Of course. Are you still banking with the same bank?"

"Yep."

"And is your account number the same?"

"Yep."

"I've got all the information in my file. Consider it done, my friend!"

With a simple shake of hands, the deal was completed. Hap signed the offer, Pete counted out a thousand dollars in cash, which Hap folded and stuffed in his pocket. Hap trusted Pete completely to transfer the balance as he had promised. After all, he had been doing this for Hap for a quarter of a century! And Hap's bank balance was already quite impressive for a man who made his living trapping.

"Well, I gotta git goin'," said a beaming Hap, "Goin' over ta Clarence Johnson's place and buy me some new pups fer sled dogs. I'll stop by and let ya know when I'll be back with the rest a my furs before I head back ta my cabin tomorra."

"Pick out some good ones Hap. As always, it's nice to do business with you.", replied Pete.

Hap walked back into Jacque's store to do one final bit of business before he went off to purchase his new pups. Jacque was still at his check out counter watching his two new customers.

"I'm a headin' fer Clarence's place ta take a look at what kind a pups he's got fer sale, now that I'm a rich man.", began Hap. "I'm gonna leave my list a stuff I need ta re-supply myself fer the next few months. You kin start pilin' my order in bags or boxes. I'll stop by later this afternoon when I get done over at Clarence's and settle up. I plan on leavin' fer my cabin bright and early tomorra mornin. I'll be back in town in about a week or ten days with the rest a my furs, and then pick up my new pups I'm hopin' ta pick out today. Then I gotta get back home again and a start trainin' um."

Hap produced a long shopping list from his jacket pocket and handed it to Jacque.

"Sounds like a plan to me Hap. I'll have your provisions ready for you by sometime this afternoon. Stop by when you get back from the Johnson place and we'll make arrangements to move your supplies down to your canoe tomorrow morning. I'm sure we can find someone who'll help. Good luck on your shopping for pups!"

Hap smiled and started for the door, unaware that the two strangers had been listening intently to every word!

Part Six: "Johnson's Pups"

Clarence Johnson, and his wife Waneta, lived nearly a kilometer northwest of Nitchequon. A narrow, well traveled path swung west off the main street of the village, right next to Edna's, and meandered through a thick forest of second growth spruce and tamarack to the Johnson home. Several other rural families lived further west and north along the same path, but Clarence and Waneta lived in the first house on the right.

Like many of the long time citizens of Nitchequon, and it's surrounding area, Hap had known the Johnson's for many years. Hap had bought nearly a dozen and a half different pups from Clarence, all of which turned out to be outstanding sled dogs. Four of the five dogs that Hap lost during the aftermath of the nor'easter in March were his most recent purchases, only four years earlier. Hap obtained Aurora, who had been his lead dog, six years ago. Aurora was the best sled dog Hap ever owned or worked with.

Clarence Johnson was a true native of the area. His grandfather, Christian Johnson, moved from Arizona to Canada in the mid 1890's, after he had read an article about the life of a trapper. Prior to his move, Christian spent eight years in the U.S. Army. He had been assigned to a detachment of cavalry in the desert southwest. His unit was given the task of rounding up Apaches and settling them on reservations. The assignment sickened Christian on a career in the military, and he immigrated to Quebec.

Upon settling near Nitchequon, Christian married a full blooded Cree squaw named Who-shon-nee, which means "October moon". Three children resulted from this union, Clarence's father, Arnold, an older brother Thomas, and a younger sister, Virginia.

Thomas moved to the United States about 1914, enlisted in the army, and was killed fighting the Germans while stationed in France during World War One. Virginia died from scarlet fever when she was only eight years old. Arnold stayed in the Nitchequon area and trapped with his father up until the old man was unable to continue the rugged life of a trapper. That was in 1929.

Christian died in 1948 at the ripe old age of 83. Clarence's grandmother died years earlier, trying to deliver a fourth child.

Arnold Johnson was forty years old when he married the young widow of a trapper who had fallen through the thin ice of a beaver pond and drown. Arnold and Anna Johnson had but one child, Clarence, who was born in 1939.

Clarence worked at just about every job one could do, trying to make a living in the wilderness. Like most men who lived in the region, he did a lot of trapping during his younger days, but never really took to liking the lonely life of a dedicated trapper. He worked for a time in the logging business, and did some guiding on week ends for the dribble of sportsmen who occasionally ventured into the Nitchequon area to fish or hunt.

Early on in his life Clarence met Waneta, the half breed daughter of neighbors who lived several kilometers west of the Johnson homestead, and they eventually wed. For reasons unknown to Hap, the couple had produced no children.

Clarence and Waneta were two people who just naturally loved dogs. They got into the dog raising business by accident. Stray dogs or unwanted pups would somehow seem to end up at their home, and the steady accumulation of more dogs resulted in more pups. Clarence decided to breed sled dogs, first as a hobby, and then realizing there was a demand for good sled dog stock, made a business out of it. And now that racing sled dogs had become a fashionable pastime all across North America, Clarence and Waneta often had a tough time keeping up with the demand. By advertising in several outdoor magazines, many wealthy sled dog enthusiasts flew into Nitchequon to purchase pups from the Johnson's. Their success was indeed a storybook story!

Hap set a rather brisk pace for himself, as he strolled through the pristine forest, following the worn path that would take him to the Johnson's home. The day had warmed considerably, and Hap found it hard to believe that the weather had stayed so warm and pleasant for such a long time. Very unusual for this time of year in Quebec. Birds serenaded his passage. A pine squirrel looked down from it's high perch and scolded him as he passed. A male spruce grouse drummed his courting music from deep within the forest. Dozens of different varieties of wildflowers bloomed all along the edges of the trail. Hap thought his route looked somewhat like the road to the Emerald City in the Wizard of Oz. The air was laced with the delightful smells of spring. Yes sir, today life was exceptionally good.

It was nearing ten o'clock when Hap arrived at the Johnson homestead. As usual, some of the adult dogs detected his arrival before he even reached the gate in the fence that surrounded the Johnson's compound. A din of barking erupted from numerous dogs, which intensified as additional dogs and pups decided barking was the thing to do. Hap grinned. Dogs, he thought, often acted a lot like people. Many just followed the leads of the leaders.

Clarence looked up from his current chore, which was doing some minor fence mending, to see who or what was coming down the path. He recognized Hap almost at once. Immediately a broad smile crossed Clarence's face and he met Hap at the gate.

"Hap! I was hoping you'd stop in and pay us a visit. I figgered it was about time you showed up in town with your annual catch of fur. Good to see ya!", greeted Clarence.

"Good ta see ya too! Ain't this a wonderful stretch a spring weather we've been havin'? How ya been?", replied Hap.

"Come on in.", said Clarence, as he opened the gate and ushered Hap inside. The barking increased a notch or two. "Shut up you mutts!", yelled Clarence at his noisy companions. A few obeyed, but the majority kept yapping.

"They'll shut their traps in a bit," offered Hap, "soon as they see I'm friendly."

Waneta appeared from behind the house, her fingers covered with dirt. A small garden spade in her left hand told Hap what she had been doing.

"Hey Waneta!', called Hap. "Got that garden planted yet?"

"Well, I'm working on it," replied Waneta, "but I think it's a tad too early to put any seeds in the ground just yet." And then she added, "Hap Larson, what a sight for sore eyes. You're as punctual as the ground hog. Show up just about the same time every spring! Good to see you survived another winter!".

As usual, the normal chit chat took place, as each was brought up to date as to what had transpired in their lives during the months since Hap had last visited the Johnson's. Like Edna, Waneta shed a couple of genuine tears as Hap related the story which led to the telling of the tragic death of his dogs. It was then that Clarence and Waneta realized that Hap's visit was more than just social in nature.

Hap was invited into their cozy log home where Waneta put on a fresh pot of coffee and produced a plate heaped with fresh baked cookies. Another half hour evaporated as the three refreshed themselves with drink and snacks, plus jibber jabbered about this and that. The Johnson's were a wonderful couple.

"Well." Hap said, finally working up to the main reason why he was here, "let's take a look at yer pups. As I told ya, gotta buy some new ones and git started on their trainin' The snow'll be flyin' in a few more months and I gotta new sled that needs ta be pulled."

As Hap and the Johnson's returned to the yard , barking once again began in earnest. But as Hap went from pen to pen and dog to dog, tails began to wag and the barking and yowling ceased. Dogs have the uncanny ability to sense whether a person is dog friendly or not. It was easy for them to detect Hap was a dog lover.

It took Hap nearly an hour to make his choices. There were so many good looking pups. The decision as to which five he wanted was not an easy choice, but an hour well spent. In each pen Hap squatted on the ground and let the pups roll and tumble all over and around him. He loved it! Hap watched for the pups who exhibited lots of spunk and signs of independence. The ones who strayed from the pack to sniff and explore the far corners of their pens. These were the pups Hap would choose. These were the strong ones, and the ones with brains. The ones that a man often needed to depend on for his survival in the bush!

Hap had put his stamp of approval on four pups, but hesitated about number five. He was torn between a silver colored male malamute with one brown eye and one blue eye that seemed to be bigger and stronger than most of the pups. Hap thought this one might make a good lead dog. But another pup in another pen also held his interest. This pup didn't look like your traditional sled dog breed. Hap asked Clarence about the pup's ethnic backgound.

"Well Hap," began Clarence, "the bitch, as you can see, is the biggest female husky I own. She's four years old, and very friendly and strong. She got out of our fence a while back and was gone for almost two months. Have no idea where she was. But one morning, there she was, back laying by the gate. And she was pregnant. Gave birth to but three pups. One died at birth and I already sold one to the Omstead's in Nitchequon. So, I don't know who or what the male was that mated with her. But it looks to me like whatever breed or mixture it was, it was a very big dog. Or wolf! I wouldn't rule out the possibility she mated with a wolf. Happens ya know."

Hap scratched his chin and pulled aimlessly on his beard, deep in thought. "O.K., I'm gonna take a chance on the big one who had the mystery daddy. He's gonna be a big one, and I'm gonna gamble he's the one ta be my new team leader. I'll take him. And that makes five."

"Hap, once again I think you've made some good choices.", remarked Clarence. Waneta nodded her head in agreement.

"One more thing." added Hap, I'm gonna be takin' a sizable load a supplies back ta my cabin when I leave tomorra mornin'. I'm gonna be back in a week or so with another small load a furs. Can you hang on ta my pups till then? I'll pick 'um up then when I' got enough room in my canoe fer five squirmin' pups."

"Not a problem, Hap. We'll keep 'um as long as it takes for you to get back.", replied Clarence.

"Now comes the nasty part.", joshed Hap. "I suppose ya want some money fer this bunch."

Clarence looked at Hap and grinned. "Tell ya what Hap. I'm in a good mood today, and I really feel sorry about what happened to your team. They were all fairly young dogs, still had a few good workin' years left in 'um,......so I'll toss in one fer free. Give me two hundred dollars instead of two fifty. Does that sound fair?"

"More than fair.", answered Hap. "Ya don't have ta give me no deals ya know. I didn't come here a beggin' and looking' fer any special favors."

"I know," replied Clarence. "But you've been a good customer, and I know you treat your dogs very well,....... and oh what the hell, I count you as one of my best friends. And friends need to do something nice for friends once in a lifetime."

Hap and Clarence gave each other a short hug and Hap started to pull his wad of bills from his pocket. Clarence stopped him with another announcement.

"Hap, before you go, I want you to take a look at another batch of pups I've got in a new pen out back by the garden. I know how you love dogs, and, ...well, I just want you to see them."

"Sure, I'll take a look. Why didn't you show me these before I picked out my new team?", asked a bewildered Hap.

"Cause these ain't sled dogs. They're huntin' dogs. And they're wonderful dogs.", explained Clarence.

Actually, there were two new pens behind the Johnson's home. And Hap recognized the breed almost at once. He had owned a dog of this breed when he was a youngster back in Newberry! Best hunting dog he ever saw. The pens contained two adults and six pups. Black Labradors!

"What ya doin' raisin' Black Labs?" asked a puzzled Hap.

"Well, it's a long story, Hap. Two years ago Jacque talked me into guidin' a couple of city dudes from Quebec to do some duck huntin'. They flew up in a fancy new Otter with more gear and expensive huntin' stuff than I'd ever seen. One was a big shot real estate developer from Quebec by the name of Blakely. The other one was some high roller client that Blakely was tryin' to butter up for some big deal. They were both a couple of real assholes. They didn't know nothin' about huntin' either. They also brought these two Black Labs." Clarence pointed to the two adult dogs. "After a couple of days the two decided they didn't like gettin' up early, sittin' in a cold duck blind, and missin' lots of easy shots, so they checked out of Edna's and flew home."

"So, how did you come by gettin' their dogs?", asked Hap, still puzzled.

"Well, I could tell right off they didn't really like dogs.", replied Clarence, "Treated 'um real rough and uncaring, if ya know what I mean. And when they left Nitchequon, they abandoned the dogs! Flew off and left 'um on the bank of the river! People like that got no business even ownin' a dog!"

"And you offered to take 'um in." guessed Hap.

"Yep. You know Waneta and I are softies when it comes to dogs. Well, one bein' male and one bein' female, you know what came next. A litter of beautiful pups. And we ain't havin' any trouble getting rid of them either. This is their second litter. Lots of folks around here hunt ducks, geese and grouse, and Black Labs are as good as it gets if ya want a good huntin' dog. And they make good house pets too! Good with kids. Ya get the best of both worlds. Good hunters and good companions. They're smart too. Police use 'um to sniff out drugs. They're one of very few breeds that can be trained as seein' eye dogs. Wonderful dog, these Black Labs." Clarence looked at Hap and knew he had made another sale.

"Ya, I know all about Black Labs. Half the folks back in the U.P. own one. I did too, when I was a teenager.", remembered Hap

Hap spent another fifteen minutes playing with the six rolly, polly pups. He picked out the smallest female, as she was the pup that seemed to be the most energized and independent dog in the litter. And Hap knew that females usually made better hunters and were easier to train. Also, he remembered his mother's opinion that the males of all species, including dogs and men, were generally more bull headed than females. It had taken Hap a few years before he realized his mom had been right, as usual.

As Hap settled his account with Clarence and Waneta, he was happy, even though his final selection added another hundred dollars to his bill. Hap considered the expense to be a genuine bargain!

"This Lab pup has changed my thinkin' a bit, now that ya talked me inta buyin' one.", said a grinning Hap. "I'm still countin' on you folks to hold onto my sled dog pups fer a week or two, but seein' as the Lab is old enough to be taken away from her mother,......well, I'm gonna take her along with me today. It'll be somebody ta keep me company on my trip back ta my cabin and then back ta Nichequon again with the rest of my furs."

"Hap, that's up to you. But if it were me making that decision, well....I'd do the same thing.", agreed

Clarence, showing a wide smile. Waneta nodded in agreement.

After a few parting words were exchanged between the Johnson's and Hap, a light hearted old trapper headed down the path which would lead him back to Nitchequon. And a small black shadow tagged along behind.

Part Seven: "Delayed "

Hap couldn't remember a time in recent history when he had felt so wonderful. His new purchase romped and frolicked along beside him, sniffing every flower, stone and stick along the trail. Just watching a new puppy investigate it's strange new world was enough to excite any dog lover's heart. The beautiful sunny spring day had gotten even more beautiful!

Hap took his time heading back towards the village, as it was only a little past one o'clock, and he was totally enjoying watching his new pup explore the sights, sounds and smells along their route. A wisp of blue smoke curled from Hap's pipe, a permanent smile was pasted on his lips, and between puffs of his Bond Street, he whistled "Blue Skies, Smiling at Me, Nothing But Blue Skies Do I See". Yes sir, Old Hap Larson felt like a young man again!

By the time Hap and his new companion had traveled about half the distance to Nitchequon, Hap noticed the pup was beginning to tire. Hap kneeled down and picked up the pup, unbuttoned a couple of the buttons on his wool coat, and slid the tired pup inside. Almost immediately her dark brown eyes closed and went sound to sleep. Hap smiled deeply and whispered, "Dang it, you're sure one little cutie pie."

Before moving on Hap needed to stop and release some of the coffee that he had consumed at the Johnson's. It was then the old woodsman detected something wasn't normal. All the animal and birds sounds he had been hearing had stopped. Only a slight moaning in the tree tops from a gentle southwest breeze disturbed the forest's stillness.

Hap looked around. Nothing seemed out of place. Maybe the critters had just decided to shut up and take a mid day nap, he thought. He resumed his journey.

Just ahead was a sharp bend in the trail. As Hap reached the bend he stopped short and looked ahead in disbelief! About ten meters in front of him was the still form of someone sprawled face down in the dirt. As Hap quickly walked to the side of the lifeless individual he wondered what in the world had happened to this stranger! He saw it was a man. A man wearing a dirty baseball cap. Hap noticed the man was breathing, as his back was moving slowly up and down. The mystery deepened.

Hap knelt down by the man and slowly and gently rolled him over. Hap stared at the face of the prostrate stranger. Somehow he looked vaguely familiar. Suddenly the man's eyes shot open, and an evil, toothless grin crossed his lips. He stared up at Hap for several seconds and then whispered, "Got ya, old man!"

In an instant Hap recognized the stranger. It was one of the men who had arrived in Nitchequon by canoe early this morning. One of the men whom he had seen shopping in Jacque's store. Hap sensed a slight sound of movement behind him. He suddenly realized he had stepped into a trap! Instinctively Hap reached for his .44. But then he remembered he had left it in his room at Edna's. Hap's head had turned but a few inches when something thudded on the top of his skull. The impact created a hollow sound in his brain like a rotting pumpkin being smashed against a stone wall. Bright red and yellow lights, interspersed with shooting stars, flashed across his eyes. And then Hap's beautiful sunny spring day turned black.

It was nearing four o'clock before the old woodsman began stirring back into semi-consciousness. His first faint sensation was a feeling of something warm and wet caressing his right cheek. Hap tried to pry open his eye lids, the right one fluttered partly open, which let in a dazzling brightness that touched off terrible shooting pains in his head. His left lid started to open and then a grinding pain caused him to close the eye lid once more.

Slowly his mind began to recall the events that had transpired just before his sunny spring world turned black. Hap touched his right hand to his cheek to see what the wetness was. His fingers bumped into something furry. He opened his right eye wider, and tried to focus his blurred vision on what he had touched. As his sight slowly cleared, he saw a small black puppy sitting by his face and wagging it's tail.

The memories of buying his new pups and leaving the Johnson's came quickly hurtling back. Then the realization that someone had bashed his head with something that was now causing his brain to throb. The face of the toothless man with the dirty baseball cap came flooding back. And the memory of the sickening sound in his head when he was struck from behind.

Then all the pieces of the mystery fell quickly together. Hap knew full well before he thrust his hand into his pants pocket that it would be empty. His seven hundred hard earned dollars would be gone! And he was correct in his assumption!

Hap rolled over on his back and rested until the relentless throbbing in his head subsided a bit. Then he forced his left eye lid open. Again be felt a grinding pain. He brushed the left side of his face with his hand and found it to be covered with crusty mixture of dried blood and sand. The left side of his head had been resting in the dirt for nearly three hours, and a trickle of blood from the whack on his head had mixed with the sand and dried on his face and beard. Some of it had worked itself into his left eye.

By gently rubbing his eye and making it water, the discomfort diminished somewhat. But the eye still felt scratchy. Hap surmised his eyeball must have been slightly scratched by the sand and dirt.

After a few minutes of lying on his back, he forced himself into a sitting position. Once again pain shot through his head and the world began to spin. He gently felt the top of his head. A lump the size of an egg pinpointed the exact spot where he had been clubbed.

An examination of his fingers showed that the bleeding had stopped. That was a bit of good news. A small whine from his new puppy brought his attention back to his comrade.

The pup was still sitting on her haunches, looking up at Hap, as if to ask, "What happened to you?" Hap reached over and gave the pup a friendly pat on the head and said weakly, "Thanks for the face wash, but ya only got half of it." Despite the pain, Hap still managed a tiny grin.

Very slowly, Hap got back on his feet. The pain returned in force each time he moved. The world still was revolving slowly, but seemed to be slowing down. Gradually, the world corrected itself and Hap looked around where he had been laying for the past three hours.

His wool Kromer was lying by the side of the trail. It had possibly cushioned the blow slightly, and may have prevented even a more serious injury, or worse! He bent over slowly to retrieve it. Once again shafts of pain punched through his head. But at least this time the world did not spin. Carefully replacing his cap, as not to rest it against the painful lump on his head, he looked around again. Just off the edge of the path he spied the weapon that had been used to knock him unconscious . It was a limb from a tree, about three feet long and as big around as his wrist. It had been as though he had been bushwhacked with a Louisville Slugger!

It was almost four thirty when Hap and his puppy began a slow, painful trek towards Nitchequon. Although the distance was less than a half kilometer, it took Hap nearly a half hour to reach his destination. He wanted badly to sneak into his room at Edna's and clean up his face and injured head, but Hap knew he needed to alert the village that two outlaws were somewhere in their midst. So his first stop became the Nitchequon General Store.

Jacque was just getting ready to close for the day when Hap stumbled into the store. Jacque starred at Hap with a facial expression that resembled half disbelief and half horror. Had Hap been able to see himself in a mirror, he would have understood Jacque's look.

"Hap! What in the world happened to you?", Jacque exclaimed as he rushed from behind the counter to reach Hap, who was leaning against the door jam.

Hap's eyes burned with anger as he replied. "A couple a sleezebags delayed my arrival!"

Part Eight: "Revelations and Recovery"

Jacque, with a questioning look of fear on his face, steered a woozy legged Hap Larson to the nearest chair. His face looked a mess, although the injury to his head was still hidden from view by his wool Kromer. The blood that had oozed from his scalp, and bonded the sand and dirt to his face and beard as it dried, left Hap looking like the entire left side of his face had been ripped open.

It took but a few minutes for Hap to relate the unfortunate episode that had befallen him as he was returning to Nitchequon from the Johnson's home. However, in his slightly dazed condition, he had neglected to inform Jacque as to the identity of his attackers. After looking at the lump on Hap's head, Jacque realized the blow had quite possibly caused a concussion. Someone with a knowledge of medicine was needed to examine Hap and render an opinion. And there was only one such person in Nitchequon.

Jacque poked his head out the door and looked up and down the main street of the little village. The nearest persons were the group of children that had helped Hap carry his furs to the General Store. As usual, they were at play, chasing one another around is some sort of semi-organized game.

"Hey!" Jacque shouted at the top of his lungs. "Hap Larson is hurt. Run as fast as you can to Edna's and tell her to get over her." In mass, the children headed for Edna's at a full run. "One more thing!", Jacque bellowed after them, "Tell Edna to bring her first aid kit!"

Jacque's booming voice caught the attention of several other Nitchequon residents, and within minutes a small crowd began to gather in the store to see the injured man and find out what had happened. Violence and bloodshed were things not often associated with living in or near Nitchequon!

Jacque quickly drew a small pan of warm water and began to clean the dried dirt and blood from Hap's face and whiskers. Hap pushed Jacque's hand away and said, "I kin clean myself up. I ain't no basket case yet! But ya kin do me a favor Jacque. My new pooch ain't been fed nor had any water fer about five hours now. Kin ya round up somethin' fer the little gal?"

"Of course I will. Sure is a good looking Lab. I guess Clarence found another soft spot in that hard old heart of yours.", Jacque replied with a good natured grin.

By the time Edna arrived, Hap had cleaned up his face enough that he looked almost normal. Except for the egg sized lump on the top of his head.

It was a very concerned Edna that gave Hap's injury a very close inspection. She took time to look into his eyes and wave one finger back in forth to check on his eye coordination. Edna was so close to him that Hap could smell her perfume. It had been many years since he had received such close attention from a woman. And he was rather enjoying it! After a few minutes Edna gave her professional opinion.

"Hap Larson, you're one lucky man. Oh, I don't mean you're lucky someone bashed your head with a club!", explained a slightly embarrassed Edna. "I mean you're lucky you weren't killed! I'm sure you have a slight concussion, but a few days of rest in bed will probably bring you back to normal, except for that knot on your head. It'll take a week or better for that to disappear. The cut in your scalp is fairly deep, but if we keep the wound clean it'll heal up o.k. without stitches. There'll be a scar after it heals, but with that thick head of hair you've got, it won't show."

Hap shifted his body in the chair and looked at Edna saying, "Thanks fer yer help Edna. I'm sure glad ta hear I'm not as bad off as my head feels. How long did ya say I gotta take it easy?"

"At least two days. Three or four would be better.", answered Edna, with a smile.

Gosh, Hap thought, she sure is pretty when she smiles! But then he responded, "I ain't gonna be able ta hang around here for no three four days! I gotta get back ta my cabin and bring the rest a my furs ta Pete before he leaves."

"Hap Larson, you're going to stay and rest until I tell you you're o.k. to leave. I'll tie you into your bed if I have to. And that's final!", said a determined Edna, with her hands on her hips.

Hap looked at her, grinned and just shrugged his shoulders. Hap Larson wasn't used to taking orders from anyone, let alone a woman! But he knew he had met his match!

Another voice sounded from the small crowd that had assembled. It was that of Peter Mackenzie. "Hap, don't worry about me leaving town without your furs. I'm sure there will be a few more trappers trickling in with their stash. I can stick around for at least another couple of weeks if need be. So you mind the good Dr. Edna and get yourself healthy before you take off for your cabin. We wouldn't want you falling out of your canoe into the river and polluting our clean water."

A smattering of mild laughter rose from the onlookers.

Hap turned his head to look at Pete and responded, "Looks like the whole bunch a ya has ganged up on me. Maybe you're all in kahoots with those two lowlifes that bushwhacked me on the trail.", joked Hap.

Hap's remark suddenly reminded everyone that there were two unknown outlaws on the loose somewhere nearby. It was now Hap's chance to identify his attackers.

"Hey Jacque," he began, "remember them two yahoos who were hangin' around yer store jist before I headed out towards Clarence's place?"

"Ya, I sure do. They left shortly after you did, and then came back in my store to buy some more stuff about two a'clock.", replied Jacque.

"Well, them's the two creeps that ambushed me! They tried ta knock my brains out, and stole my seven hundred dollars!, exclaimed a now irritated Hap. "They musta followed me down the trail, but because I was hightailin' it fairly fast, they probably didn't catch up ta me until I was already ta the Johnson place. Once they seen where I went, they musta figgered I'd head back ta town sooner or later, and set up their little ambush. Now that I think about it, they heard me tell ya I had some money on me."

"I'll be danged!" began Jacque. "Now it all makes sense! When those two left right after you did, about nine a'clock, they only bought a few cans of beans, a summer sausage and a box of crackers. Didn't look like they had much money. When they came back at two, they had a wad! Bought a whole bunch of stuff, some rain coats, pants, boots, a small tent and some cooking equipment, lots of food, blankets, and an old second hand single shot twelve gauge I had for sale, along with a couple of boxes of buckshot and slugs. The total bill came to a little over four hundred dollars! Now I know who's money they spent!"

"Ya, mine!", grumbled Hap.

Jacque continued. "They left in a big hurry. Looked real nervous. I followed them to the door and watched where they went. Loaded everything in a canoe and headed downstream as fast as they could paddle. Hard tellin' where they was headed."

It was Pete's turn to speak again. "I'll get my radio phone and call the Mountie Headquarters in Chibaugaman and see if we can get some help in this matter. These guys have to be caught and stopped. Hard telling who might be their next victim."

Little by little the curious crowd melted away. Everyone gave Hap some positive words or gestures prior to departing. This was more evidence that Hap Larson was well liked and respected by everyone in and around Nitchequon. Except the two strangers who had waylaid him. And no one knew exactly where they might be at the moment.

Finally, only Pete, Jacque and Edna remained. Hap looked tired. His new pup had curled up in a corner and was taking a nap. Edna picked up the drowsy dog, took Hap by the arm and together they walked down the street to Edna's Boarding House. Hap was in the first stage of being nursed back to health.

Edna was able to keep Hap fairly inactive for three days. He did rest in bed quite a bit, although he complained long and hard about his confinement. Although even while he was ranting and raving, he smiled and looked happy. The gash in his scalp was healing nicely, showing no signs of infection. Thanks to the tender loving care of Edna.

Many of Nitchequon's citizens visited Hap to wish him well and check on the pace of his recovery. Among them were Jacque and Pete, who made it a point to visit their old friend at least twice a day. Hap arranged to have Pete take enough money out of the amount he was still owed for his furs and pay his bill at Jacque's store. Pete replied that he had already set that amount aside before he transferred the balance to Hap's bank account in Val d'Or. Hap thanked him for his thoughtfulness.

The time passed quickly for Hap. All too quickly he thought, as he turned in for the night after his third day of rehabilitation under the care of Nurse Edna. Hap lay in his bed for nearly two hours before he fell asleep. Even though he wished to get as much rest as possible before he began his return trip to his cabin in the morning, there was much on his mind.

The three days under Edna's care had left Hap with mixed emotions. Emotions that he had forgotten he had. Also some that he didn't even know he had! The two of them had spent a lot of time together the past three days, and although Hap had known Edna for many years, he hadn't really known her. They shared many stories about their individual lives. And the more they talked, the more personal their stories had become. Hap never confided in anyone enough to talk in depth about his childhood. Or his teen aged years. Nor the seven winters he had spent with Charles when they trapped together at The Cabin. And certainly he had not shared any of the details of his failed marriage with anyone. Not even to Bill Osborne. But all this he had shared with Edna. And more. Why, he asked himself, had he done so?

But there was more. Something else troubled him deeply. It was not understanding WHY he felt as he did whenever Edna was near. Often his palms grew moist. His stomach would twitch and turn. His heart would race. Oh God he thought, maybe my heart is failing.

There certainly was a different feeling in Hap's heart, but it definitely was not failing!

Hap slept fitfully all night. And he had dreams. Dreams such as he had never had before. In his dreams he was a young man again, and he lived in a beautiful wonderland with a red haired Irish lass with snapping blue eyes.

Edna had taken it upon herself to organize several volunteers to help Hap carry all his provisions from the General Store to his canoe. Jacque agreed to open his store at seven o'clock, rather than the usual eight. That would give Hap an extra hour of daylight to begin what would certainly be at least a four day trip back to his cabin. The return trip from Nitchequon was ninety five per-cent all upstream, and he would have a heavily loaded canoe, plus he would be required to portage all his provisions over three major portages.

Both Hap and Edna were up by five. Hap packed his meager belongings, cleaned up his room and then ate breakfast with Edna. Neither of them said much. To Hap, Edna seemed sad and depressed. He wondered why, but didn't ask.

A few minutes before seven they walked slowly down the short street to Jacque's store. Hap's new pup raced ahead, checking out all the smells along the way. The volunteers were already assembled at the General Store ready to assist helping Hap carry his supplies to his canoe and pack it. Within a half hour the canoe was crammed with provisions and ready for departure.

Hap shuffled his feet awkwardly and thanked everyone for their help. Even Pete arrived a few minutes early to see Hap off and once again tell him to take his time in returning with the rest of his furs. Hap made it a point to single out Edna for some special thanks for all the time and effort she had put in to get him back in shape again. To Hap, it appeared her face flushed just a tiny bit, but then again, maybe it was just the way the morning sun was reflecting off her cheeks.

Hap was about to step into his canoe when Edna suddenly stepped forward and gave him a kiss on his cheek. Now it was Hap's turn to find his face flushing. Edna whispered, "Now take care of yourself and don't try and set some new speed record in getting back to your cabin. The rivers are still running high, so take your time and don't take chances. I'll see you again in a few days."

Before Hap could reply, Edna spun around and hurried towards her Boarding House. Hap was unable to see the tears that trickled down her cheeks.

One more round of "good-byes" were repeated and Hap settled down in the rear seat of his canoe and took the first of what would be many strokes with his paddle. He didn't look back, although his friends who had come to see him off kept waving until he disappeared around the bend.

Part Nine: "Return to the Cabin"

Once leaving Nitchequon, Hap paddled west, heading downstream on the Grande Riviere, for about three kilometers. This would be the easiest part of his trip home. Then he would swing north, into the mouth of the Caribou River and fight upstream currents, on this and three other rivers, for the remaining 60 kilometers to his cabin. The trip would include three portages, the shortest being about four hundred meters and the longest being nearly a kilometer. The first portage would bring him to Wolf River, the second portage would lead to the Mineral River and the final portage would locate him on Otter Creek, which flowed past his cabin. Between Nitchequon and home was nothing but wilderness.

There was another route that could be taken which would shorten the distance between his cabin and Nitchequon by nearly 20 kilometers. But that route contained a half dozen roaring rapids that required more long portages. The longer route was the quicker route.

By mid afternoon of the first day the weather began to change. The spell of warm, sunny days began to show signs of coming to an end. High cirrus clouds began to cover the sun, greatly reducing it's intensity and the temperature began a slow, steady drop. By mid-afternoon, the sun was nearly obscured and the western sky had darkened considerably, promising rain. By five o'clock it began to drizzle.

Although there were several hours of good daylight remaining, Hap knew the conditions would continue to deteriorate. He pulled ashore near a thick stand of spruce and quickly make camp. First off, he donned his rain suit. Next he cut a ridge pole from a small sapling, suspended it between two trees, and stretched his plastic tarp over it. He secured the corners of the tarp to the ground with short sharpened stakes made from sections of tree limbs.

His ground pad and blanket, plus his small bag of personal belongings were tossed into the shelter. Within another fifteen minutes he had collected a sizable pile of dry wood that would keep his fire burning for several hours. Lastly, he emptied his canoe of it's provisions and piled them neatly in a long narrow pile. A can of beans, several generous thick slices of smoked ham and several homemade biscuits, compliments of Edna, plus several tea bags were set aside for supper. He and his pup would eat well tonight. Then the canoe was turned upside down over his supplies to keep them dry. Grabbing his small bag of cooking equipment, and filling his coffee pot with river water, he retired to the comfort of his shelter. Looking at his curled up pup he proclaimed, "Let it rain, we'll sleep real good with rain drops drumming on our rain fly."

By building a fire just under the outer edge of his shelter, the overhang would prevent the rain from putting out the flame, plus allow him to be safe and dry under the tarp while he cooked and slept. Hap put several tea bags in the coffee pot and placed it beside the fire to heat. He knew it would take at least twenty minutes or more for the cold water to reach the boiling point, and then he'd need to let the tea seep for another ten minutes before it was ready to drink. This gave him at least a half hour to relax and smoke his pipe.

Hap cut up about half the ham, and broke up a biscuit on a tin plate. The pup wolfed it down in several gulps, licked her chops and looked for more. "I'll have some left overs when I get done with my share. But you're gonna hafta wait a while." The pup licked the plate clean and ran to the river for a drink. In less than a minute she returned and shook the rain water off her coat. Then she sat down and looked at Hap as to question what was next on the agenda.

"Well, little gal," said Hap as he gently stroked the pups head. "I gotta start thinkin' about a name fer ya. Can't keep callin' ya little gal ferever." The pup wagged her tail and curled up next to Hap on his blanket and licked his hand.

"You and me are gonna get along jist fine. Now let me do some thinkin' I'm gonna come up with a good name before that pot a tea boils." The pup looked up at Hap and tilted her head, as though she understood every word. Hap fondly patted her head and scratched her ears. The pup closed it's eyes in complete contentment.

Many different names for dogs filtered through Hap's mind during the next few minutes. Several times his thoughts drifted back to Nitchequon and the name of "Edna" popped into his mind. Mumbling to himself he grumbled, "Heck, ain't even gone a day yet and I'm thinkin' about that woman already." Once again Hap felt that strange twitch in his stomach.

Hap kept playing with the idea that because his dog was a female, which in human form would be considered a lady, he needed to come up with a name befitting her gender. And he felt his pup needed a dignified name to fit the beautiful lady she was sure to become. "Sadie the Lady", he thought. "Yep," Hap said out loud, "That's it! Sadie the Lady, and Sadie for short." The pup opened one eye and looked at Hap. He patted her head once more and said, "I hereby christen you Sadie!" The pup closed her eye as if in agreement.

By seven thirty Hap had cooked and eaten his dinner. He sat crossed legged on his blanket and starred at the glowing fire as he sipped his third cup of tea and puffed a bowl of Bond Street. The rain had settled into a soft and steady, drizzle. To Hap, it looked like one of those spring all night soakers. Good sleeping weather he thought.

Finally settling into his bedroll for the night, with Sadie snuggled beside him, Hap lay quietly thinking about Edna, and listening to the pitter patter of soft raindrops as they lulled him into deep sleep.

Morning dawned gray and dismal, but the rain had ended. A cool, fresh breeze from the northwest signaled the rain was totally over and the sky would probably begin to clear soon. Hap quickly made his breakfast out of some warmed over tea and two of Edna's biscuits heaped full of smoked ham. Sadie also received a generous portion. Within another twenty minutes the shelter was dismantled, the canoe reloaded, and by six fifteen Hap and Sadie were back on the river.

Day two on the river passed without incident. The spring run off had receded considerably and the current was not as heavy as it had been a few days earlier when Hap had made the downstream run from his cabin to Nitchequon. The all night drizzle had not been heavy enough to raise the water level in the river much either, so Hap and Sadie made good time. And by ten o'clock the sun broke through the overcast. By eleven, the skies were once again clear.

They arrived at the first portage about four thirty in the afternoon, and Hap decided he would carry all his supplies and the canoe to the Wolf River before making camp for the night. That way he'd once again get an early start in the morning and possibly be through the second portage by nightfall tomorrow. This portage was the longest one, and Hap was anxious to get it behind him.

Hap removed the cargo from his canoe and was getting ready to hoist the craft onto his shoulders when his nose detected the distinct aroma of wood smoke. A check of the wind indicated the smoke had to be coming from the direction of the Wolf River. Someone else had probably already set up camp for the night on the very spot where Hap was headed.

"Wonder who in the heck it could be?", Hap questioned silently. "Maybe it's Gus Lindstrom. Pete said he hadn't brought his furs into Nitchequon yet. Then again, maybe it could be Bill Osborne. He's about due for his spring swing through this neighborhood. Maybe some early season fishermen were air lifted into Ketchekan Lake and are floating down the Wolf to be picked up in Lake Chimabogama. Guess there's only one way to find out."

Hap lifted the canoe onto his back, and with Sadie following close behind, they headed down the portage trail to see who was camped at the other end.

About half way through the long portage, Hap stopped and rested the bow of his canoe against a large spruce tree so he could take a short rest. The smell of smoke was stronger now and his well tuned sixth sense rang a caution signal in his head. He took a deep breath and realized the smoke he was smelling was being produced by the burning of green wood. The smoke was heavy, and highly scented with the odor of spruce pitch. Nobody burned green firewood when there was so much dead, dry wood laying all over the forest floor. At least nobody who knew anything about the out of doors. Hap left the canoe leaning against the tree and eased ahead to check out whoever it was that was burning green wood.

Within ten minutes he neared the end of the portage trail. The distinct gurgle of the Wolf River could be heard faintly. He slowed his pace and peered down the trail towards the source of the smoke. Cresting a small ridge that crossed the portage trail, Hap spotted the campfire. He was now only a little over a thirty meters from the camp site, but drooping limbs from the trees that lined the path did not allow him a clear view of the area around the fire. Heavy black smoke was billowing skyward and very little flame was evident. Then there was movement, as someone walked to the fire and piled more wood on it. After giving the smoldering fire a couple of kicks with his foot, the stranger sat down on the ground and began talking to someone who was out of Hap's line of vision. Now Hap knew at least two persons were present, and although the conversation was muffled, both voices sounded angry. Hap's caution signal changed to danger!

Ducking into the trees that lined the path, Hap began a slow, stealthy approach towards the camp site. Moving within less than ten meters from the unsuspecting strangers, Hap was finally able to make out their conversation. It wasn't like him to be sneaking around listening to people's private dialogs, but his sixth sense kept telling him that something was very wrong, and he hesitated to make his presence known just yet.

Peering through the thick branches of the tree that concealed him from view, Hap was able to make out the features of two men who were having a very loud and angry argument. Both were dressed in what looked like fairly new jackets and hats. Other than that, Hap was not able to distinguish any facial features that might give him a clue as to whom these persons were. A small tent was situated a short distance from the smoldering fire. A rifle or shotgun was also visible, leaning against a tree a several meters from the fire. Hap's little inner voice told him to stay hidden and listen to the angry conversation a bit longer before deciding his next move.

"Shoulda killed him right off, like I wanted, but no, you wouldn't let me!", snarled one of the men.

"Look a here, we're already in deep trouble. Killing somebody ain't gonna help us none if we get caught!", snapped the second man in response.

We ain't gonna get caught! We've already agreed we're gonna hide out up here in the bush till fall and by then the law will have given up on us. We'll just filter back to some big town and nobody'll be the wiser!", responded the first speaker.

Then a third voice interrupted the violent conversation. "You both better think long and hard about killing a Mountie, because if you do, the entire force will not sleep until they catch you both. You're already in deep enough trouble for breaking out of prison."

Hap was jolted by the voice of the third, yet unseen, individual. There was no mistaking who had uttered those words of warning to the two quarreling strangers. It was the voice of Sergeant Bill Osborne!

Hap blinked his eyes and swallowed hard in disbelief. The shorter of the two strangers then got to his feet and walked a short distant from the fire. Hap changed his position slightly and was finally able to see Bill Osborne. He was seated at the base of a tree with his arms tied behind his back. Another rope had been placed around his neck and then around the tree. Sergeant Osborne was a captive of two violent men!

As the stranger reached Bill's side he spoke to the helpless man, his voice swelled in anger as he roared, "Shut your stinkin' mouth, you damn Mountie, of I'll blow your brains out right here and now!" And he gave his defenseless captive a sharp kick in the ribs.

As the cowardly captor turned towards Hap to return to the fire, Hap saw he had a pistol in his hand. Then a flicker of flame illuminated the stranger's face. An evil smile had spread across his face and lips which outlined a nearly toothless mouth. In an instant Hap recognized the face! It was the man whom he had thought was hurt on the trail when he was returning to Nitchiquon from the Johnson's home! It was one of the men who had bashed his head with a club and robbed him of seven hundred dollars!

Hap was instantly gripped with nearly uncontrollable anger. His hand quickly withdrew the .44 revolver from his holster and he began to consider what his next move should be. But then Sadie, who had been sitting quietly behind Hap, quickly put an entirely new chain of events into motion!

Part Ten: "Payback"

The inquisitive pup let out a shrill "woof". The two men were instantly on their feet and whirling around, looking in the direction where Hap and Sadie were concealed. Hap remained motionless, still hidden behind the bushy spruce. His mind was racing, asking himself, "Now what do I do?"

"Somebody's out there!" hissed the toothless escapee. The second man made a lunge for the gun that Hap had seen leaning against the tree. As he stumbled past Sergeant Osborne, Bill stuck out his leg and tripped his captor. The man fell face first, sprawling in the dirt. A lifetime of acquired instinct took control of Hap's mind and he reacted quickly.

Swinging his .44 with a two handed grip, he quickly but accurately took a bead on the gun which rested against the tree. With a crisp squeeze of the trigger a deafening roar engulfed the forest. The 250 grain bullet struck the action of the convict's gun and sent it spinning off into the dirt. The impact of nearly 1500 foot pounds of energy rendered the weapon inoperative.

Hap then began to swing his weapon towards the second man, but to his horror he saw the muzzle of a revolver pointed right at him. Hap dove to his left, just as the outlaw pulled the trigger. A whizzing sound passed within inches of Hap's ear. As he hit the ground he rolled over quickly, and in one smooth continuous motion aimed his revolver squarely on the center of his attacker's chest. Hap then jerked off his second shot.

The .44 magnum's slug struck the toothless man square in the chest, sending his body crashing backward to the ground, his weapon flying from his lifeless hand. Hap was already on his feet to meet the second attacker, who had retrieved his useless shotgun, and was rushing at Hap with the intent to once again bash in his skull.

Hap tried to aim his revolver at the onrushing attacker, but the enraged man was already swinging the shotgun at Hap's head.

Hap ducked just in time. The momentum of the man's swing began to carry him past Hap. As he stumbled by, Hap landed a well placed boot square in his groin.

The man dropped his weapon and fell to his hands and knees, groaning in agony. But fighting back the pain, he whirled around and tried to tackle Hap. With all his might, Hap swung his revolver, and smacked the attacker on the side of his head. Every muscle in the man's body went limp, and he slumped to the ground. Hap bent over his unconscious foe and hissed, "Payback time, sleezeball!"

Hap quickly checked the man he had shot for any sign of a pulse. There was none. The entire front of the dead man's coat was soaked with blood and more was trickling out on the ground from the exit wound in his back. The man had probably died instantly.

Next Hap quickly untied Sergeant Osborne. After Bill reassured him that, despite the kick in the ribs, he was physically O.K., Hap slumped to the ground and leaned against a tree. The events of the past few seconds replayed in his mind several times. And then he looked at the Sergeant and said, "Oh my God Bill, I've killed a man!"

Sergeant Osborne walked to Hap's side and sat down beside him. "It was self-defense Hap. You didn't have any choice. Good thing you acted so quickly the way you did. Had you hesitated, they'd have killed us both. These two guys are the worst. You should have been in my position for the past few hours. I heard enough horror stories about stuff these two have pulled that'd make your hair stand on end. I'd say you're a hero, Hap!"

"Just who are these two anyway?", asked Hap.

"From what I gathered from their ranting, raving and bragging, they have been breaking the law for quite a few years. The one you killed was named Luke Stillwell. He seemed to be the so called brains of the two. At least he usually got his way. He's the one who wanted to kill me as soon as they got the drop on me. But that's another story! The other one laying over there with the knot on his head, is George Klosinski. Both of them have robbed banks, gas stations, convenience stores, you name it, they're robbed it. They also broken into houses, beat people up, raped several women, and did just about everything else that's illegal, except murder. Or at least they didn't admit to any murders. That's why they had a major disagreement about doing me in. Lucky you happened along when you did!"

"But why did they tie ya up in the first place and then threaten to kill ya", asked a puzzled Hap.

"I came over the portage from Otter Creek after stopping at your cabin and finding the note. Then I went down the Otter and portaged over to the Wolf. I had to paddle downstream past this portage to visit Gus Lindstrom. I spent a couple of days at his cabin, just visiting and helping him get his furs organized so he could take them into Nitchequon. Then I came back upstream to this portage and found these two crooks camped here. I thought they were fishermen or sight seers. When they saw I was the law, they figured I was on their trail, and they got the drop on me, with that old shotgun you put out of commission, before I even got out of my canoe. Then they took my service revolver and tied me up. That was the gun that almost killed you, Hap. Good thing you dove to the side just as Luke fired. That's about the end of the story. I was only tied up for about three hours, but it sure felt like a lifetime. I sure owe you one Hap.", concluded Bill.

"Naw, no big deal. But I'm sure glad everything turned out o.k. fer you, Bill.", answered Hap.

Then Hap told Bill his story about being waylaid by these same two crooks when he was returning from the Johnson's.

Bill shook his head in disbelief, and all he could think of to say was, "Unbelievable!"

Hap and Bill dragged the unconscious convict to the very tree to which he and his former partner had tied the Sergeant, and did likewise. Once their prisoner was securely restrained, Sergeant Osborne tossed a bucket of cold river water in his face. Sputtering, the now captured outlaw returned to the land of the living.

Once the cobwebs had lifted from the captured man's mind, Hap, with a look of hatred on his face, squatted down in front of the man who had attacked and robbed him. Hap had several questions to ask.

"Do you remember me, you slimy bastard?", snarled Hap. The man's face took on a flush of fear, but he did not respond.

"Remember how you snuck up behind me and whacked me with that club? You coward!" The tied up man began to tremble.

"Remember how you and your dead buddy over there, took my seven hundred dollars, and then spent over half of it at the Nitchequon General Store? You lowlife!" The man's lips began to quiver.

"Well, maybe I'll jist get my friend here, Sergeant Osborne, ta take a little walk in the woods fer a bit ta give me enough time ta get seven hundred dollars worth of beatin' the hell otta ya!", growled Hap. The captive decided to talk.

"It, it, it," he stammered, "was all Luke's idea. He heard you tell that store keeper that you were a rich man. So Luke made me help him follow you down that trail, but you were walking too fast for us to catch up and stop you."

"So then ya two yellowbellies decided ta wait along the trail and bust my head! Didn't ya?", bellowed a still furious Hap.

"Ya, that's right. But it was all Luke's idea.", pleaded George.

"But yer the low down snake that hit me in the head!", screamed Hap, his face but a few inches from that of his former attacker. "Where's what left of my seven hundred dollars?"

"Luke's got it. It's in one of his pockets. He's the one who spent it. It was all his idea." , continued George with the same line of defense.

Sergeant Osborne interjected. "O.K. Hap, cool down, don't kill this one too." George's face looked like something you'd see in a wax museum. Bill continued, "Let's take a look in poor old Luke's pockets and see what we can find.

In Luke's right hand front pocket was two hundred and seventy two dollars. Bill handed it to Hap. "I can't do anything about the rest right now Hap, but when I get this bum, George, back to Nitchequon I'll call for a plane to haul him and his buddy's dead body back to Chibaugaman. When I file the paper work on this case I'll see if there is any money for victim compensation. Can't promise anything, Hap, but you've got my word I'll do my best!"

"Fair enough," Hap replied, "at least what I got now is better than loosin' the whole seven hundred.

Nearly an hour had passed since Hap left his canoe leaning against the spruce tree on the side of the portage trail. And he still needed to move all his provisions across the portage. When Hap indicating his desire to resume his journey back to his cabin, the Sergeant had an idea.

"Moving all your supplies will go a lot faster if you had some help, don't you think?", Bill inquired.

"Sure would." Hap agreed. "But you autta stay here Bill, and watch George, so he don't squirm out of them ropes he's tied up with."

"What I meant Hap, was to have George help with the hauling. All three of us can grab a load and I'll walk behind George with one hand on my pistol. I'm sure he'll stay in line. "Won't you George? Or would you like to return to Nitchequon in a body bag like your former buddy, Luke?"

George's eyes grew to the size of golf balls, and he quickly nodded his head in agreement with Sergeant Osborne's plan.

It took but another hour for all of Hap's supplies and his canoe to be toted to the banks of the Wolf River. By six o'clock a cooking fire, made with dry wood, was blazing away and dinner was being prepared by Chef Larson. George was once again tied securely to a tree, and Sergeant Osborne was preparing the body of Luke Stillwell for transport to Nitchequon.

Sergeant Osborne rolled Luke's body in a tarp and tied it tightly. Then the encased body was stuffed in a sleeping bag, zipped up and tied shut. This would be the makeshift body bag in which Luke would take his final canoe ride.

After supper, plans were made as to how the trio would spend the night. Bill suggested that Hap sleep in the small tent the outlaws had erected. After all, it really was Hap's tent, as it had been purchased with his money. George would be stuffed in his sleeping bag and his hands tied together after his arms had been stretched around a small tree. Although he might not be real comfortable, he'd still be present in the morning. Bill would sleep in the out of doors near the fire and keep one eye on George. If somehow George got loose and caused any trouble, either Sergeant Osborne or Hap would shoot him. The look on Georges's face indicated he'd do as he was told.

Hap and Bill were wide awake well before sunrise. They quickly dressed and began making final preparations for their departures. George, who complained he had slept very little, was untied from his night time prison. As Hap stood guard, Bill tied a long rope securely around George's neck, and then allowed him to walk a short distance into the forest so he could take care of a much needed nature call. However, George was not allowed to walk beyond Sergeant Osborne's eyesight.

After all three men, plus Sadie, had eaten a substantial breakfast, George and Sergeant Osborne, with Hap assisting, carried Luke's body, Bill's canoe, and all Bill's personal baggage to the Caribou River. The sergeant was nearly ready to depart on the downstream voyage to Nitchequon.

Looking at Hap, Sergeant Osborne had some additional suggestions. "Well Hap", he began,

"I hope you don't run into anymore situations like the one you blundered into here. All that stuff we left behind that these two crooks bought with your money is yours. Do with it whatever you wish. I know you can use all those canned goods, and the tent. Leave that old beat up canoe on the bank and I'll see if I can find out who the owner is, and also find out if he wants to come and get it. It isn't really worth much."

"Ya, I kin use most of what they bought. I'll stash most of it in the woods and pick it up when I come back from my next trip into town. I really don't have room fer much now with the load I'm carryin', plus my dog.", replied Hap. "But say Bill, how ya gonna get George back to Nitchequon without him trying to get away, or somethin' worse?"

"Got that all figured out, Hap. George is going to sit in the front of my canoe and paddle. I'm going to tie one end of that long rope around his neck and the other end around the body of his former buddy. If he tries anything, I'll either shoot him or tip the canoe over and let both him and his former partner go to the bottom of the river. I don't think George is going to give me any trouble." George shook his head, indicating he wouldn't.

"But what about when ya gotta stop fer the night?", questioned Hap.

"We're not going to stop for the night. Seeing as we'll be going downstream all but the last three kilometers, I figure we can make Nitchequon in about twelve or thirteen hours. We'll only have to stop a couple of times to get out and stretch. And I've got the gun this time."

Hap and Bill shook hands. "I'll be waiting for you in the village, Hap.", added Sergeant Osborne. "You said you'll be back in a few days. There will probably be some formal inquest into Luke's death. It's possible you may have to be questioned. But don't worry. There won't be any charges against you. As I said, it was self defense, plus you were acting to save the life of an officer."

The two friends warmly shook hands once more, and Hap helped Bill shove off. He watched until Sergeant Osborne and his human cargo disappeared around the bend. Hap leaned over and gave Sadie a pat on the head. "Come on, little gal, it's time we went home."

(Chapter Three)

A New Beginning

Part One: Return to Nitchequon

It was late afternoon on the twenty first of May when Hap and Sadie finally arrived at the cabin. After parting company with Sergeant Osborne and his human cargo, the remainder of Hap's journey had been anti-climatic. For that he was thankful!

Hap carried all his provisions to the cabin and his root cellar, arranging everything in a semblance of order. He then wasted no time in preparing supper , as he intended to go to bed early and get a good nights sleep. Hap already had decided he would begin his return trip to Nitchequon early next morning.

He was somewhat apprehensive about the possible inquest into the death of Luke Stillwell. Even though Sergeant Osborne has assured him no charges would be forthcoming, Hap was worried. He had killed a man, and hoped to close that chapter of his life as quickly as possible. Also, he was anxious to pick up his new pups, get back to his cabin, and begin their training sessions. And even though he tried not to think about Edna, deep down inside he missed her dearly.

Up well before dawn, Hap once again packed a meager amount of equipment and supplies for the downstream run to the village. He was determined to make Nitchequon in three long days of paddling and portaging. And hopefully there would be no extra curricular adventures, like meeting up with more characters like Luke and George!

Leaving the cabin, just as a gloomy dawn began extinguishing the darkness of night, Hap and Sadie began their journey. During the entire three day trip the weather continued to be cool and cloudy, but only during the second day on the river did a small amount of rain fall. Nothing else out of the ordinary took place, and just like clockwork the two travelers were in sight of Nitchequon by mid afternoon on the twenty fourth of May.

But the sight that greeted Hap's eyes, as he and Sadie rounded the final familiar bend in the river, made his mouth drop open in utter surprise! The quiet little village of Nitchequon he was so used of visiting was bustling with activity.

No less than three seaplanes were tied up at the docking area! One was a large twin engine Otter with an insignia of the Royal Canadian Mounted Police, plus four large red letters, "RCMP", on it's fuselage. A second smaller single engine Beaver was likewise marked. The third plane was a new twin engine Piper Seneca V, which carried bold blue letters, "CCN", the call letters of the Canadian Communications Network. It was Canada's largest and most popular television network!

Several dozen people were visible near the river front, and the din of dogs barking, people talking, and children yelling could be clearly heard for several hundred meters. Hap was mystified as to what might be creating all the commotion.

He was still over a hundred meters from the beach when someone on the dock spotted his canoe. Hap could easily hear the individual's voice as he yelled, "Here he comes now! Here comes Hap Larson! And a throng of persons quickly gathered at the water's edge and began cheering and clapping their hands.

Hap slowed his paddling and continued to view the activity ahead of him with an ever growing feeling of apprehension. Why were so many people waiting for him? Why were they so excited? His mind had already concluded the reason the RCMP planes were here had something to do with the Luke Stillwell and George

Klosinski incident. But why were representatives of CCN here? What could have happened to bring a TV crew to a small, remote village like Nitchequon? Hap briefly considered turning his canoe around and heading back to his cabin. But then, right in front of the crowd, he saw a woman with long red hair and a beautiful smile on her face, waving her hand franticly at him. Hap's stomach gave a little twitch as he dug in his paddle and headed for the beach.

Part Two: "The Celebrity"

Hap Larson was one of the last persons on earth who would attempt to seek out fame and notoriety. But in this case, the fame and notoriety sought out Hap! As flashbulbs flared and TV cameras recorded his arrival, Hap stepped ashore before a cheering crowd, Edna moved quickly forward to meet him. She threw her arms around his neck and kissed him firmly on the lips. The crowd's cheering increased. Hap' beard helped somewhat to visibly reduce the deep red blush that spread across his surprised face.

Still holding her arms around his neck, Edna spoke to Hap in rapid, but somewhat subdued tones. "Oh Hap", she began, "thank God you're safe! Sergeant Osborne told just about everybody in town about his ordeal at the portage between the Wolf and Caribou Rivers. And, and, and, how you just came along out of nowhere and saved his life! And, and, and, how you almost got shot by that awful man who robbed you!" Edna had to stop for a moment to catch her breath. "You're a real hero Hap! The people of the town have been waiting for your return. They want to hear the whole story from you, too! So much has happened here in Nitchequon the past few days. You'll be so surprised! Oh Hap, I'm so proud of you! And I'm so glad you're safe!" At that, two small tears ran down Edna's cheeks, and she gave Hap another tiny kiss. And all Hap could do was look into those snapping blue eyes and continue to blush. He had always been a man of few words, but now he was totally speechless!

Then others began to step forward to shake his hand and offer warm words of welcome and congratulations. First in line was Sergeant Bill Osborne. Hap was very pleased to see he was present. The line of well wishers continued. Jacque, and Pete, and even an old fellow trapper like himself, Gus Lindstrom, who lived in a cabin on the Wolf River. Next came Clarence and Waneta, plus numerous other individuals, who's faces were familiar, but who's names escaped him. There were even total strangers who shook his hand and wished him well. Hap was totally overwhelmed by the accolades he was receiving!

The cheering and clapping slowly subsided as the crowd parted to allow a smartly uniformed Mountie to step forward. The officer appeared to be in his mid fifties. He was wearing a Mountie's traditional ceremonial full dress uniform, which included the bright red jacket, black pants tucked neatly into gleamingly polished knee high leather boots, and a Smoky the Bear hat. "Mr. Larson, I feel privileged and honored to finally meet you! I'm Commander Wilber Cunningham, Royal Canadian Mounted Police", began the distinguished looking Mountie. "Sergeant Osborne has told me quite a bit about you and I'm very happy to make your acquaintance." With that he extended his right hand. Hap swallowed hard and accepted his hand shake.

Hap's inability to think of anything to say continued. In fact, he was having trouble just plain thinking! Never before in all his sixty years, had he encountered a situation such as this. And he was sure of one thing, he really wasn't enjoying himself, except maybe the attention he had received from Edna.

Commander Cunningham continued. "We've set up our official welcome station in the General Store. I'd like you to come along with me, that is if you are finished with greeting all your friends here at the beach. We don't have to hurry."

Hap looked all around at the sea of smiling faces surrounding him. Hap finally mustered up his voice and answered the Commander. "Ya, I guess I'm done here. But first I gotta carry this load a furs up ta the General Store.", said Hap, pointing to the stacks of pelts in his canoe.

"I'm sure we can make short work of that, Mr. Larson.", replied the Commander. "Who would like to give Mr. Larson a hand in moving his furs to the Nitchequon General Store?"

More than a dozen volunteers quickly moved forward, each snatching up a bundle of furs, and a procession of humanity headed towards Jacque's store.

The entourage slowly wound it's way down Nitchequon's only street. The line of Hap's friends, well wishers, and the TV camera crew, resembled a scene in the movie, "The Pied Piper of Hamlin". Never, had the village of Nitchequon been host to such a gathering of people!

Reaching the General Store, Hap looked up to see a large banner suspended over the door, which proclaimed; "Welcome Hap Larson! The citizens of Nitchequon and Quebec thank you!" Hap swallowed another lump in his throat and followed Commander Cunningham into the store.

A small table occupied the usually vacant area in front of Jacque's check out counter, and a half dozen chairs had been placed around it. Three red coated Mounties occupied three of the chairs. As the Commander and Hap entered the room, the three quickly stood and snapped to attention. Tiny beads of sweat popped out on Hap's brow. "Oh, oh", he thought, "this don't look good!"

Commander Cunningham took control of the situation. "At ease gentlemen." he commanded the three junior officers. "Looking at Hap, but addressing the others in the room, the Commander continued. "Let me introduce you to our honored guest." Pointing at each of the rigid Mounties, he introduced them to Hap. "Mr. Larson, meet Lieutenant Richardson, Captain Montcalm, and Sergeant Smitters." The three Mounties smartly clicked their heels together and saluted Hap. Turning and pointing towards the door, the Commander continued. "You already know Sergeant Osborne over there, and standing next to him is Corporal Jenkins." The two Mounties, which seemed to be guarding a closed door, smiled and nodded.

Not knowing what he should do next, Hap allowed his instinct to take over. Extending his right hand and moving forward, he shook hands with the three Mounties who were standing by the table. "Glad ta meet ya's. Why don't you guys relax and have a seat?", offered Hap.

The officers looked nervous, but quickly seated themselves when Commander Cunningham motioned with his hand for them to accept Hap's offer. Hap and Commander Cunningham took two of the three remaining vacant chairs. A sixth individual , a shapely young dark haired woman dressed in smartly tailored business attire, stepped forward and filled the remaining chair. Hap looked all around the room. What he saw did little to ease his continuing feeling of apprehension. Hap guessed correctly some sort of official meeting was about to take place!

Part Three: "Surprises"

Mr. Larson, I'd like you to meet Miss Noland. She is an employee of the Department of Taxation and Revenue for the Province of Quebec. Hap nodded politely and said, "Pleased ta meet ya mam." The young woman gently took Hap's hand and gave it a short shake.

"Nice to meet you too Mr. Larson.", replied Miss Noland.

Hap looked around, figgiting with his Kromer as he held it in his hands. "Ya kin all call me Hap, that'd be o.k. with me", he suggested.

"Now Mr. Larson," continued Commander Cunningham, "let me put you at ease and begin by saying, the reason we are meeting with you in what may appear to be a very formal manner, is,.... well it's just the way we do business. Official rules you know. You are in no way in trouble with the government of Quebec." Hap gave an audible sigh of relief. "Sergeant Osborne's official report on the incident which resulted in the death of Luke Stillwell has completely satisfied the Board of Inquest that your actions were entirely justified. You acted in self defense. Plus, without question, you saved Sergeant Osborne's life, to say nothing of your own."

Hap's entire body relaxed and he emitted a second, and more vocal, sigh of relief. A small smile even spread across his lips. "Thank you sir!", was all Hap could say.

"But there is one more thing regarding this incident, no, actually there are two more things.", said the Commander, as he thoughtfully rubbed his chin. Hap's eyes suspiciously locked on those of the Commander. "It's been hinted that you own a .44 magnum handgun, which you used to kill Mr. Stillwell. Is that correct?"

The lump in Hap's throat was back again. He knew, all too well, that handgun ownership by private citizens was illegal in all of Canada. And the penalty for possessing one was quite severe. Sergeant Osborne and many of the Mounties assigned to policing the wilderness areas just looked the other way and ignored the law. The law officers knew that the folks living in the savage wilderness often needed the help of a handgun to survive. But for individuals who were found to possess such weapons in more civilized areas were apt to be in a heap of trouble. Hap looked around the table and nodded his head in the affirmative. His apprehension had also returned!

Commander Cunningham looked sternly at everyone at the table. He cleared his throat, and looking at Hap saying, "Well, Mr. Larson, I'm glad to learn you DO NOT own such a firearm. I know all of us here at the table are likewise happy to know you don't own one." Then looking at the other four subordinates seated at the table, the Commander asked, "AREN'T WE?" In unison, there were four affirmative responses.

There was a third sigh of relief from Hap.

"Now moving on to the final item on my agenda concerning the late Luke Stillwell and his accomplice, George Klosinski." began a smiling Commander Cunningham. "I know Sergeant Osborne told you a bit of background information about those two vicious outlaws. But the Sergeant, being isolated from the outside world for long periods of time, was not totally aware of the entire story." The Commander paused to pour a glass of water from the pitcher that had been placed on the table. He took his time ingesting several small sips. "Those two ruffians had been terrorizing the good citizens of this Province for over twenty years. Of course, that does not count the seven and a half years they spent behind bars in several different jails and prisons. Their rap sheet includes armed robbery, assault, rape, arson, fraud, and list of misdemeanors as long as your arm. And something else that Sergeant Osborne was not aware of at the time he spoke to you, was the murder of the owner of a small marina outside of Keyano." The Commander took another sip of water. "After breaking out of prison near Mont-

Laurier, Mr. Stillwell and Mr. Klosinski broke into a sporting goods store, taking a rifle which wasn't locked up and some shells, and several hundred dollars. Next, they stole a pick up truck, and by sheer luck made it all the way to Keyano! There they were caught in the act of trying to steal a boat and motor, with the intent to use it to disappear into the wilderness. They shot and killed the marina owner. In desperation they grabbed a small canoe and some meager provisions, then fled eastward on the river towards Nitchequon. While trying to navigate a rapids, the canoe tipped over and they lost the rifle. Mr. Kolsinski states the two didn't even know where they were going, but just panicked and paddled east. I guess you know the rest, Mr. Larson.", concluded Commander Cunningham.

Hap reverted to his speechless condition once more. He felt slightly numbed by all he was hearing, and just sat looking at the Commander and his staff.

"There is one more item, Mr. Larson." began Commander Cunningham once again, a wide smile finally softening his stern face. Miss Noland has something to add before we adjourn this informal meeting. Miss Noland, if you please."

All eyes in the room focused on the next speaker. "Mr. Larson. The crime spree, and subsequent fruitless search for Mr. Stillwell and Mr. Kolinski resulted in a very generous sum of money being raised and offered for the arrest and conviction of the two criminals." Miss Noland glanced at a piece of paper that rested on the table. "The Province of Quebec offered a reward of $50,000 dollars, and combining the donations of several additional private organizations brings the total amount of the reward to a bit over $70,000 dollars." Miss Noland paused and looked at Hap. The room was as silent as a tomb.

Hap glanced around and noticed that everyone in the room was looking at him and smiling.

"What's everybody lookin' at me for?", asked a still bewildered Hap.

"Well," replied Miss Noland, "The reward goes to the person who captured, or in the case of Mr. Stillwell,..... ah,.... how shall I say it,......disposed of his threat to society,......and Mr. Kolinski. That's you, Mr. Larson! A check for $71,250.00 will be sent to you after I return to my office in Quebec with the proper papers, which you will need to sign."

At that, everyone in the room stood and once again began clapping. Hap's face had turned ashen, and all he could say was, "Oh my God! What'll I do with all that money?", but then quickly added, "Anybody got a pen?"

Miss Noland produced several sheets of official looking documents, which Hap nervously signed without reading what he was signing. Besides his body feeling numb, the affliction seemed to have spread to his brain. A smiling Miss Noland filed the signed papers in her leather brief case and once more shook Hap's hand. This time with a bit more enthusiasm.

Commander Cunningham had one more announcement to relay to Hap. "Now Mr. Larson, the easy part is over. What is going to happen to you next is anybody's guess." Hap looked blankly at the Commander, as if trying to figure out what could be more draining on one's mental energy as what had taken place during the past forty five minutes. "The media people are demanding an interview with you and I am sure you are not aware of how ruthless these modern news hounds can be. I would suggest you insist the interview be held right here in this room in order to keep the nosey public at bay. Just dealing with the TV people from CCN will be a big enough challenge. I'll have my officers prevent the interview crew from entering until you have had time to regain your composure. You do look a bit shaken, old chap! If you'd like to invite any of your friends to be present during the interview, please do so. They might help to give you some moral support. Believe me, you'll probably need it. Good luck Mr. Larson, and in behalf of the citizens and government of Quebec,......Thank you once again for your heroic action. We do indeed owe you a great debt of gratitude."

Hap's face continued to contain a blank look, but he managed to blubber out a short reply,

"Thanks, Commander,....... thanks fer everything!"

Part Four: "CCN"

Before leaving the store, Commander Cunningham and his staff shook hands with Hap one final time. Only Sergeant Osborne remained behind to restrain anyone from entering the room until Hap gave the word. The two old friends finally had time to chat in private.

"How are you holding up, Hap?", asked a grinning Bill Osborne. "You look a little pale."

"If I live ta be a hundred and sixty, I hope I never have ta go through somethin' like that again", sighed Hap. But quickly added, "Unless somebody's got seventy thousand ta give me!"

The two chuckled at Hap's last remark and the small bit of laughter did wonders to relax Hap a bit.

Then his face became serious. "Bill, old buddy, I know you musta moved heaven and earth ta get the Commander ta overlook the fact I own a pistol. How'd ya pull that one off. I figgered maybe you'd tell him I shot Luke with my rifle."

Bill thought for a few seconds and then replied. "Yes, I thought about leaving out the part about you doing Luke in with a .44 revolver, and just letting the medical examiner and the Board of Inquest assume he was shot with a rifle. But those medical people are pretty sharp. They've seen all kinds of gunshot wounds and a .44 magnum with hollow points really makes a messy exit hole. I don't know of any standard rifle bullets that make an exit hole that large. I decided to be honest and see if I could pull some strings down at headquarters and allow this scenario to end as it has. It sounds corny, but usually honesty is the best policy."

"I sure am grateful ta ya Bill. I figgered I was dead meat if the question of my pistol came up during an inquest, or whatever ya call this ordeal I jist went through. But I can hardly believe the Commander let it slip by. He looked ta me ta be a real straight shooter." responded Hap.

"Let's just say, the boss owed a few favors to his old Sergeant , so I collected a bit of the debt." Bill smiled as he put his hand on Hap's shoulder. The issue was settled.

"Bill." began a thoughtful Hap. "Do I hafta get interviewed? Can't I jist sneak out the back door and hide in the woods till the whole bunch leaves town?"

"Well, I suppose you could refuse. But you won't. Might as well get it over with. Beside, maybe you'll like being on TV and become some big, wealthy star!", teased a smiling Bill. "Besides, these news people got noses like bloodhounds and they'd probably sniff you out, even hiding in the woods."

"O.K., Bill," agreed Hap, "give me time ta go out back and take a leak and then we'll let the wolves attack the lamb. But I'd like ya to let Jacque, Pete and Edna inside before ya open the cage door and send the predators in."

"I'll make sure your friends are here. But I don't know about you being a lamb. This crew from the city just might find out they tried to bite off more than they can chew. Even if you were a lamb, you wouldn't be tender", replied Bill.

Hap headed for the back door. "Hey Hap," Bill called after him. "Don't get lost and forget how to get back in here!"

Hap turned and smiled, and then gave his friend an obscene gesture.

The CCN crew consisted of six people. Hap wondered how their Piper had been able to haul six people and the pile of equipment that was being dragged into Jacque's store. And all this time and effort had been spent just to interview Hap Larson! Hap was mystified.

It took nearly a half hour before all the video and recording equipment was set up. There were banks of lights powered by several large marine type batteries. The floor was covered by a jumble of cables, wires and cords. A tripod on wheels held a camera of some sort.

And there were thing a ma jigs and what ya ma call its that Hap had no idea what they might be or what purpose they served. And while all this preparation was taking place, Hap and his friends were ignored by the entire crew.

Huddled around Jacque's check out counter, Jacque, Pete, Edna and Hap watched the CCN crew organize their equipment. The half hour allowed Hap to fill his friends in on the specifics as to what had happened during the closed session with the Mounties. Many people in the town already knew about the reward, including his three friends, so that aspect of his story was received by, "We already knew that." from Edna. Actually, there was very little new information Hap could tell them as to why the Mounties had flown to Nitchequon to meet with him.

News of Sergeant Osborne's arrival in the village, with Luke's body and George as his prisoner, had spread quickly. Bill's account of what had taken place at the portage trail spread like wildfire throughout the sparsely settled area. Interest in the event grew quickly, as graphic details of the shoot out appeared in newspaper accounts and on radio news broadcasts throughout Canada and the U.S. Generally, life in and around Nitchequon was usually peaceful and quiet. An event such as this was bound to create a multitude of excitement in the community!

"Say," exclaimed Hap, suddenly remembering something he had wondered about during his interview with the Mounties. "Does any of ya know what happened ta my dog durin' all this 'citement?"

"It's all taken care of Hap," responded Edna with a soothing smile, "I fed the little rascal and those children who helped you carry your furs up from the river are playing with her right now. She's having a ball. She's in good hands."

Finally the flurry of activity by the CCN crew came to a halt. All the equipment was in place and ready to record the interview with Hap. One member of the crew was standing behind the TV camera turning knobs and flipping switches. A blinking red light indicated the power had been turned on. Two other men were adjusting the angle of the lighting on two banks of flood lights. The lights were so bright, they made Hap squint. A fourth person, this one being female, was putting makeup on a fifth person, also female. It looked to Hap like the interview he was dreading was drawing near.

A short balding man in his forties, carrying a clipboard, walked to where the foursome were chatting . He extended his right hand to Hap and announced, "Hello. I'm Harry Timmermann, the news production manger for CCN News. Sorry for the delay, Mr. Larson, but we're now ready to begin." Hap noticed the lump in his throat had returned, so he just nodded his head and seated himself in one of the two chairs that had been positioned in front of the camera.

The second chair became occupied by a stunningly beautiful blond woman, probably in her late thirties. But with all the TV makeup, her age was difficult to determine. She crossed her long shapely legs and adjusted her short skirt. Hap took a second look at the woman seated across from him and thought to himself, "Well, at least the scenery is nice!" Mr. Timmermann proceeded with the introductions.

"Mr. Larson, this is Jacqueline Bower. She is one of our anchor persons on the evening news show from WQEB in Quebec, which is one of our affiliate stations." Jacqueline extended a perfectly manicured hand, tipped by long artificial cherry red fingernails.

Smiling sweetly, Ms Bower shook Hap's hand and said, "I'm so pleased to meet you Mr. Larson! You probably are not aware of the fact that you have become quite a celebrity in Quebec. In fact, the story of your heroic deed has been picked up by the international news services.

Newspapers, radio and TV stations throughout the world have reported the events concerning your shootout with Luke Stillwell and the capture of George Klosinski. And the fact that your swift action prevented the death of a law enforcement officer has resulted in your being named "Citizen of the Month" by the International Fraternity of Law Enforcement Officers!" Hap's face looked pale again.

Jacqueline continued, "However, as of this moment, no news gathering agency has been blessed with a personal interview with the "Hero in the Wilderness", as one newspaper headline billed you. And I feel honored that CCN reached you first, and I am delighted to have been chosen to do the interview. So, if you are ready Mr. Larson, I'd like to get started. There are probably other reporters already on the way here."

Hap shifted his body awkwardly in his chair. Once again he found it nearly impossible to believe what he was hearing! Struggling to think of something to say in response, Hap faintly muttered, "Heck, it weren't that big a deal. I jist did what I hada do. Those two dirtbags didn't give me much choice." Hap noticed a green light was blinking on and off on top of the camera and it was making a low humming noise. What he was saying was being recorded! Beads of cold sweat popped out of his forehead.

The interview lasted over an hour. Besides answering questions pertaining to the shoot out with Luke and the capture of George, Ms Bower spent considerable time dragging information out of Hap about his youth, why he chose to move to Quebec, what prompted him to become a professional trapper, and vivid descriptions of life while living alone in the wilderness. She was especially interested in recording the gruesome details about Hap's dog team drowning in the river. And even more interested in hearing Hap tell of his unbelievable struggle to reach the safety of his cabin. In other words, Ms Bower had succeeded in capturing on film many highlights of Hap Larson's life story.

To Hap, the interview seemed to pass more quickly than the actual time that had elapsed. And once the camera stopped recording, and Ms Bower and Harry

Timmermann gave Hap their sincere thanks, the entire ordeal did not seem as bad as he envisioned it would be. Being the professional she was, Ms Bower's technique of questioning had put Hap at ease, and he had not ever noticed that his fear and apprehension melted away during the first few minutes of the interview. But Mr. Timmermann had one final surprise for Hap.

"Mr. Larson," he began, "We at CCN, and our affiliate station WQEB, can not thank you enough for giving of your valuable time to allow this interview. And as a final thank you we'd like you accept this check for one thousand dollars. However, there is one small stipulation. You'll be required to sign a simple statement swearing you will not grant any other interviews to another news agency nor individual independent reporters pertaining to the subjects that were covered in your interview with Ms Bower." Mr. Timmermann extended his clipboard and a pen.

Hap blinked several times, looked around the room at the CCN crew and his three friends, and managed a squeaky voiced "Sounds like a good deal ta me! Best offer I've had in quite a while. Besides, I ain't real anxious ta go through another one a them interview anyway." Hap quickly signed the document and was handed a check for one thousand dollars. Maybe, he thought, being a celebrity wasn't so bad after all!

Part Five: "More Surprises"

Twilight was settling in by the time Hap emerged from the General Store. Between meeting with Commander Cunningham and his staff, plus the interview with the crew from CCN, nearly three hours had passed. A few of Nitchequon's citizens were still wandering around in the street, or conversing in small groups. Most paused and waved at Hap, or gave him a "thumbs up" as he and Edna walked towards the river's docking area.

Sadie was still running and playing with the children that had volunteered to take care of her while Hap was detained in his meetings. At the sound of her name, she romped to Hap's side, tail wiggling at full speed, obviously happy to see her master. Hap stopped and picked her up. His reward was receiving a good face washing from Sadie's tongue.

The two planes that had carried the Mounties to Nitchequon had departed, but the CCN Piper was still tied to the dock. Walking to where he had left his canoe, Hap discovered it had been dragged ashore and tipped upside down, just as canoes should be when not in use. But his small waterproof bag of personal items was missing, as were his camping and cooking equipment.

"Don't tell there's a couple more thief's in town. All my stuff is missin' and somebody has been foolin' with my canoe". Grumbled Hap, his anger beginning to rise.

Edna giggled. "I thought you might be in that meeting with Commander Cunningham for a long time, so I cleaned out your canoe, tipped it over, proper like, and carried your bag of clothes, or whatever you carry in that little yellow bag of yours, up to your room. Your camping and cooking equipment is stored in the shed in back of the store. You know, the one that Pete works out of. So cool down Hap. You've had enough excitement for one day. Come on, I think it's time for me to fix you some supper. I've got a ham baking in the oven. The dining room is going to be crowded this evening, as the CCN crew is staying over one more night. Plus, Bill Osborne is renting a room right next to yours and he'll be eating with us. They all seem to be nice people, should be a fun evening"

"Best offer I've had in the last few minutes, Edna, and thanks fer takin' care of my stuff. Ya didn't hafta do that ya know.", Hap said shyly.

"I didn't do it because I had to, I did it because I wanted to. Do you think for one minute a woman can't do things most men think is just MEN STUFF?", replied Edna with a wink.

"I know ya good enough ta know ya kin do anything ya puts yer mind ta.", Hap answered as he returned Edna's wink.

Then he gently took Edna's hand and together they, along with Sadie, strolled down Nitchequon's main street to Edna's Boarding House.

Hap slept well. The fear and apprehension he felt ever since he killed Luke Stillwell had drained away. And the worry concerning the interview with CCN had likewise dissolved. Dinner had been a gourmet masterpiece, as always, and the after dinner conversations with the rest of Edna's guests were superbly stimulating. Harry Timmermann was a bit stuffy, but the remainder of the TV crew were very friendly people. Hap noted that once Jacqueline was free of her TV makeup, she did look a bit older than he had earlier estimated. But still, she was a strikingly beautiful woman. In fact, Hap had not seen such a good looker since the time when he was in high school and one of his classmates brought a copy of "Playthings" to school.

Edna had breakfast ready promptly at seven o'clock. Bill and Hap once again ate with the CCN crew, who finished their breakfast quickly. They had a schedule to keep and Harry was anxious to return to Quebec with the tape containing Hap's interview. The taped interview would need to be edited prior to it's showing on TV.

Jacqueline took time between sips of her coffee to inform Hap as to what was going to be done with the taped interview..

"Mr. Larson, it's really too bad you folks don't have television reception here in Nitchequon. But that's understandable seeing your community does not have electrical power. Your story that we recorded is scheduled to be aired as an hour long special in about a week. All twelve of the CCN affiliate TV stations all across Canada will be broadcasting the program. There will of course be many Americans who live close to the border that will also be able to view the telecast. Besides that, I have no idea how many potential viewers are connected to cable or a dish provider. Your face and your story will be quite familiar to many millions of people. You should be proud."

Hap fiddled with his coffee cup, still in a daze about all the changes that had taken place in his life in such a short period of time. Looking up at Jacqueline and the other members of the CCN crew, he replied, "I jist can't believe all of this is really happenin'. I mean, whoda thought an old codger like me would ever have all this stuff happenin' to 'um? I sure thank all of ya nice folks who took the time and cared enough ta listen ta an old geezer who lives in the woods blab about his life. I never figgered anybody'd give a hoot. Thanks again!"

"We'll send you a copy of the tape in care of Edna's here in Nitchequon. Maybe somebody has a generator and a VCR. You'd enjoy watching yourself.", added Harry. With that, the crew excused themselves from the table, gathered up their suitcases, and headed for the Piper that would fly them back to civilization.

Edna, Bill, Sadie and Hap walked to the docking area to see the film crew off. Their equipment was already on board, having been loaded a short time after the interview had been completed. A dozen or more citizens of the village were also on hand to watch their departure. Planes coming and going to and from Nitchequon was not unusual, but a plane carrying a group of people who were going to put Nitchequon on the map was unusual.

As the Piper taxied down the river into the wind, everyone waved their good-byes. Within seconds, the plane was airborne and banking towards the south, heading for Quebec with it's valuable cargo.

"Well," offered Hap, not thinking of anything profound to say, "there they go. I guess now maybe things'll quiet down around here and life'll return ta normal."

The group of well wishers began walking toward Edna's, when the sound of a plane coming in for a landing drew their attention back towards the docking area. A blue and yellow Caribou, of nineteen fifties vintage, bounced down on the waters of the Grande Riviere and taxied to Nitchequon's docking area. Faded red letters informed the onlookers the plane was offered for charter by "Wilderness Flight Service, Charters to anywhere. Gagnon, Quebec".

"Maybe we got some more news people pokin' around fer an interview.", surmised Hap, a grin on his face. "Well, if it tis, they took a long trip fer nothin'."

The pilot, who looked to be about eighteen years old, opened the cockpit door, and nimbly jumped to the dock. He quickly secured the plane to the dock with a stout rope, and opened the passenger door. Two individuals stepped out of the plane unto the dock. The young pilot jumped back into the plane, and removed two suitcases, a large green canvas duffle bag, and a cylinder shaped carrying case about six feet in length. The pilot then jumped from the plane to the dock and conversed with his passengers for a few seconds. The older man, who appeared to be about Hap's age, handed the pilot a wad of bills. The three shook hands, and the pilot quickly untied his plane, jumped back into the cockpit and started the motor. Within seconds the ancient Caribou was skimming over the water's surface and was once again airborne.

The older man and his partner, who looked to be in his mid thirties, spoke to each other briefly and then picked up their luggage and walked towards Bill, Edna and Hap. The older gentleman stopped a few feet from where the trio stood and asked, "By any chance, do any of you know a man by the name of Hap Larson?"

Part Six: "The Reunion"

Hap's eyes jerked wide open in surprise at the sound of the man's voice. It was a voice that Hap had not heard for over a quarter century. It was a voice from the past, a voice that he thought he would never again hear. Hap answered the man's question.

"What's the matter, Charlie, don't ya know yer old trappin' partner when yer lookin' right at 'um?"

Charles looked at Hap, his eyes attempting to recognize the face from which the familiar voice had come. He dropped his suitcase and in two long strides seized Hap in a firm bear hug. Hap hugged him in return, as the two long lost cousins were once again reunited.

Stepping back, the two looked at each other, as though each was waiting for the other to say something. Hap found his voice first.

"Charlie Baldwin! If you ain't a sight fer sore eyes! What in the world are ya doin' back here? And how'd ya know I might be around here someplace?"

"Hap, Hap, Hap! God it's good to see you again! Up until a few days ago, I wasn't even sure if you were still alive! I haven't heard from you in over ten, no, maybe fifteen years! The reason I didn't recognize you is because of all those whiskers on your face. But your voice is still the same! I'd never forget that voice.", replied an excited Charles.

"Yer voice gave ya away right off.", countered Hap. "I'd probably figgered out who ya was by yer face too, once I got a good look at it. Ya don't look so bad fer an old fart. Father Time ain't treated ya too bad, by the looks a things."

The second new comer finally found a pause in the conversation, and was able to speak. "Dad, are you going to introduce me to your cousin, or do I have to do it myself?"

"Oh excuse me," apologized Charles, "I was so surprised to find Hap so quickly....., Hap, this is my oldest boy, Jason. He's heard so much about you and couldn't pass up the opportunity to come with me and try to hunt you up. That is, once we found out you were still alive and kicking."

Hap and Jason warmly shook hands. "I'm so glad to meet you, Mr. Larson. Or can I call you Hap?" I never thought I'd meet a genuine celebrity, especially one who is a member of our family. This is exciting!", grinned Jason.

"Jist call me Hap. And I don't know about all that celebrity stuff. I sure don't feel like no big shot. Don't look like one neither." Hap chuckled as he said it. "How'd ya find me? How'd ya know I was still in these parts?"

Charles picked up his suitcase. "Hap, there's so much I need to tell you. So much has happened that you probably don't even know about. Is there someplace we can talk? Maybe a motel or something. Or is that old boarding house still in business? Jason and I need a place to stay. We'll get settled and then you and I have a lot of catching up to do!"

"Boy, have I got a deal fer you two!", Hap answered. "This here good lookin' woman is Edna. Edna Sullivan. She owns and runs the old boarding house, and jist happens to have a couple of rooms to rent. Her cookin' ain't the greatest, but it'll stick ta yer ribs."

Edna gave Hap a good natured punch in the arm and then shook hands with Charles and Jason. Then she finished off the introductions.

"This gentleman here is Sergeant Bill Osborne of the Royal Canadian Mounted Police. But you probably already guessed his occupation by looking at what he's wearing." More hand shakes took place. Edna continued. "Why doesn't everyone follow me. I'll get you two settled into a nice clean, comfortable room and then feed you some of my not so great food that your cousin here seems to consume in great quantities at regular intervals." Edna gave Hap another playful punch in the ribs and lead the group up the street to her boarding house.

By eight o'clock, Charles and Jason were registered at Edna's. Having taken their suitcases to their room and freshening up a bit, they seated themselves at a table in the dining room and poured a hot cup of fresh coffee. Edna was in the kitchen preparing their breakfast order. Bill had stopped off at the General Store to stock up on some necessary supplies. He would be heading out on his patrol route in a day or two, and wished to give Jacque time to get his order organized. Hap, having already eaten his breakfast, poured a cup of coffee and joined Charles and Jason at their table. He figured there was no time like the present to begin finding out what Charles and his son had come to tell him.

It took nearly twenty minutes for Charles to bring Hap up to date on what had happened in his life since the two had parted company in 1956. Hap did know that Charles had married his high school sweetheart, a perky Italian brunette named Shirley Lotti. He also knew that the couple had produced two children, both boys. Jason, who was now enjoying a plate of pancakes smothered in warm maple syrup, and a younger brother named Bret. Hap was also aware that Charles and his wife had purchased a hardware store and evidently had done well financially. The two cousins did write a few letters to each other up until the early 70's, and then for reasons not known to either, they simply stopped communicating.

Hap listened while Charles told him the single hardware store he had purchased in Sept Iles had expanded into a small chain of eight stores! The business had made him a lot of money. And only last year Charles and Shirley turned the business over to their two sons, and retired.

Then a week ago, the Sept Iles Daily Independent had run a syndicated story about an old trapper who had single handedly ended a violent crime spree, by killing one of the perpetrators and capturing the other. And in doing so, he saved the life of a Mountie the two criminals were holding captive and mistreating. When Charles finished reading the story, he knew that his cousin was still alive and still living in the same old cabin their grandfather had built. Jason arranged for a bush pilot to fly them to Nitchequon, and here they were, reunited once more!

Hap had a lot less to tell about his life, as the story never changed much from year to year. By the time five minutes elapsed, Hap brought Charles and Jason up to date. Of course, Hap Larson was a man of few words and he was prone to leaving out all but the most major details.

Edna cleared the table of the dirty, but empty, breakfast dishes and poured everyone a fresh cup of coffee. Charles slowly stirred a tad of cream into his cup, and starred vacantly at the brew, as though deep in thought. After a few seconds he looked up at Hap, and stated, "Hap, the rest of the news I must tell you is not good news." And just by the tone of his voice, Hap knew what Charles was probably going to tell him.

Part Seven: "A Change in Plans"

"When was the last time you visited your parents back in Newberry?", Charles asked.

"Too long ago, I suspect.", replied Hap. "They're dead ain't they?"

"Yes, Hap. Your dad, Ole, died four years ago. He had a massive heart attack and was dead before they got him to the hospital. After that, your mom Martha, just gave up wanting to live. She died about a year and a half later. You didn't even know about it, did you Hap?"

Hap starred at his feet and shook his head, "no".

Charles spoke again. "Both my folks are gone too. Your Uncle Ed passed away nearly six years ago, and my mom, your Aunt Bertha, was buried just last fall. At least our parents all lived to a ripe old age, and were blessed with good health almost all their lives."

Hap looked up, two small tears had streaked his ruddy cheeks. "Don't know why I quit visitin' my folks. Used to go home at least once in a blue moon. Guess I jist got old and lazy. Never did care to write neither. But you already know that, Charles. I don't know what else to say,....except ta thank ya fer takin' the time ta come and tell me."

Edna had walked to where Hap was seated and had begun gently stroking his head. He looked up at her and said, "Bet ya thought a tough old buzzard like me couldn't shed a tear." Edna just smiled and kissed his cheek.

Charles took a long sip of coffee, and continued. "Being an only child, Hap, you of course were willed all your parent's property, both the land and their personal property. Also, they had a small nest egg in the bank, and that goes to you too. The State of Michigan won't wait forever for an heir to show up, so I'd suggest you take time and return to Newberry and get all the paper work straightened out. Whatever you want to do with the property is up to you. I paid the back taxes on the place, so you don't owe the government any real estate tax. You can pay me back whenever it's convenient."

Hap looked stunned. This turn of events had thrown him a real curve ball. His mind shifted into overdrive as he sought to re-arrange his plans. After nearly a minute of awkward silence, Hap lifted his eyes and looked at everyone around the table. "Guess I ain't got no choice. I gotta go. But all this sure puts a crimp in my plans."

Hap explained his dilemma to Charles and Jason. He informed them about purchasing five new pups to replace his team that had drown in the river over two months earlier. He needed to return to his cabin with the pups and begin training them as soon as possible. Even though his new dogs wouldn't be fully developed nor able to run a long trap line, he could at least do some trapping during the coming winter season. Charles listened intently as Hap poured out his frustration and then supplied a partial solution to his problem.

"Hap, I think Jason and I can help you solve your problem. You see, we didn't come here JUST to see you. We didn't even know if we'd find you. So our plan was to rent a canoe and journey upstream to your cabin, and surprise you. We brought along our fishing equipment and planned to do some fishing along the way and after we got to your cabin. Otter Creek is still full of trout I hope." Hap nodded, "yes". Charles continued. "So here's my idea. You head on out to Newberry and take care of the business you need to take care of. Jason and I will pick up your pups, buy some supplies, and head to the cabin. When you get back from Michigan, we'll already have started training the dogs. I was a trapper once upon a time, if you remember, and I do know how to train sled dogs. What do you think Hap. Is that a plan or what?"

Hap blinked his eyes several times, and then a wide smile spread across his face. "Danged if it ain't a good idea. Wished I'd thought it up myself. I guess things are gonna work out o.k. after all. Well, time's a wastin', I got a lotta stuff ta do before I leave fer Newberry, and there's no time like the present ta git started."

Hap's first order of business was to visit Jacque. All of the merchandise that Jacque sold in the General Store came to Nitchequon by plane. Hap needed to know when the next flight would arrive so he could make arrangements to fly out. The freight hauling airline, which flew out of Montreal, also carried passengers if there was space available, and generally little or nothing was shipped out of Nitchequon. Jacque informed Hap the twin engine float plane would be delivering an order day after tomorrow. From Montreal, Hap could catch a commuter flight to Sault Ste Marie, Michigan. Once there he could either hire a cab or catch a bus to Newberry. His first problem was solved.

Next he walked to the Johnson's and informed Clarence and Waneta that his cousin, Charles, would be picking up the pups in a day or two. Hap sent an hour filling his friends in on the news that Charles had delivered, and his revised plan of action.

It was early afternoon when Hap returned to his room at Edna's. He began organizing what he would be packing for his trip to Newberry. There was a tap on his door.

Expecting a visit from Charles and Jason, Hap was surprised to see Edna. "May I come in Hap?", Edna asked. Hap nodded and stepped back to allow Edna to enter. As she walked through the door she added, "We have to talk!"

Part Eight: "Newberry"

Edna took a seat on the edge of the bed, folded her hands on her lap and looked at Hap, a tiny smile curled the corners of her lips. Hap stood by the door, a puzzled look on his face, wondering what in the world it was Edna needed to talk to him about. After all, she could have spoken to him at breakfast or down by the river when they saw the CCN crew off. Edna began.

"Hap, I know you're going to think I'm crazy, but,.......well,........ I want to go with you when you leave for Michigan!" Hap's jaw dropped open in surprise. Edna continued. "Don't say no Hap! Please! It's been,.... oh such a long time since I've gone anywhere. I'd love to go with you and see where you grew up. You've told me all about Newberry, and how pretty the country is. Besides, you could use some company on a trip like this. I can help you get through the rough spots. And,.... and,......I already talked to Betty Synstad and Alice Hamilton. They'll take care of my boarding house till we get back! Please! I'll pay my own way!"

Hap walked to the bed and sat down beside Edna. He took her hand in his, and looking into those snapping blue eyes, said, "Can't do that Edna. No way!"

Edna lowered her eyes and pulled her hand away from Hap's.

"No way I'll let you pay yer own way! Guess I better git back over to Jacque's and tell him to save two seats on that plane."

Edna's face lit up like a Christmas Tree. "Oh Hap, I'm so happy! I can't wait to get going!" And with that she grabbed Hap and gave him a warm tender kiss, causing both of them to topple over backwards on the bed. Hap looked at her and said, "Might as well haul ya along. All I'd do is think about ya the whole dang time I was gone."

Edna giggled, gave Hap another short kiss and headed for the door of Hap's room. Framed in the doorway, she turned and lovingly looked at him, one hand on her hip. "I better start packing. Takes us women a long time to pack. Oh, and one more thing. I love you!"

The plane from Montreal arrived in Nitchequon mid morning the following day. It was only an hour late. Hap, Edna and their baggage were waiting. Charles, Jason, Pete, Jacque, Bill, Sadie and a dozen or so others had likewise assembled to see the pair off. Several had some parting words.

From Bill came, "Now don't you two run off and get married!"

Jacque took the cue. "Hope the motel in Montreal has adjoining rooms!"

Pete was more gentle. "Never mind these smart asses, just have a safe trip and enjoy civilization. See you both in about a week."

Hap and Edna both blushed like two teen aged lovers on a first date. Neither had suspected that the growing affection they had been showing towards each other had been so noticeable to their friends. The only thing Hap could think of to say was a "good-bye" to Sadie, who had been placed in Jacque's capable care. With hand shakes all around, the couple climbed aboard the twin engine Cessna, and waved to their friends as the plane taxied away from the dock. By two thirty they were in Montreal.

Jacque had used his radio phone to call ahead for reservations at the Best Western, which was near the Montreal airport. On Hap's and Edna's orders, he reserved but one room. Unknown to Hap and Edna, Jacque had reserved a room with a hot tub. Of course, Jacque knew Hap would have no idea what a hot tub was, and smiled inwardly as he envisioned Hap's reaction when Edna told him what it could be used for. Jacque also requested a chilled bottle of champagne be waiting for the two senior love birds when they arrived in their room.

Hap and Edna checked into the motel shortly after three, only to find their room was not quite ready. Feeling rather hungry, they ordered a light lunch in the hotel restaurant and then took the elevator to their third floor room.

For Hap, it had been over twenty years since he had stayed in a motel. And nearly double that amount of time since he had stayed overnight with someone of the opposite sex. Nearly the same could be said for Edna.

Once they set down their suitcases, and checked out the accommodations, both once again assumed the role of teenagers on a first date.

"Ah, what the heck is this?", asked Hap, pointing at the large hot tub in one corner of their room. "Looks like a big bath tub. Why da we need two.? There's a tub and shower in the bathroom!"

Edna explained what a "hot tub" was, and glossed over it's various applications and special uses. Hap blushed a bit and exclaimed, "Well, I'll be damned, What'll they think a next?"

After the two had taken showers individually, they relaxed and turned on the TV. As afternoon melted into early evening, Edna and Hap slowly allowed nature to take it's course. They watched TV, exchanging small talk, plus mixed in some tender kissing and caressing, which eventually resulted in their rediscovery how wonderful it was making love to someone special. Special to each other. During their moments of pure ecstasy, even the word "love" was whispered. Hap was introduced to the hot tub, and marveled at it's therapeutic value,..... to both body and soul. The champagne was consumed slowly, and supper was ignored. Early evening gave way to night. And all it's splendor!

It was nearing midnight, their energies finally exhausted, before the two lovers fell asleep.

Cuddled together, both slept with smiles of satisfaction plastered on their faces.

By two thirty pm the following day, a DC 9 carrying Hap and Edna touched down on the runway at Sault Ste. Marie International, right on schedule. Upon inquiry, Hap and Edna were informed a bus was not scheduled to make a westward run down highway 28 until the next day, so they opted to rent a cab for the 65 mile trip to Newberry. By four forty five they were checking into "Sportsman's Bar, Supper Club and Motel". Hap was back in his hometown.

After dining in the motel's supper club, Hap took Edna on a walking tour of Newberry. Pleasant memories from his youth were shared with Edna as her tour guide pointed out various landmarks of interest and places Hap had spent time while growing up. They walked at a leisurely pace for over an hour, hand in hand, enjoying a perfect spring evening. Even the normal hoards of mosquitoes kept their distance. Edna seemed as excited about the tour as though she might have been visiting Paris for the first time.

Before retiring to their motel room, the couple stopped off in the bar for several small glasses of wine. Hap kept glancing around, expecting to see someone he knew, and was relieved he was unable to do so. He had had enough excitement for quite a while, and was completely content with the quiet time he and Edna were sharing together. God, he was a happy man!

The second night together was even more romantic than the first. The wine had relaxed the two new lovers, making their acts of love even more pleasurable. Edna made one minor complaint, as she giggled girlishly, "Hap honey, I wish we'd rented a room where the bed doesn't squeak". Hap hadn't noticed.

Promptly the next morning, shortly after the First National Bank of Newberry opened for business, Hap and Edna were seated in the office of the bank's president, Gino Vernetti. His father, Alfonse, had been the president of First National when Hap was a youngster, and of course Gino knew Hap's parents very well. Quite typical of small town banking.

The bank officials had received notification from Mr. & Mrs. Larson's attorney and the probate judge that the Larson's son, Hap, was the sole beneficiary. Therefore, he was entitled to the entire amount in his parent's accounts, plus their home, land and personal property. The paper work had been finalized some time ago, and all that was required of Hap was to sign the legal documents.

A final accounting of the Larson's savings, checking and CD accounts came to a grand total of a bit over twenty seven thousand dollars. Hap placed twenty five thousand in a CD and took the balance in cash and travelers checks.

Before leaving the bank, Hap asked Mr. Vernetti if there might be someone he and Edna could hire to drive them to his parent's home. A quick phone call produced a willing volunteer. Joe Hilgala arrived at the bank ten minutes later, driving an old rusty Ford pickup. He appeared to be in his early twenties, and worked for the bank as a part time janitor and all around handy man. After a short session of introductions, Hap and Edna piled into the cramped interior of the old truck for a twenty minute drive to the Larson homestead.

Mother Nature provided Hap and Edna with another beautiful spring morning. Robins were visible in nearly every yard, scratching for worms. The air, fresh from Lake Superior on a gentle northwest wind, was laced with the smells of dandelions, cherry blossoms and moist earth. A few puffy cumulous clouds floated slowly southward, outlined against a royal blue sky. Two bald eagles soared high overhead, riding the air currents with their long, powerful wings. And the dirt road was devoid of traffic.

Hap took time to fill their driver in on the general details of why he and Edna were in Newberry. Joe, of course, had known Hap's parents and also knew that they had a son who hadn't been around Newberry to visit in quite some time. When asked what he intended to do with his parent's house, Hap replied, "Ain't had time to figger that one out yet."

The Larson's owned eighty acres of mostly forested land that straddled the upper region of the Tahquamenon River. Their home sat upon the crest of a small hill that overlooked the pristine waterway just a few hundred yards downstream from where Sixteen Creek deposited its water into the larger river. The house faced east, and had a commanding view of the river valley. There were no neighbors for several miles in any direction.

Edna was awestruck by the magnificent setting. "Oh Hap, it's even more beautiful than I imagined! It's like looking at a painting! I can see why you have such fond memories of growing up here."

Joe settled down in a lawn chair that sat on the porch which overlooked the river, while Hap and Edna walked down the path that lead to a small pier. An old rowboat rested upside down on two saw horses next to a tiny storage shed which housed a pair of oars, an old Johnson motor, anchor and several fishing rods. Joe watched the couple as Hap pointed this way and that, obviously relating some sort of information to his companion.

In a few minutes the couple returned to the house. Hap unlocked the front door with a key Mr. Vernetti had given him and gave Edna and Joe a tour of his former home. Made of logs, the building was typical of many such homesteads which were built in the 1920's and 30's. Vertical white cedar logs formed the exterior walls, which were set on a foundation made of cement and stone. A small basement had been dug under half of the house that served mainly as a root cellar for storing canned goods, vegetables, and smoked meats. From the front door, a short hallway ran between two bedrooms. The hallway lead to a large room overlooking the river, that served as a combination kitchen, dining and living room. A bathroom had been added just off the kitchen. A large split stone fireplace graced one wall of the living room, and in one corner a spiral staircase lead to a small loft area, which had been converted to another small bedroom. Looking at the river valley from the large picture window in the living room, all Edna could say was, "Oh Hap, I've never seen such a beautiful place. I'd just love to live here!"

Hap smiled, and replied, "Forgot how dang nice it really is myself."

Next Hap unlocked the garage door. The single stall held a 1957 Chevrolet Nomad Station Wagon in nearly mint condition. The tires were almost flat, but an inspection of the odometer indicated the vehicle only had forty eight thousand miles on it. Hap's parents had never strayed far from Newberry.

Returning to the old pickup, the trio headed back towards Newberry. Hap asked Joe if he could drop he and Edna off at the County Court House. Within twenty minutes Hap and Edna were on the sidewalk in front of the court house, shaking hands with their chauffer and thanking him for the transportation. Hap left a folded up fifty dollar bill in Joe's palm.

The Registrar of Deeds Office was on the first floor, just across the hall from the County Clerk's office. Hap went through the process of proving who he was, and then changing the deed of ownership to the property on the river from his deceased parents to himself. Now all Hap had to do was decide what he wanted to do with the land and the home.

After dining on a meal of broiled shrimp with all the trimmings, plus a glass of after dinner wine, Hap and Edna once again retired to their motel room for what would be their final night in Michigan. Having completed all necessary tasks, Hap's business in Newberry was done. Tomorrow a taxi would be returning them to Sault Ste. Marie for a flight to Montreal. And by day after tomorrow, they would once again be back in Nitchequon.

The hands of the clock were nearly nudging seven when Edna turned on the TV set. Flipping through the channels she suddenly stopped and looked at an announcement about a special program to be aired in a few minutes. The station was WSUD, a CCN affiliate broadcasting out of Sudbury, Ontario. A pretty blond woman, named Jacqueline Bower was making an announcement. This station, along with another dozen CNN Network stations would be airing an hour long special. The documentation would feature the life story of an old trapper named Hap Larson, who lived in the Quebec wilderness. The hour special was entitled, "LAST OF A DYING BREED".

For the next hour, Hap, Edna and somewhere around fourteen million other viewers watched and listened to an old woodsman tell of a lifestyle hardly imagined by most. A lifestyle that in the minds of most viewers had ended decades ago.

One of those millions of viewers was a college professor of Canadian History and Culture who taught at the University of Quebec. Within minutes after the conclusion of the broadcast, Professor Pierre LeBlanc picked up his phone and excitedly made a phone call. A phone call that would alter the course of Hap's life one more time!

(Chapter Four)

The World Turned Upside Down

Part One: "The Meeting"

By the time the plane carrying Hap and Edna back to Nitchequon had landed, the meeting that was initiated as a result of Professor LeBlanc's hurried phone call, had already taken place.

Besides teaching a course in "Canadian History", and "Cultures and Lifestyles of Quebec" at the university, Professor LeBlanc was serving as president of an organization known as "The Society to Preserve Quebec's Culture and Heritage".

Foremost on the Society's current agenda was financing and planning the development of a Historical and Cultural Park, which would house original, or replicas, of buildings and objects depicting historical and cultural events connected to Quebec's past. Several large grants had already been secured from various governmental departments, plus Professor LeBlanc and the Society's Board of Directors were successful in obtaining substantial financial backing from nearly a dozen corporations.

One important era, pertaining to Quebec's early history, was the role played by trappers and the trapping industry. Very little serious trapping took place anymore, and the Society was having a great deal of difficulty obtaining first hand information or any authentic "hands on" materials for inclusion in it's Historical and Cultural Park. While viewing CCN's documentary, "LAST OF A DYING BREED", Professor LeBlanc realized he had located an individual who might be the answer to the Society's dilemma.

The meeting had taken place in a conference room at the University of Quebec. Besides the Board of Directors representing the Society, the President of the University and several key individuals connected with major corporations backing the Historical Park were also present. Only three of the eleven persons present at the meeting had viewed the CCN interview with Hap Larson, so Professor LeBlanc secured a copy of the tape from WQEB.

The first order of business for the assembled representatives was to view the tape. The program easily sold everyone on the Professor's belief that someone who might assist the project fill in some of the gaps for the trapping display, had been identified. The next step was to send someone to find Mr. Larson, and seek his assistance.

By unanimous vote, it was decided that Professor LeBlanc would be the logical person to meet and talk with the old trapper. Plans were laid to send the Professor and a small support staff to Nitchequon as soon as the University's spring semester ended in early June, which now was only a little over a week away. It sounded like a simple plan to complete.

Part Two: "Dilemmas"

The day following Hap and Edna's arrival back in Nitchequon was spent getting Hap ready to return to his cabin for the summer. It was also a day of mixed emotions for both. Hap tried to conger up some valid excuse for staying in the village a bit longer. And he knew why. But he also knew there was much to do back at his cabin to prepare for another long sub-arctic winter.

For the past thirty years Hap had always looked forward to the winter trapping season with a great deal of anticipation. However, now that something besides trapping had entered his life, the feeling of anticipation was sadly lacking. And the more he thought about being away from Edna for months on end, the greater became his frustration. But he had to leave. He had no other choice.

Hap's departure from Nitchequon on June 2nd could best be described as "gut wrenching".

Edna was unable to hold back her tears and it took all of Hap's will power to keep from doing the same. Besides the deep gloomy feeling of depression in Hap's belly, a dark, dreary day, complete with periods of cold rain, made his departure even more difficult.

Besides Edna, only Jacque ventured to the river bank to see Hap and Sadie depart. Hap pulled himself away from a sobbing Edna, kissed her tear stained cheek, and shoved off. He turned and looked back briefly and saw Edna blow him one last kiss. Hap quickly turned his back and began to paddle with all his might. He didn't want Edna and Jacque see his own tears that were streaming down his face.

Hap's journey back to his cabin was one of pure misery. The weather remained cold and windy, with intermittent showers. The second night on the portage trail, between the Caribou and Wolf River, it even sleeted and snowed! Typical spring weather in the far north. Before leaving his campsite, Hap gathered up the supplies that had been left behind after the incident with Luke and George. Reliving the memory of the shoot out, as he spent a cold night in his small tent, only caused a deepening of his already sagging spirits.

Hap and Sadie arrived at their destination about noon on June 5th. Charles and Jason were happy to see their relative arrive safe and sound. At about the same time Hap was pulling his canoe ashore, a plane carrying four representatives from The Society to Preserve Quebec's History and Culture were stepping out of a plane onto the dock in Nitchequon.

"You mean to tell me he's no longer here?", asked Professor LeBlanc.

"You're four days too late.", answered Jacque. "He's probably already at his cabin, or at least getting dang close.

"How far away is this cabin of his, by air I mean?", inquired the Professor.

"Well, as the crow flies, I'd say forty, maybe forty five kilometers. But there really isn't any place to land a float plane on Otter Creek. It's too narrow. There is a lake about five kilometers upstream with some long Indian name. Hap calls it Misty Lake. He says it's not very big. It's the headwaters of Otter Creek. May not even be big enough to set a float plane down on it. And even if you could, you'd have to carry a canoe tied to the pontoons and paddle from the lake downstream to the cabin, and then back to the plane again. I think Hap said there were a couple of bad rapids between his cabin and the lake.", replied Jacque.

"How then do you suggest we might reach Mr. Larson? It's very important that we see him.", continued the Professor.

Pierre told Jacque about the Society's Historical and Cultural Park project. And how after viewing the CCN program, he and his committee decided Hap Larson was the person who could be of great assistance in solving at least part of their dilemma. The store owner listened intently.

Jacque thought for a few moment after Professor LeBlanc had finished his explanation, and then gave the committee his suggestions. "No doubt in my mind that Hap Larson is the man you're looking for. Nobody that I know of knows as much about trapping as he does. And his skills of living and surviving in the wilderness are legendary in these parts. Now, there are several ways you can accomplish your mission. One, I can find a guide who can take you to Hap's cabin by canoe. However, if all of you intend to go there, you'll need several canoes. It's a tough trip. Ninety five percent all upstream, with three long portages tossed in to go with the paddling. That trip will take a minimum of four days, if all of you are strong paddlers. Two, if somehow you could get a helicopter to fly you to Hap's cabin, I think there is enough open space between the creek and his cabin to land a chopper. Three, you can come back in September when he makes his final trip to our village for his winter supplies. I could give you a call on my radio phone when he arrives."

The four members of the committee fell silent and just looked at one another for a few seconds. The Professor spoke. "Suggestions one and three are definitely out of the question. I haven't ridden in a canoe since I was a teenager. I doubt if I could paddle a canoe for an hour without having a heart attack . And I also doubt that my three colleagues here are in any better shape than I am." Three heads nodded in agreement. "And we can't wait till September, as we hope to get our project started as soon as possible. We must take advantage of the summer weather to begin construction of the Historical and Cultural Park. So it appears your second suggestion is our best bet. We'll call our friends at Canadian Petroleum and have them send up one of their Bell Jet Rangers."

Jacque had one more additional suggestion. "Before you do that, I'd suggest you have your pilot fly to Hap's cabin to see for sure if you'll have enough space for a chopper to set down. I've got a quadrangle map of the area and I can show you exactly where the cabin is located."

"Professor LeBlanc nodded in agreement, and turning to his committee members said, "Let's do it. We've got plenty of daylight left."

Charles and Jason were showing Hap how well his five growing pups were taking to their sled pulling lessons. One by one, the young dogs gave a short demonstration by pulling a four foot log around the cabin. Hap was impressed. Dog number four had just completed its circuit when the sound of a low flying plane caused everyone to look skyward. A single engine Otter came into view, following the course of Otter Creek at tree top level. It passed Hap's cabin, banked sharply and circled the cabin several more times before retracing it's route back down the course of the creek.

The three bewildered spectators on the ground looked at each other as if waiting for someone to offer an answer as why a plane was checking out Hap's cabin.

Hap shrugged and said, "Probably a bunch a fishermen lookin' fer a place to set down and fish. Ain't anywhere near here they gonna be able ta do that. That's what I like about this spot. Lot's of peace and quiet."

Part Three: "Visitors"

A week passed since the Otter had paid a visit to Hap's domain. The incident was all but forgotten. Hap immersed himself with chores and training his new team from daylight to dawn. Keeping busy helped to keep his mind from constantly thinking about Edna. And his future.

There were several minor leaks in the roof that needed attention. Sphagnum moss was gathered from the forest for fresh chinking, which was inserted between the cracks of the ancient black spruce logs that formed the walls of Hap's cabin. There was lots of wood to be cut, split, and piled to dry for heating and cooking during the long eight months of snow, cold and ice. Having Charles and Jason as his guests and helpers made Hap's days somewhat more pleasant. It was after the kerosene light was extinguished, and Hap lay in his bunk that the thinking took place. And there was much to think about. Sound sleep became harder and harder to find.

"You know Hap, Jason and I came here to visit and do some fishing. I forgot how much work there is to do when everything has to be done by hand." Charles took the last bite of his breakfast pancake, pushed back his plate and sipped a tad of hot tea."

"Ya, you two have been workin' up a sweat all right. And I appreciate yer help. When ya git ta my age, stuff don't git done as fast as it did years back." Hap chuckled at his own remark.

"This is the greatest adventure I've ever encountered", interjected Jason. "I'm having a ball. I can't thank dad enough for allowing me to come here and experience living in the boonies. I'll remember this trip for the rest of my life!"

"And I'm dang glad ya came. But you two have helped me enough. Why don't ya pack up a canoe and

136

head up ta Misty Lake and camp out fer a few days. The brookies and lakers should be jumpin' in the boat this time a year. You remember that little island off the north shore, don't ya Charlie?" Charles smiled and nodded. Hap continued. "We got things pretty well shaped up around here, and I kin get by without the both of ya looking over my shoulder. Take a break and do some fishin'. Besides, a nice stringer of lakers would look dang nice hangin' in my smoke house out back. Ain't had any smoked laker since way last fall."

"You know Hap, I was thinking that very thing. Mentioned our old camping spot on Misty to Jason on our way to Nitchequon. It's one of the most beautiful places on this earth and the trout are so thick they have to take turns swimming." More chuckles from Hap and Jason.

An hour later Hap was waving good-bye, as his two helpers disappeared upstream, heading for a small island on a tiny lake in Quebec's pristine wilderness.

Professor LeBlanc was becoming more and more frustrated. His call to Quebec on Jacque's radio phone had been successful in gaining support from Canadian Petroleum for his plan on how best to contact Hap Larson. However, at the moment all the company's helicopters were presently on assignment. It would be at least a week before one could be freed to fly to Nitchequon. Plus another problem with the Professor's plan had surfaced. Pierre was unaware of the relatively short flying range of most choppers. He was informed that a support plane would need to accompany the Bell Jet Ranger to Nitchequon. Extra jet fuel for the helicopter would need to be flown in, along with a service mechanic. And all of this would take time to plan and accomplish. And valuable time was being wasted! All the Professor and his committee could do was sit in Nitchequon and wait. The only thing on the plus side was having clean, comfortable accommodations. And although the owner, a woman named Edna, seemed depressed and sullen, the food was excellent.

Charles and Jason were on their third day of fishing and enjoying the beauty and solitude of Misty Lake when Hap received a visitor. Sergeant Bill Osborne was passing through Hap's territory on his routine spring and summer tour. Since leaving Nitchequon nearly two weeks ago, the Sergeant had visited two more old trappers, like Hap, who still clung to a way of life that was rapidly ending. Some people suggested the ending of old fashioned life styles was "progress". Bill Osborne was one person who disagreed.

Hap was splitting and piling some firewood when Sadie's barking alerted him that someone or something was coming up river. Hap put down his splitting mall and removed the corncob pipe from his mouth. Hap recognized the canoe and it's occupant as soon as it came into view around the bend of the creek. Bill Osborne was early. He usually didn't show up until late June or early July. But it mattered not, Hap's old friend was more than welcome anytime.

Part Four: "Some Call It Progress"

Once ashore, Hap wasted no time in showing Bill his new trainees. The pups, now growing like weeds, were already starting to look like real dogs. They woofed and smelled Bill up and down, soon realizing that he was definitely an o.k. person. Next Hap showed off his growing wood pile and the new chinking job he and his two helpers had completed.

Hap invited his visitor to enter the cabin where Hap had a kettle of home made moose stew simmering on his small kitchen cook stove. Jabbering away as he did so, Hap filled his coffee pot with water and set it on the stove to heat. Lunch was still a half hour away.

The weather had returned to more normal conditions, and the day was mostly sunny and warm. The two old friends returned to the out of doors, sat down on a couple of rickety homemade log stools, and resumed their conversation.

Hap filled Bill in on his trip to Newberry, excluding his romantic interludes with Edna, and in general let Bill know about all that had happened to him since Bill had left the village of Nitchequon. Bill seemed to be deep in thought as he listened to Hap's story.

"Glad to hear your trip went so smoothly. Often in cases such as yours, some sort of unseen problem crops up.", began Bill. He paused and looked at the ground. Hap seemed to detect Bill looked troubled. Looking up at Hap once more, Bill continued.

"You've probably wondered why I'm here so early on my summer swing through the area. It's not even officially summer yet. I visited Henry Bodine and Larry Ramsdell at their trapping cabins over on Papoose Lake and the Cree River. I had some urgent news to deliver. Bill hesitated briefly and then continued once more.

"Hap,....... I'm bringing news that you aren't going to like hearing." Hap's body stiffened. He suspected Bill was going to tell him there was still some sort of problem concerned with the shooting death of Luke Stillwell. But what Bill was about to tell him was even worse!

"Shortly after you left Nitchequon, on your trip to Michigan, a plane that delivers mail and supplies to the village arrived. There was a packet of information for me from the RCMP Headquarters in Ottawa. They routinely send me information pertaining to orders, rule changes, new laws, etc. But there was information in this delivery that is upsetting to me, and it will be to you also. In fact, the news is beyond upsetting, it's downright disgusting."

"What the heck is it?", asked Hap, his voice mixed with fear and apprehension.

"A logging company has purchased the rights to log off a considerable portion of this very area where your cabin is located, and much of the land to the north, west and east." Bill paused.

Hap was stunned. His eyes met Bill's, and searched Bill's face, not believing what he had heard. Hap thought possibly Bill was joking. But the look on his friends face assured Hap that Bill was not joking.

"How,.....how,......how the blazes," Hap stuttered, "are the loggers gonna git here ta cut. How they gonna get the timber ta the mills. There ain't no road within a couple hundred kilometers a here!"

"Early last summer the Department of Transportation, with financial help from several large lumber and pulp wood corporations, began building a logging road west out of Fermont. I wasn't aware of that until I received my packet of information from headquarters a couple of weeks ago. As of right now, the road is nearly half finished, and if we have decent weather this summer and fall, well,...... you'll probably be able to hear the bulldozers by October. I'm so sorry Hap.", concluded Bill.

Hap knocked the ashes from his pipe and shook his head in disbelief. Slowly he lifted his head and looked at the forest that surrounded his cabin. The forest was his world. The creatures that inhabited it's woods and waters sustained him. The wilderness was his life. Now, that would all be taken away. The animals would be gone. The once gin clear creeks and rivers would become clouded with silt and mud. "Progress" was coming!

Part Five: "Proposals"

There was little sleep for Hap that night. And what little sleep he was able to get was wrought with distorted nightmares laced with bizarre visions of trees falling, fleeing animals and dying fish. And between the awful dreams he lay in his bunk and thought.

Hap dragged himself out of bed well before daybreak. Why lay in bed and torment yourself, he thought. "Might as well git up and make some coffee." As dawn began to inch its way towards becoming daylight, Hap fed his dogs and consumed several cups of strong, black coffee.

Back in his cabin, he sat slumped in a chair at his crude table, sipping coffee, scratching Sadie's head,......and thinking. Funny, he thought, thinking is always a much clearer process during daylight hours. Especially during very early morning.

For nearly an hour he sat. Alone with Sadie, and alone with his thoughts. Over and over he sifted his options and ideas through his thought process. Finally, convinced he had decided on a sensible course of action, he took out paper and pencil and jotted down some numbers.

Account balance in bank at Val d'Ore,	$ 82,000
Money coming for catching George and killing Luke ,	$ 71,250
CD at First National in Newberry	$ 25,000
Market value of land and house in Newberry	$150,000

Hap studied the numbers for several minutes, then neatly folded the paper and tucked it away in a small ledger. Looking at Sadie he told her, "I guess you and me ain't so poor after all."

Hap and his dogs were in front of the cabin dozing in the warm mid morning sun when Charles and Jason returned from their four day fishing trip on Misty Lake. Amidst barking dogs, the pair dragged their canoe ashore and began unloading gear. Hap rolled over on his side, propped his head up with one arm and asked, "Well where's my trout?"

Jason, grinning from ear to ear, hoisted a stringer out of the water. It was heavily laden with fish. "Is this enough for you Hap?"

Hap got to his feet and came to admire their beautiful catch. "Looks like a dozen ta me. Glad ta see ya stopped at yer limit. Let me git my fillet knife and I'll git these beauties cleaned while they're still fresh. We'll save a couple fer supper and I'll soak the rest in salt brine and smoke 'um tomorrow." Charles and Jason smiled in agreement.

As Hap filleted the lake trout, he told his two companions about Bill Osborne's visit and the terrible news he had brought. Like Hap, Charles and Jason were devastated by the realization that this pristine, virgin wilderness was scheduled to be slashed to the ground.

"Once the loggers get here..." Charles stopped in mid sentence as the roaring sound of a helicopter shattered the peace and quiet of the forest.

Hap's prediction that life in Nitchequon was going to return to normal, once all the excitement concerning his encounters with Luke and George had died down, did not come to pass.

Since Hap's departure from the village on June 2nd, there had been a nearly continuous parade of planes, boats, and even a helicopter coming and going from Nitchequon. More reporters had arrived looking for "The Last of a Dying Breed". Even though Hap Larson was the man they were looking for, the news hounds were content interviewing other citizens of the village in order to create a story for whatever type of media they represented.

There were also planes carrying site seers, real estate brokers, fishermen, and of course employees of Canadian Petroleum, plus staff persons from the University of Quebec. Edna's Boarding House was doing a land office business! Edna should have been ecstatic. But her loneliness and discontentment continued to grow.

Like Hap, Edna's nights were spent in fitful sleep, interspersed with much thought. And also like Hap, Edna gradually developed a course of action. The citizens of Nitchequon were surprised one morning to find a large sign in front of Edna's Boarding House. It simply read: "FOR SALE, by Owner".

The Bell Jet Ranger circled Hap's cabin, hesitated in mid air, and then landed gently in the open area between his cabin and Otter Creek. The dogs howled in terror and fled for the forest. The prop wash from the rotor blades made small, loose objects skitter across the ground. Some were blown into the side of his cabin, others into the trees or into the water. Dust, twigs and other assorted flying objects peppered the three bewildered onlookers.

Through squinted eyes, Hap and his two companions read the inscription of the chopper's side. "CANADIAN PETROLEUM, Inc." The doors opened and four well dressed men stepped cautiously onto the ground. One carried a large brief case. As the dust was settling, one of the men stepped forward with his hand extended, walked towards Hap and greeted cheerfully, "Good morning Mr. Larson, I'm Professor Pierre LeBlanc."

Blair Blakely arrived in Nitchequon on his private plane about the same time Professor LeBlanc and his committee were landing at Hap's cabin. He was not a total stranger to the area. Several years earlier, he had brought a prospective client to Nitchequon on a duck hunting trip. For several days and nights they had rented rooms at Edna's Boarding House.

Mr. Blakely owned a real estate company in Quebec that specialized in developing large parcels of land for recreational purposes. Having visited the area, the recent flurry of news covering the events surrounding the little village of Nitchequon had brought back memories of how wild and beautiful the area was. And the President of Blakely Enterprises had plans to make a lot of money on a enormous real estate deal near Nitchequon.

Blakely Enterprises had discovered there was a large tract of land for sale nearby and acted quickly. The company discretely purchased nearly a mile of shore line on Lac Nichicun, just a few miles from Nitchequon. It was the intent of Blakely Enterprises to construct a large, luxurious, fishing and hunting resort. The scope of the plan would be to offer on site fishing and hunting packages or more expensive "fly in" adventures to any number of remote lakes and streams. The sporting world was filled with individuals willing to pay big money to be pampered and coddled, but yet experience the so called rugged life.

What Blair Blakely now desired, was a place to house his architects and work force in order for his proposed resort project to get off the ground quickly. And later, when his resort was completely developed, property values in the village would soar. And any property he owned could be sold for a substantial profit. The "For Sale" sign in front of Edna's Boarding House caught his eye. The building and its location looked like it might be exactly what he was looking for!

As Hap numbly shook the Professor's hand, Pierre introduced his colleagues. "This is Mr. Wayne McDonald, Assistant Dean of Curriculum at the University of Quebec. Next to him is Mr. Myron Silverman, President of Canadian Petroleum's Community Relations Department, and over here is Mr. Conrad Davidson, Executive Director of The Society to Preserve Quebec's Culture and Heritage."

Hap blinked and looked blankly at each individual, as they lined up to shake his hand in greeting.

Charles, sensing that Hap was dazed and speechless, introduced himself and his son to the new group of visitors. Another round of handshakes took place.

Hap emerged from his bewildered state and finally thought of something to say. "Who are you guys and what ya doin' here?"

Pierre laughed politely and answered, "Mr. Larson, we have something to ask of you,......and it's all rather complicated and lengthy. Could we possible go inside and chat?"

Hap looked at Charles and Jason, glanced back at the Professor and said, "Ya, I guess so. Come on in, but I'll warn ya in advance, it ain't fancy!"

"Hello! I believe you're the owner of this establishment, aren't you?", began Blair Blakely as he entered Edna's Boarding House and spotted Edna sitting behind the front desk.

"Yes,", replied Edna, "I'm Edna Sullivan, what can I do for you?

"My name is Blair Blakely. A friend and I stayed here for several days a couple of years ago. Do you remember me?

"Well", began Edna, "So many people have stayed here over the years, it's hard to remember them all. No, I can't say I do remember you, but your face does seem somewhat familiar." Edna knew people liked to hear things like that, even if they weren't always true.

"My wife and I are thinking about moving out of the city and buying a little business that's away from all the hustle and bustle of urban life. I just happened to be in Nitchequon with a friend of mine, who has some minor business to attend to. I was walking around your quaint little village and saw your for sale sign. Thought I might as well come in and have a look around.", explained Mr. Blakely.

"Oh!", gasped Edna. "I put that sign out just yesterday morning. I certainly didn't expect anyone to show any interest in this place so soon. Come on in and I'll take you on a tour of the building."

"That would be so nice of you, Ms Sullivan. It appears that although the building is quite old, it's been taken care of very well."

Twenty minutes later the tour ended in the dining room. Edna poured two cups of coffee and produced a plate of chocolate chip cookies. She joined Mr. Blakely at a small table. The negotiations began.

"You certainly have a lovely little boarding house here, Ms Sullivan. It's very simple, but functional!", said a smiling Mr. Blakely.

"Oh thank you! This place has been my life for over fifteen years, ever since my husband passed away. I've taken very good care of it.", countered Edna.

"Could you tell me why you wish to sell your business?", asked a still smiling Mr. Blakely.

"Well, as you can see, I'm no spring chicken anymore, and.......well other things have come along in my life and I just feel I'm ready to change my life style. Business is still good. I've been able to make a comfortable living,......but,......I've just had enough. It's hard work you know. Cleaning, cooking, and fixing up things all the time. I just want out.", Edna finished with a sigh.

Blair Blakely had heard just what he wanted to hear. A widow who was anxious to get out. He smiled inwardly as he skillfully played his next card.

"Have you set a price for the property? Could you tell me what you're asking?", prompted Brian coyly.

"Oh dear", stammered Edna, "This is all happening so quickly. I really don't know. My husband and I bought the property way back in 1958. It was quite run down. We did put a lot of money into fixing it up. But, my,..... that was such a long time ago. I'm really not sure how much it's worth. I haven't really had time to think about a price."

"To be totally honest, Ms Sullivan, my wife and I have looked at several other small business opportunities in other small villages and I would need to bring her here to look at yours so she could make a comparison. You understand, I'm sure. My friend, who was good enough to let me ride along with him, will be leaving Nitchequon in less than an hour. But he will be returning in a couple of days. I'm sure he'll let Cheryl, that's my wife, and I fly back here with him when he returns.. That will give you some time to think and come up with a fair price. Then when my wife arrives, she can look your place over, and if she is interested in buying your business, we can talk about price, terms and etc. How does that sound to you?", asked a smooth talking Mr. Blakely.

"That would be just fine! I doubt if anyone else is going to pop in during the next few days looking to buy my place. I'll be looking forward to meeting your wife.", answered Edna.

The two shook hands and Mr. Blakely left smiling politely. Little did Edna know Mr. Blakely did not have a wife. She had divorced him five years earlier.

Professor LeBlanc and his committee members followed Hap into the dimly lit interior of the old trapping cabin. Once their eyes grew accustomed to the new light conditions, the Professor let out a soft whistle. "My, my, my!", he began. "I must say, this is wonderful! I never would have believed I'd ever see such a well preserved piece of history. Why,.......it's like stepping back in time about a hundred years! Isn't this a treasure?" The three committee members nodded in agreement.

Hap heard the words, "wonderful", "well preserved", "piece of history", "treasure". These guys must be joking or they've been a drinkin' jungle juice on the way here, thought Hap. How could they be making such a fuss over an old log shack with a dirt floor and a tin roof?

As the foursome poked around the interior of the old building, ooouuuing and aaahhhhing as though they were enjoying an eight course meal, Hap set a fresh pot of coffee on the stove.

After the self-guided tour of Hap's cabin had ended, the Professor got down to making his proposal.

"Mr. Larson, why don't you and I sit down here at your table so I can explain exactly why we are here and why we feel you can be of tremendous assistance in helping us solve a huge problem that has us quite perplexed.", began the Professor. "Conrad, could you hand me that brief case please?"

As the Professor opened the leather case and began sorting through a ream of papers, Hap attempted to be the perfect host. "I gotta apologize fer my lack a furniture and chairs, but generally it's jist me who lives here. Some of ya kin sit on my bunk over in the corner,......and,.....hey Jason, go outside and bring in them two old stools. That'd be better than makin' my guests stand. And cut out that Mr. Larson stuff. Ya kin jist call me Hap."

Jason and Charles quickly brought in Hap's yard furniture and everyone somehow found something on which to seat themselves. The Professor continued speaking.

"Mr. Larson. We represent an organization called The Society to Preserve Quebec's History and Culture." For the next twenty minutes the Professor explained the Society's plan to build a Historical and Cultural Park. Hap gazed at a set of blueprints that included areas that would house the replica of an old Viking settlement, French and English forts, various old and ancient sailing ships, a fur trading post as it may have been during the time of the Voyageurs, a typical trapper's cabin, displays honoring the Royal Canadian Mounted Police, and more. When the Professor concluded his explanation, Hap was still not quite sure where he, Hap Larson, fit into the scheme of things."

"Now I listened ta ya real close, but I still don't quite understand 'zactly what ya want from me." Hap began slowly. "Now if I heard ya right, ya want me ta help you guys build a cabin like this one of mine at that park of yers? And ya want ta take me, my dogs and my sled someplace and make a movie of me settin' out traps? And ya want ta take movies of me trappin' some critters and skinnin' 'um? And then yer gonna show them movies at yer new park and ta kids and put it on TV so people can see what we old time trappers did? And then yer gonna pay me big bucks fer doing all that stuff?"

"That's correct Mr. Larson. In fact, the figure I suggested we'd be willing to pay you for helping us get all of this accomplished is not set in stone. It is a negotiable amount.", responded the Professor rather quickly.

"Oh heck, it ain't the money that bothered me. I think that number ya threw at me was jist fine. Oh ya, jist fine and dandy! I jist couldn't figger out why ya'd pay so much fer me doing so little.", said a grinning Hap.

The Professor looked at his companions and shrugged, thinking possibly he should have quoted Hap's payment at a much lower number.

"Does this mean you'll do it? Do we have a deal?", asked a very excited Professor.

Hap sat starring out the small dust covered window, as if in deep thought. He sat silent for nearly a minute. The Professor, getting nervous, cleared his throat.

"Ah hem. Is something wrong Mr. Larson?"

"Naw, nothin's wrong. Jist doin' a little thinkin'." Hap paused again. "About me helpin' to build a cabin jist like this one." Another pause. "Too bad we jist can't move this one to that park of yers. Then ya'd have the real McCoy. But I suppose that ain't possible."

Part Six: "The Sale(s)"

The plane owned by Blakely Enterprises taxied to the dock in Nitchequon, two days after Mr. Blakely had first talked to Edna about the possible purchase of her boarding house. Besides the pilot, Mr. Blakely had brought along his personal secretary, Tiffany Torkelson. As the two exited the plane, Blair spoke briefly to his pilot.

"Ross, don't go too far from the plane. I don't think this is going to take very long. I need to get back to Quebec by this afternoon and meet with the architects. I really must get this project off the ground and running as soon as possible." Mr. Blakely then turned to Tiffany and said, "Now remember, your name is Cheryl. All you have to do is act somewhat interested in this building we're going to look at. But find as much fault with it as you can. And don't say anything stupid that'll get the old woman mad at us. Do you think you can handle this?"

Tiffany chewed her gum and tossed her bleached blond head sideways towards her employer and answered, "Ya sweetie, no problem."

"Now spit out that wad of gum and try to act like you're my wife!", commanded Blair.

The trap was set and baited!

The interior of Hap's cabin became as silent as a tomb, after his suggestion that the cabin should be moved to the Society's park, if possible. The members of the Professor's committee looked at each other in stunned silence. If Hap Larson was serious about what they had just heard him suggest, their mission would be successful beyond their wildest dreams!

Myron Silverman was the first to find his voice. "Mr. Larson, are you suggesting you would be willing to allow this cabin to be moved from here to our park's location outside of Quebec? That CAN be done rather simply you know."

Hap looked at Mr. Silverman, stood up and shuffled his feet aimlessly. "I got some real bad news a few days ago. Seems like the government and a couple a lumber companies are punchin' a road towards my trappin' grounds. By this comin' fall they'll be knockin' on my door. That is if there's still a door here ta knock on." Hap chuckled at his own remark. "I've been doin' an awful lot of serious thinkin' since I got the news." There was a pause as Hap took out his handkerchief and wiped his cheek. Looking at everyone in the room he quietly said, "My trappin' days are over."

Charles stepped to Hap's side and gently placed a hand on his cousin's shoulder. "Hap, are you sure you've given this enough thought? If you get rid of your cabin, where will you live? What are your plans? Are you SURE you want to do this?"

"Yep, no more to think about. It's over and done.", replied Hap. "Maybe this loggin' company is doin' me a favor. Ya don't live forever ya know. I still got a few good years in this old body yet,.....at least I hope so." Hap chuckled again. "Besides, I got a few ideas up my sleeve and some other stuff I'd like to try before they stick me in the ground. If I jist walk away from this old cabin, those loggers will jist knock her down anyway. That'd be the wrong way for this old friend of mine to wind up."

Charles smiled broadly and asked, "Do any of your future plans include that red headed gal named Edna that runs the boarding house back in Nitchequon?"

Hap's head jerked up to look into his cousin's eyes, and with a gleeful smile spreading on his face, answered, "Yer gittin' a little nosy, ain't ya cousin? You'll find out in due time."

The Professor, who had quietly taken in the recent conversation interjected. "Mr. Larson.

This turn of events is beyond anything we had expected. Mr. Silverman is correct, moving this cabin would be,.....or may I say, will be, a fairly easy task. With today's technology, a team of craftsmen can dismantle this building in a couple of days. By marking each log and each individual piece of the cabin, it can be put back together exactly as it was and no one would be the wiser. The pieces can be air lifted out of here and flown to Nitchequon with the aid of a larger helicopter. Then everything would be transferred unto a plane and taken to the site of our park. And Mr. Larson, all we would ask of you is to be present as an advisor to supervise the dismantling, shipping and re-assembly of your cabin."

Hap simply nodded in the affirmative, and added, "Best offer I've had in a couple of weeks!"

"Hello again, Ms. Sullivan. It's me, Blair Blakely." Edna appeared, wiping soap suds off her hands with a small towel that was tied to her apron.

"Oh, Mr. Blakely. You did come back.", greeted Edna. "Lots of times people tell me they'll be back and I never see them again."

"Well, I'm a man of my word. When I tell someone I'm going to do something, I do it. Honesty is the best policy I always say.", boasted Blair.

"I suspect this is Mrs. Blakely." inquired Edna, looking at the woman clinging to Mr. Blakely's arm.

"Yes,...Yes. This is my wife, ah, Cheryl. "Cheryl, meet Ms Sullivan. She's the nice lady I told you about who is interested in selling her business."

The bogus Mrs. Blakely extended her hand, and giving Edna's a limp shake, responded, "Glad to make your acquaintance, dearie."

Edna's eyes quickly scanned the woman's fingers. She wore no wedding ring. Shifting her eyes quickly to Mr. Blakely's hands, no wedding ring was visible either. A warning flashed through Edna's head. Something wasn't right here. Why would a married couple not wear their wedding rings?

Quickly regaining her wits, Edna continued. "Well, I suppose you didn't come all this way to just chat with me. Let me show you around. If you have any questions, please feel free to ask. Like you said Mr. Blakely, honesty is the best policy.

As the trio toured Edna's establishment, Edna took every opportunity to study her two prospective buyers. And the more she looked, the more she assured herself the couple were not married. Mr. Blakely looked to be in his late forties or early fifties. Cheryl Blakely, or whoever she really was, looked to be in her late twenties, perhaps younger. The two just didn't look legitimate.

And Edna began to feel that Blair's smooth, easy manner was a cover up for whatever his real disposition and motive might be.

Finishing the tour, Edna invited the couple to have a seat in the dining room, while she went to the kitchen for coffee and snacks. However, before returning to the dining area, Edna positioned herself just out of sight behind the open kitchen door and listened for a bit to the hushed toned conversation between Mr. Blakely and his make believe wife.

"Tiffany, did you notice anything on our tour that you didn't like? Something that you can complain about? I mean, if we can act like we really aren't sure we like the place, she'll drop her price.", asked Mr. Honesty is the Best Policy.

"That'll be easy. I didn't see anything in this crummy hole I did like.", sneered Tiffany.

"O.K., O.K., good, but don't piss her off. We want to do this gentle like. She wants out of this place real bad and if we play our cards right we can get this dump for a song.", whispered Blair.

Edna gave a cupboard door a kick to let her visitors know she was returning. A smiling Edna poured three cups of coffee and set down a platter of fresh peanut butter cookies. "Well, how do you like my boarding house?", asked an innocent looking Edna.

Tiffany, filing one of her nails and crossing her slender legs, whined, "Welllll,.....I suppose I could get used to living here. We'd have to paint all the rooms a different color. It's all so,....so,.... old looking. And not having real electricity. I mean,......having to listen to that noisy generator all day. And Blair, darling, how much would new furniture cost? I mean,......I'm not into antiques. Most of this stuff must have come over on the Mayflower."

"Now, now dear, it isn't that bad." remarked Blair, shooting his secretary a nasty scowl. We could fix everything up the way you like it. What do you think. Should we make Ms Sullivan an offer?"

Tiffany looked first at Blair, and then a still smiling Edna. "Oh, I suppose. You're the one who really wants to move up here to this God forsaken place. I'll just be a loyal wife and do what you wish."

Edna thought she might vomit, the acting was so terrible, but still remained her smiling innocent self.

A beaming Mr. Blakely popped the question. "Well, Ms Sullivan, did you come up with a fair figure? I mean,....did you arrive at an asking price for your property?"

Now it was Edna's turn to spread the bull. After all, she thought, turn about is fair play, so let's fight fire with fire. "Why yes, I have. After you left, I talked to one of my neighbors about it. He's a retired real estate broker and has kept abreast of what property is worth. He spent quite some time looking my building over and was amazed at what wonderful shape it's in." Edna closed her eyes briefly and offered a silent prayer. "Please God, forgive me."

Blair's face began to pale.

Edna shifted into second gear. "Of course I realize I could get much more if this property were located in a more populated area, but then again, my friend said that there is presently a skyrocketing interest in places like Nitchequon, as more and more people, just like you and your lovely wife, seek to escape from the insanity of living in the larger urban areas."

Blair was now holding his head in his hands and Tiffany was looking in a small pocket mirror, freshening up her lipstick.

Edna eased off a bit and asked, "Are you feeling alright Mr. Blakely? You look a bit pale."

"Ah, naw, I'm ok, just a slight head ache.", replied Blair weakly.

"So, anyway,....where was I? Oh yes, you wanted me to come up with a price. My friend, the very successful real estate broker, who is now retired,......I believe I mentioned him to you. All things considered, the rising property values here in Nitchequon, the excellent condition of my property, the fact it is making money, and the building's historic value, oh,.... but you probably didn't know, it's the second oldest building in Nitchequon. Built in 1879 I believe." Edna paused and smiled sweetly at her prospective buyers.

"So how much do you want?", growled a frustrated Mr. Blakely.

"One hundred and seventy five thousand dollars,..... American dollars.", chirped Edna, still smiling sweetly, "My friend, the retired real estate broker, well, he said it was worth at least two hundred thousand, but I just want to be fair. Honesty is the best policy you know!"

"Oh my", mumbled Blair. I didn't expect the asking price to be so inflated. Would you consider a counter offer?"

"I'll be willing to listen. What is the property worth to you?", asked Edna, turning her smile up a notch.

Blair looked at Tiffany and asked, "Well darling, what do you think? How much are you willing to offer. This would be your home too, honey."

Tiffany opened a fresh stick of gum, and shoving it in her mouth replied, "It's your money and your idea to move here. After all, I'm just trying to be a good, loving wife."

Mr. Blakely stiffened and glared at his secretary. Then, looking back at Edna's smiling face said, "I'll give you a check, to be drawn on an American bank, for one hundred thousand, even."

"Oh heavens!", exclaimed a surprised acting Edna, as she gasped for effect and put one hand over her mouth in faked surprise. "That would be giving it away! But,......how should I say this?, If that's all my business is worth to you, or perhaps that's all the cash you can come up with, I'll wait until I meet with the other interested party later this evening, and if they don't give me a better offer, I might consider counter offering your counter offer, ...or whatever you'd call it. I'm not real knowledgeable about this real estate language."

"What other interested party?" barked a now deeply concerned Mr. Blakely. I thought you said there wasn't any one interested in this place, ah, er, business."

"Oh at the time I said that, there wasn't.", explained Edna. "But a VERY interested group arrived this morning and are waiting for one of their top executives to arrive for a meeting with me at seven o'clock this evening. I'm sure you saw their plane when you and your friend arrived earlier. You had to see it tied up at the dock. The new one with Canadian Petroleum, Inc. printed on it's side."

Blair slumped back in his chair, looking even more pale. "Why would Canadian Petroleum what to buy this place?", asked a now sweating Mr. Blakely.

"Well, as I understand it, talking to several members of the company's drilling crew, they are going to do some extensive exploration for oil deposits in this area and the company needs a headquarters of some sort with the capacity to house and feed their employees. They seemed VERY excited to find such a PLACE for sale right in the middle of the area they are going to explore."

"Ah,....why don't you give me your counter offer right now, and maybe we can come to terms, Ms Sullivan.", asked a now slightly shaken Mr. Blakely.

"As of now, I'd be foolish to lower my asking price until I meet with the executives of Canadian Petroleum..." Edna never got to finish her sentence.

"OK, OK, YOU WIN", shouted Mr. Blakely. Then regaining what was left of his composure, added. "I guess your business is worth one seventy five."

"Actually", added Edna, still smiling sweetly, but giving the knife in Mr. Blakely's ribs one more little twist, "It's worth two hundred thousand. But I'm only being fair. I promised I'd be honest!"

The President of Blakely Enterprises rapidly wrote a check for one hundred and seventy five thousand dollars, on City Corp, Bank of America in New York City. Edna penned out a bill of sale, which would serve as a temporary legal document.

"My attorney will be flying in tomorrow, or the following day at the latest, with all the necessary legal documents to make this transaction strictly legal.", barked a beaten Mr. Blakely. "I'm sure you're a woman of your word and will not back out of our deal."

"Oh my gracious no!" squeaked a giggling Edna. I'm an honest person, just like you said you were. I'm sure we can trust each other. However, there is one final item I'll need your attorney to include in the terms of the sale."

"What now?", asked a scowling Mr. Blakely.

"You'll have to give me a month to get out. I'll need to look for another place to live.", asked Edna sweetly, with a bit of a pout.

"OK. But if you can find something sooner, I'd like you out as soon as possible.", answered Blair.

"Oh thank you Mr. & Mrs. Blakely. You're so kind.", cooed Edna.

Blair scowled, grabbed his temporary wife by the arm and headed for the front door. Edna followed them and waved good-bye as the two quickly headed for their plane, which was waiting at the dock. Edna couldn't resist one final insult.

"Good-bye Mr. Blakely. Nice to have done business with you. Enjoy your new life here in Nitchequon with Tiffany."

Blair spun around, glared at Edna and uttered several four lettered words usually only heard in a low class saloon.

Edna laughed, folded her check and safely tucked it in her bra.

Part Seven: "Loose Ends"

The meeting inside Hap's cabin finally ended, and it's seven occupants moved out of doors into brilliant afternoon sunshine. Professor LeBlanc took several deep breaths of fresh spring air, liberally laced with the scent of spruce and tamarack. "Ah, Mr. Larson. It's easy to see how someone like yourself has become so attached to a place like this. It's so beautiful and peaceful."

Hap put a match to the bowl of his corncob pipe and nodded in agreement.

"Well gentlemen," said the Professor, speaking to his committee members, "We really should be going. By the time we reach the village, check out of the boarding house, and get back in the air,.....well, we'll have to hurry to reach Quebec by nightfall." Then looking at Hap, he added, "Do you have any final thoughts or questions, Mr. Larson?"

"Jist two that I can think of right off." replied Hap, scratching his chin. First off, when my cabin gits tore down, and I gotta move, well,.......my sled dogs are gonna need ta be moved too and taken care of till I find a new place ta live."

"I'll take care of that for you Mr. Larson." responded the Professor. "We can fly your dogs out on the helicopter when we move the components of your cabin. There are any number of fine boarding kennels in and around Quebec where your dogs can be housed and cared for until we find suitable housing for yourself. And we'll pay the bill for their care until you get settled."

"Well, that's mighty nice of you fellas," responded a thoughtful Hap, "but first I'd like ta check with Jacque. He's got a fenced in area behind his store where my dogs could stay fer a while. I don't think he'd mind takin' care of 'um fer a bit. My cousin and his son will be headin' back to the village in a few days. I'll have them ask

Jacque. If he'll take 'um, ya can leave 'um there. If not, well then I'll take ya up on yer first offer."

"Whatever is best for you Mr. Larson. Either way will be entirely acceptable with us.", smiled the Professor.

"My second question is this.", added Hap. "Could ya give me a rough idea when your crew is gonna git back here ta start tearin' down my cabin? I gotta a few things ta do before the old shack gits moved."

"Myron, you'd be the one to address Mr. Larson's question. You're the one who will be scheduling the work and securing a suitable helicopter to move Mr. Larson's cabin to it's new location.", suggested the Professor.

"Yes, I suppose it would be nice if Mr. Larson had some idea of when his home is going to be moved some eight hundred kilometers." A bit of mild laughter rose from the listeners. Mr. Silverman continued. Our biggest chopper, a Sikorsky DH/MH-53 model, is usually available on fairly short notice. I would think we'd be able to organize a work crew and arrive back here in less than two weeks. However, we will need to send a couple of men here with chain saws to enlarge the area next to your cabin to accommodate the much larger Sirkorsky. A chopper of its size will need at least twice the space to land and take off than the area here in front of your cabin where we landed with this Bell Jet Ranger. If we could find someone in the village willing to spend a few hours doing the clearing, under your supervision or course Mr. Larson, well, that much could be accomplished in the next day or two. The four of us will be flying back to Quebec in our float plane that's waiting for us in the village. We'll leave this Ranger and the pilot in Nitchequon to bring the men who will be doing the cutting here and back. Do you think there might be two or three men in the village willing to fly here and work for a day? They will be paid well."

"Heck yes!" responded Hap. "When ya git back ta the village, stop fer a minute and talk ta Jacque. He owns the Nitchequon General Store. He'll find a whole bunch willin' ta make some money."

"Alright," concluded Mr. Silverman, "That's what we'll do. You can expect your work crew here as soon as, what's his name? Jacque?, Yes that was it, as soon as Jacque lines up two or three reliable men."

"That'll probably be day after tomorra. Jacque'll get right on it. Jist tell him Old Hap needs some help."

With that, the committee representing The Society to Preserve Quebec's History and Culture shook hands with Hap, Charles and Jason. And several minutes later the Bell Jet Ranger had cleared the tops of the spruce and tamarack that lined the banks of Otter Creek and was heading southwest towards Nitchequon.

"And if you'll sign this last final legal document, Ms Sullivan, the sale of your establishment will be final, and you can begin spending your one hundred and seventy five thousand dollars,...American." concluded Attorney Leonard Pesman, forcing a smile.

"Oh, I'm really not in a big hurry to spend it yet. But the check is already on it's way to my bank in Montreal. It went out on the mail plane early this morning.", replied Edna, forcing a smile in return. "And besides, as you well know by the terms of the sale, I do not have to move out for another month. I really must start looking for a place to live."

"Well, thank you so much for your hospitality, Ms Sullivan. I must get moving along. I have another meeting scheduled with my client, Mr. Blakely, later this evening. And the plane trip takes almost two hours."

"I'd like to ask one more question, Mr. Pesman. Just why does Mr. Blakely want my property?", asked Edna.

Leonard Pesman stiffened. "Oh, he and his wife, Cheryl, plan to continue to run your business as it has been, as a boarding house."

Edna folded her arms across her chest and looked Mr. Pesman square in the eye. "Mr. Pesman, don't try to pull the wool over my eyes. I wasn't born yesterday. Mr. Blakely isn't married and the woman he brought here, trying to pass off as his wife CHERYL, is someone named TIFFANY.

Leonard Pesman's jaw dropped and he blinked his eyes several times, as he attempted to think of a reply. Then he quickly picked up his briefcase and coat and headed for the door.

As he stumbled out Edna's front door heading for the river, Edna called after him, "Have a nice trip Mr. Pesman. And tell Blair and Tiffany hello for me."

The citizens of Nitchequon were getting so used to planes and helicopters coming and going from their little village, that only a few children ran outside to watch the Bell Jet Ranger carrying Professor LeBlanc and his committee land next to Edna's.

It took less than twenty minutes for the four committee members to quickly gather up their belongings and pay their bill at Ednas. Wayne McDonald was assigned the task talking to Jacque and making arrangements for him to hire several woodsmen to fly to Hap's cabin and clear an area large enough for the Sikorsky to land and take off. Myron Silverman talked to the pilot and the maintenance mechanic of the Ranger, filling them in on their new mission. They would continue to stay at Edna's and fly the work crew to and from Hap's cabin. When that project was completed, they would return the Ranger to it's home base in Quebec. Several containers of jet fuel would be unloaded from the company's float plane and left on the beach by the docking area.

As Professor LeBlanc finished thanking Edna for her hospitality, and was preparing to leave her boarding house to catch the plane back to Quebec, Edna had one request.

"Mr. LeBlanc, I've got one really big favor to ask of you."

Part Eight: "Dismantled"

Later that evening, Charles and Jason would dine like kings on a gourmet dinner of fresh lake trout, prepared by Chef Larson at his outdoor fire pit. As the main course browned to perfection over a bed of glowing coals, three large potatoes , their skins blackened, baked beneath the embers. A bottle of homemade blueberry wine materialized from Hap's root cellar, which helped to stimulate their already ravenous appetites. As Charles watched the master outdoorsman work his cooking magic, he thought of a commercial he had often seen on TV. "It doesn't get any better than this!"

After sharing the meager left overs with his dogs, Hap piled more wood on the glowing coals, and the trio snuggled around the campfire, enjoying a perfect June evening. As the sun's final rays slowly slid behind the towering spruce and tamarack, a chorus of spring peepers began their evening serenade. Just upstream, a white throated sparrow sang it's farewell to another day with a wonderful rendition of "Oh, Canada". Small patches of evening mist began to rise from the surface of Otter Creek, as it's laughing babble blended perfectly with the other sounds and sights being produced by Mother Nature. Charles softly spoke what he was still thinking. "It doesn't get any better than this!"

Neither Jason nor Hap argued.

The following morning Hap began to organize his belongs for eventual transport to who knew where. Perhaps that very thought, "who knows where", was the type of anticipated adventure that caused the old trapper's sprits to begin rising once more. The expectation of what new experiences might lie ahead rejuvenated his sole. Hap Larson was again feeling alive! But, he thought, if only Edna were here.

Charles and Jason, their allotted vacation time growing short, also began organizing their belongings. They would be saying good-bye early next morning. The return trip to Nitchequon would probably take them three days, possibly four. Next would come making arrangements with Jacque to radio for a charter flight back to Gagnon, where Jason's vehicle was waiting. The drive to Sept' lies and home would take another four hours.

After lunch, Charles and Jason helped Hap mark the trees that would be cut down and removed to make room for the Sikorsky that would carry Hap's cabin, his dogs and personal belonging to a new location, and a new life. Using a can of old paint, they dabbed a small amount on the trunk of each tree that needed to be removed. The job was completed in less than an hour.

As the afternoon wore on and began to blend into evening, Charles and Jason chatted about the wonderful time they had had. Hap and Charles reminisced about their years together as young, inexperienced trappers. And Jason was successful in getting Hap to relate many stories and adventures of his years alone in the wilderness. The campfire began to die about ten o'clock. A sliver of a waning moon was beginning to cast faint shadows throughout the dark forest, as the trio returned to the cabin. And this night, sound sleep was easy to find.

As usual, Hap was awake and up before the crack of dawn. He cooked a gut filling breakfast of pancakes, fried ham and hot coffee. He also packed some smoked moose meat and several smoked lake trout for his relatives to nibble on during their voyage to Nitchequon. And just as daylight was softening the forest's darkness, the pair shoved off. For the first time in many weeks, Hap was alone with his dogs,......and his thoughts.

By eight o'clock, three of Nitchequon's citizens were loading their chain saws, axes and lunch boxes aboard a Bell Jet Ranger. Jacque had secured the unemployed loggers with a minimum of effort. Jim Simpson, Frank

Cinko and Paul Wittmann were all too happy to spend a short day cutting down trees and earning two hundred dollars each. Plus, they'd get to ride in a fancy, new helicopter! A fourth passenger was also present. A red haired woman, with snapping blue eyes, carrying a fairly large suitcase.

After Charles and Jason departed, Hap fed his dogs and then began packing his personal belongings. After all, there wasn't much else he needed to do, now that he had made a decision to give up trapping and return to living nearer to civilization. He had just finished oiling his rifle and shotgun, and putting them in their carrying cases, when he heard the whirring sound of an incoming helicopter.

Rather than getting pelted with flying objects again, he stayed inside the cabin and watched the chopper land. Three young men emerged, carrying chain saws, gas cans and axes. But then one of the workers quickly laid his equipment on the ground and turned to assist another person step from the helicopter. Hap took one look at the fourth person, felt his heart skip a beat, and raced for the door!

Hap greeted Edna with a gigantic bear hug and a kiss on her cheek. He was reluctant to overplay his emotions, with nearly a half dozen strangers looking on. All Hap could say, as a broad smile graced his bearded face, "If you ain't a sight fer sore eyes! What ya doin' here?"

"Hap, I sold my boarding house!", began Edna. "I've come to live with you,......well,......if that's ok with you."

"Oh, I guess I can find a place fer ya ta bed down. Maybe I got some space out back in my root cellar.", Hap joked, with a wink. "But why in blazes did ya sell yer boardin' house? And ta who?"

"It's such a long story, Hap. Let's wait until these men get done with their work and then we can sit down and I'll tell you all about it.", suggested Edna.

Hap nodded in agreement, hitched up his pants, and looking at his waiting crew said, "OK you fellas, let's git cuttin'!!

With Hap assisting, the trees in the marked area were felled, limbed and cut into manageable sections, which were dragged into the surrounding forest. Next, the stumps were sawed off at ground level and likewise disposed of. Edna sat on one of Hap's rickety stools and watched, marveling at how well Hap kept up a steady pace equal to his much younger counterparts. But then she wasn't really too surprised. After all, she had been witness to Hap's vitality and staying power during other types of strenuous exercise.

Even with a lunch break, which lasted nearly an hour, the new landing pad was cleared and ready for use by mid afternoon. After a brief round of handshakes and friendly parting words, the three loggers were whisked towards their homes aboard Canadian Petroleum's Bell Jet Ranger.

Hap and Edna, one arm around each others waist, waved until the chopper was out of sight. And then they quickly headed for the cabin.

In the days that followed, Hap and Edna did a lot of mostly nothing. They took walks in the forest and enjoyed watching the six dogs romp freely. They spent an entire day roaming some of the territory where Hap had trapped for so many years. Hap even re-enacted his encounter with the wolverine in front of the tiny cave where the savage attack took place. Edna giggled and laughed as Hap rolled around on the ground, reliving the fierce fight. Another full day was spent canoeing to Misty Lake. They enjoyed a noon time lunch on the island where Charles and Jason had camped. Sadie entertained them by retrieving sticks tossed into the water. And they spent their evenings sitting around a cheery campfire just talking......and planning. Then, on the morning of their eleventh day together in the wilderness, the Sikorsky arrived.

True to Mr. Silverman's and Professor LeBlanc's predictions, the cabin was completely dismantled in two days. Every log was inscribed with it's very own number, as a draftsman recorded it's exact position on a blueprint. The table, bunks, rafters, purlins. and every sheet of tin roofing was likewise numbered and recorded. Hap occasionally felt tinges of sadness to watch his home being dismantled, but at the same time he felt relieved that it's future would continue to be something functional. It was comforting to know his cabin would not simply rot away and be forgotten.

The materials from Hap's cabin were secured in bundles, wrapped in heavy plastic and sponge rubber, then placed in a large cargo net that was connected to the underbelly of the Sikorsky. The loaded cargo net would then carry it's load suspended under the giant helicopter as it was air lifted to Nitchequon and then reloaded into a large float plane.

At the end of the second day, the final components of Hap's cabin were loaded and ready for shipment. The flight crew told Hap and Edna the chopper would return the following morning to transport his dogs, sled and any personal items to Nitchequon, where Jacque would store all Hap's belongings, and care for the dogs until Hap arrived by canoe. The final plan had been set.

It wasn't until the Sikorsky vanished over the horizon that the full reality of how final this made Hap's decision. Second thoughts crept into his mind. And that night, as he and Edna cuddled together in Hap's small tent, Hap wept.

Shortly before ten o'clock the following morning, the Sikorsky left the site where the cabin had stood for over seventy years. All that remained to mark it's location was the bare, hard packed dirt floor, and the entrance to Hap's root cellar. And Mother Nature would reclaim even that in just a few short years.

Hap stood silently by his loaded canoe for several minutes. He looked for the last time on the familiar surroundings where he had happily spent a good part of his life. Then smiling at Edna and calling for Sadie to come, the three took their seats in the canoe and shoved off.

They had begun the first day of the rest of their lives.

(Chapter Five)

The Society

Part One: "Quebec"

Hap's final canoe trip, from the site where his cabin once stood to Nitchequon, was relaxing and uneventful. The most memorable event took place on the portage trail between the Wolf and Caribou Rivers. Hap, veteran trapper and recently turned actor, gleefully re-enacted the notorious shoot out with Luke Stillwell and capture of George Klosinski, at it's actual location. Edna and Sadie sat at the base of the very tree where Sergeant Osborne, and later George, spent time as prisoners. Edna giggled and clapped, while Sadie cocked her head one way and then another trying to figure out what her master was doing. Or perhaps thinking her master had gone daft. At the conclusion of the performance Hap did a deep bow, to Edna's standing ovation. The trio was having a genuinely wonderful time.

As their canoe gently floated downstream, Edna absorbed the beauty of the pristine wilderness, which lined the banks of the watery highways. Hap eagerly shared many memories of events experienced during his many journeys to and from his cabin and the village, adding yet additional enjoyment for Edna, who despite her long inhabitation in the region, had never had an opportunity to view Mother Nature in quite this manner.

Much to Edna's disappointment, the three and a half-day trip ended all too soon. The three travelers arrived back in Nitchequon on the fifth of July.

Hap spent a leisurely day helping Edna pack her personal belongings for eventual shipment

169

to.......somewhere. A second day was spent visiting old friends and neighbors to say what might be their final farewells. Waneta actually shed a few tears as Hap gave her a friendly hug after shaking Clarence's hand good-bye. And on their return from visiting the Johnson's, Hap gave another superb re-enactment where he was bushwhacked and robbed by George and Luke.

Later that same afternoon, Hap and Edna visited Jacque, who presented Hap with his reward check issued by Quebec's Bureau of Taxation, which had arrived in the mail a few days earlier. Hap looked at all those numbers on the check for nearly a minute before he realized that his net worth had increased by nearly forty per-cent with the receipt of one small piece of paper.

Having completed all their scheduled duties, Hap asked Jacque to make a call on his radiophone to Myron Silverman. It was Mr. Silverman who would make arrangements to transport Hap, Edna, all their meager personal belongings, plus the dogs from Nitchequon to......wherever the Society was going to re-locate them.

The reality of leaving their familiar, secure life styles sobered their thoughts as the couple spent their last night together in Edna's former boarding house. Tomorrow they would be introduced to a new environment and a totally new life style. Wherever and whatever it might be!

Shortly after noon on the eighth of July, the Canadian Petroleum's Sikorsky gently settled down on a landing pad at the companies headquarters a short distance outside of Quebec's metropolitan area. And waiting was yet another surprise!

As Hap, Edna, and Sadie stepped from the giant chopper, a small throng of reporters rushed forward. Hap frowned and softly muttered to Edna, "Now what the hell is goin' on?"

Leading the group was a strikingly familiar face,.....and figure! Jacqueline Bower, complete with her glowing smile, short leather skirt, and spike heels, strode quickly to where Hap and Edna were standing. With right hand extended she took total control over the situation.

"Well hello Mr. Larson! And hello to you too Ms Sullivan! Welcome to our city. Do you remember me? I'm Jacqueline Bower of CCN News. I interviewed Mr. Larson about six weeks ago in Nitchequon."

Hap, grinning like a kid with a new bike, took her hand and replied, "Dang, how could I fergit such a good lookin' gal like you?" He no more than said it when he felt a sharp jab in his ribs. Glancing sideways at Edna, Hap could tell immediately he had committed a major blunder. Those snapping blue eyes were emitting lightning bolts.

Jacqueline continued as though nothing out of the ordinary had taken place. "I know you and your lovely, ah, companion probably didn't expect a reception at your arrival, but our news staff and some other reporters from the newspapers couldn't resist the possibility of getting another interview with you. The special CCN documentary we aired about your life and your heroics was so well received by the public,..... Well, Mr. Timmermann decided to have our newsroom prepare a brief follow up story." And then after a programmed pause and a seductive smile, Jacqueline cooed, "That is if I could coax you to consent to another short interview."

Hap nervously shuffled his feet and looking at the ground answered, "Well,.....ah,.....gee,..... ah,.....I don't know,.......ah,.......o.k." Hap didn't look at Edna, but he knew her blue eyes were still snapping lightning bolts.

With Jacqueline leading, the entire group was escorted into a well-furnished reception area, resembling that of a small commercial airport. Waiting inside was Mr. Myron Silverman, and several subordinates wearing company shirts embroidered with the Canadian Petroleum logo. Myron warmly greeted Hap and Edna, and apologized for not arriving in time to meet his honored guests on the landing pad.

Then, for nearly an hour, with flash bulbs flaring and video cameras recording, Myron Silverman fielded and answered questions from the media vultures about The Society to Preserve Quebec's Culture and Heritage and their plan for developing a Historical and Cultural Park. Hap Larson explained why he had opted to give up his life as a trapper and described how his old trapper's cabin had been dismantled and flown to Quebec. For a man who had recently dreaded being the center of attention, he handled the press core with surprising ease.

"The Hero of the Wilderness" had received his welcome to civilization!

Part Two: "Riding in Style"

Following the interview, Canadian Petroleum hosted an informal luncheon in the employee cafeteria. Another hour evaporated as representatives of various news media mingled and continued to extract additional tid bits of information from Hap, Edna and Myron.

Mr. Silverman finally graciously ended the social ordeal by thanking the news hounds for their interest and coverage of, as he put it, "This exciting and extremely beneficial undertaking".

Myron then escorted Hap and Edna to a waiting limousine. The monstrous vehicle was jet black, its front doors inscribed with gold letters proclaiming *"CANADIAN PETROLEUM, INC"*. Behind the limo was a small orange and black enclosed truck, marked, "U-Haul". Within it rested Hap's sled and his dogs, plus Edna and Hap's personal belongings.

"I'm certain you and Ms Sullivan are curious as to what type of housing the Society has prepared for you.", began Mr. Silverman. The Society, with additional funding from several major corporations, was fortunate to locate a rather new home on nearly five acres of land. As a bonus, the property adjoins the two hundred acres that we purchased for development of our Historical and Cultural Park. It was previously owned by the president of a large real estate company. However, when his wife divorced him about five years ago, she ended up with the house. The x-wife found a new boyfriend in Montreal, decided to move there and sell her house here. We were able to purchase the house and property for about two thirds of what it is actually worth. Our long-range plan is to convert the building to a five star restaurant after our park is completed. So, that's where we are going to house you and Ms Sullivan until everything you have agreed to help complete is finished."

"I'm sure it will suit us just fine. It sounds very nice and cozy.", replied Edna.

"Our drivers are going to deliver you and your, what should I call it, baggage, to your new home. I'm confident both of you will find the accommodations to be quite satisfactory. And seeing you'll be living in a residence that is adjacent to our park, you'll easily be able to monitor the work to re-assemble your cabin. We have also erected a kennel behind the garage to house your dogs, which will enable you to continue with your training sessions. The cupboards and refrigerator have been stocked with a wide variety of staples, which should be sufficient to tide you over for a few days until you have time to do some shopping on your own. We'll give you a day or two to get settled and then I'll send Tim over to your residence to assist you in securing any additional items you may require." Myron paused, as if trying to remember if he had skipped anything, and then concluded, "How does that sound? Or do you have questions at this point?"

"Sounds like ya got jist about everything covered. What about you Edna? Anything ya kin think of Mr. Silverman hasn't covered?", replied Hap.

Edna shook her head indicating "no".

The limo driver opened the rear door and waited for Hap and Edna, plus Sadie to enter. Mr. Silverman interjected. "Oh excuse me! I forgot to introduce your driver. Mr. Larson and Ms Sullivan, this is Tim McKinley. He will be available to assist you folks with whatever your needs might be. You will find his cell phone number posted by all the phones in your new home. Feel free to call him at any hour."

Hap and Edna shook hands with Tim and were ushered into the spacious interior of the largest vehicle either of them had ever ridden in. Tim poked his head in the door and gave his two awe struck passengers a quick introduction to all the amenities found in a stretch limousine.

"Here's the remote for the TV, and the radio and CD player are over there. This handle opens the refrigerator. It's stocked with soda, wine and beer if you're interested. The car phone is located over there. Just lift up the padded cover and dial a number. The air conditioner and heat controls are right here and the electric window switch is the black one on the door's armrest. The green button opens the sun roof up there. If you wish to talk to me, the intercom button is that red one and the white one next to it lowers the divider window between the driver's compartment and the passenger compartment. The window itself is a one way window. You folks can look forward, but the driver can't see anything in the passenger compartment." Tim finally paused and asked if Hap and Edna had any questions. He took the blank looks on their faces to indicate there were none.

The ride to where Hap and Edna's new residence was located would take nearly twenty minutes. Afraid to touch any buttons or levers, they simply looked out the side widows and watched the scenery flow by. Hap sensed something was bothering Edna, as she stared out the window and said nothing, which was very unusual. Hap tried initiating a conversation. "What ya so quiet about honey? Don't ya feel good, or what?"

Edna slowly turned her head and looked at Hap with her snapping blue eyes. A few lightning bolts were still visible. "No, I'm just FINE!", Edna began. "AND, it appears you are just FINE too. Rather ENJOYING yourself, aren't you? I'm glad to see your EYEBALLS are finally settling back into your eye sockets where they BELONG!" Edna's voice crackled with electricity.

Hap's face reflected a questioning frown, as he asked, "What the devil ya talkin' about? Ain't nothin's wrong with my eyes!"

"WELL!", responded Edna, lightning bolts increasing in intensity, "I suppose your eyes ARE just fine. You certainly didn't take them off that blond hussy, JACQUELINE! Oh Mr. Larson, how nice to see you! Oh Mr.

Larson, would you allow me to interview you AGAIN! I CERTAINLY don't see what you find attractive about that middle aged bleached blond. If someone would scrape off all her makeup, she'd fall apart!" Edna's Irish temper was getting warmed up! And then looking at Hap she concluded, "If I had a Kleenex I'd wipe the DROOL off your whiskers!"

Hap stared at Edna for several seconds with a blank look on his face. Then slowly a grin began to spread across his weather beaten face. The grin quickly changed to all out laughter. Now it was Edna's face that reflected a blank look.

"Why gull durn," Hap chuckled, "Danged if it don't look like I got a jealous woman on my hands! I think the temperature just went up in here about a hundred degrees!"

Edna turned her head and looked out the side window. Hap quickly reached over, grabbed Edna by her hand, and jerked her across his lap. Then he quickly and firmly kissed her full on the mouth. Edna struggled to sit up, but Hap kissed her a second time, more firmly this time. Edna's struggling ceased as her anger began to subside. The couple's first "lover's quarrel" was over.

Edna returned to a sitting position and rested her head on Hap's shoulder. "Oh Hap, I'm sorry I got so angry. But the way you looked at that woman just got my dander up!"

Hap gambled as he played his next card. "Dang good thing ya couldn't read my mind as ta what I was thinkin', or ya'd really been pissed off!"

Edna eyes flared briefly and then she began to laugh as she punched Hap in the ribs one more time. "What ever you were thinking,......well,.....you can practice it on me later!"

Hap kissed her one more time and replied, "Best offer I've had in a couple a weeks!"

Part Three: "Home Sweet Home"

The intercom in the limo clicked on and Tim's voice brought Hap and Edna back into the real world. "You two OK back there? Been awful quiet." Hap and Edna breathed a sigh of relief knowing their driver had not heard their brief quarrel. Or at least Tim was pretending he hadn't. "The driveway to your new residence is coming up on the right. You'll be in your new home sweet home in a couple more minutes."

Two massive stone pillars, which supported a ornate wrought iron gate, guarded the entrance to a tree lined paved driveway that disappeared into a grove of mature maple and oak trees. The gate was open, and gracing each half of the swinging gate were two life-sized silhouettes, one of a moose and the other a caribou. Hap sucked in his breath and then let out a soft whistle before exclaiming, "Don't know what's at the end a this road, but the beginnin' sure looks impressive!" Edna's eyes had widened considerably as she strained to see what might come into view next.

The driveway took a long, curving swing to the left and suddenly a immense log home, surrounded by stately manicured evergreens, came into view. "Wow," exclaimed Edna, "I wonder who lives in that mansion?"

The limousine followed a circular drive and pulled to a stop in front of the most beautiful and gigantic home Hap and Edna had ever seen. They sat looking out the limo window in stunned silence. The rear door opened and Tim looked in saying, "Well, here we are. Hope you like it!"

As Tim ushered his passengers to the front door, his two assistants in the U-Haul truck began unloading its cargo. The five sled dogs, plus Sadie, who had not had an opportunity to roam at will for quite some time, scattered in all directions to sniff all the new smells and begin marking their new territories.

A well, but compact, manicured yard surrounded the spectacular building. Small flowerbeds, bordered by colorful stones and boulders, encased the bases of several large oaks that graced the front yard. Connected to the home was a three stall garage, and a drive through covered entrance protected the front entrance door.

Tim unlocked a varnished solid ash door, which was highlighted by an intricate stained glass window shaped like a Canada Goose. Edna, still looking stunned, led the trio into the homes interior.

A large foyer, with two huge closets paneled with knotty cedar, one on either side of the entrance, welcomed Hap and Edna to their new home. Beyond loomed an enormous room with a cathedral ceiling. The varnished log walls, which were accented with numerous expensive looking pieces of original artwork, glistened as though freshly varnished. Matching couches, chairs, recliners, end tables , coffee tables and lamps, were comfortably arranged throughout the room. Colorful shag rugs were esthetically positioned and blended perfectly with a highly polished oak floor. Brass chains from the ceiling suspended two large cut glass crystal chandeliers. In the far wall two large picture windows overlooked a spacious deck filled with padded wooden deck furniture. And just beyond the deck was a small pond on which a pair of snow-white swans swam.

Looking to her right, Edna viewed a large dining area, complete with a round oak table and eight high backed padded chairs. Beyond the dining area, an arched doorway allowed a view of the kitchen. To her left was a massive staircase that led to a wide balcony. Edna correctly assumed the upper level contained the bedrooms. And a gigantic full stone fireplace and a complete entertainment center, whose centerpiece was a fifty-two inch screen TV, graced the north wall.

Edna and Hap stood in the middle of the room, jaws agape, and looked in wide-eyed wonder. Hap finally thought of something to say. "Holdie shit Edna, would ya look at this!"

Within a half-hour Tim's assistants had the couple's baggage carried to the master bedroom and a guided tour of the building and grounds was completed. Tim reminded Hap and Edna that he was on call twenty-four hours a day and should they need anything, don't hesitate to phone. A final thank you from Hap and Edna sent the limo and U-Haul back down the driveway, and the new occupants of the magnificent log home were left still standing in a daze.

Hap rounded up his five sled dogs and placed them in the new kennel complex that has been installed behind the garage. Just inside the back door of the garage he found a large plastic container marked "Dog Food". The Society had thought of everything!

As Hap was feeding his dogs, Edna began poking around the garage's interior. An object on one of the shelves caught her attention. It was a dust-covered mailbox. And on it's side were gold colored letters, which spelled out "Blair & Cheryl Blakely".

Part Four: "The Park"

Being in such a new environment caused fitful sleep for both Hap and Edna. Even an enthusiastic round of love making in their king sized bed, which was usually better than a sleeping pill, did not help.

Next morning, while Edna tried to figure out how to adjust the temperature of the water in their bathroom shower, Hap fumbled with the automatic coffeepot in the kitchen. Learning to use everything found in their new home, as Hap put it, "these god damned new fangled gadgets" was going to take a while. Although Edna had figured out how to use the TV well enough for them to watch the evening news the night before and view Hap and Mr. Silverman's interview on WQEB.

Later, after Edna had showered and dressed, Hap attempted to cook breakfast on the kitchen range, an expensive Jenn-Air combination range and grille, fueled by propane gas. The first batch of bacon burned to a crisp and the second batch took fifteen minutes to cook.

"First thing I autta do is pitch this dang stove in that pond out there and build me a wood fire in the yard so I kin cook decent!" grumbled the frustrated old trapper. Edna giggled.

"Now Hap darling, don't get so upset. We'll figure out how to use all these modern things sooner or later. Rome wasn't built in a day you know.", said Edna soothingly.

"Ya, I know, it wasn't built in a day, but old Nero burned her down in a few hours.", Hap growled in return.

Even though Hap was not satisfied with the results of his efforts, a breakfast of scrambled eggs, bacon, fried potatoes and whole wheat toast, plus a cup of weak coffee, was enjoyed in the out of doors on their deck. And while they ate and sipped a second cup of coffee, they were entertained by a live outdoor show.

Song birds flittered from tree to tree, singing praises to a beautiful summer morning. The swans swam to the shore and accepted crusts of toast that Edna tossed to them. A mother mallard, and her half grown brood of nine, dipped for unseen delicacies beneath the pond's mirrored surface. Gray squirrels combed the oak trees, harvesting acorns for breakfast. And a doe with her fawn watched the couple suspiciously from the sanctuary of the evergreens. If it hadn't been for the sounds of heavy equipment being started to begin another day of construction in The Park, Hap might have imagined he was still living in his cabin on the banks of Otter Creek.

Edna placed the dirty dishes in the dishwasher, poured in the liquid soap and punched a button. "See darling, how easy life can be with all these modern conveniences?" beamed Edna.

"Ya, ya, ya. Big Deal. Ya pushed one button. I kin handle that. Tomorra you cook the breakfast and I'll do the dishes!", replied Hap.

A few minutes later Hap was leading Edna down a narrow trail through the woods towards the sounds of heavy construction equipment. Emerging from the trees, an unexpected sight greeted their astonished eyes. Before them lay the two hundred acres that was being developed by The Society for their park. Dozens of laborers criss crossed the landscape, as bulldozers, backhoes, draglines, bobcats, tractors, and forklifts pushed and hauled and scraped and dug. The scene reminded Hap of a colony of busy ants.

Near the center of all the activity were parked a half dozen trailers of various sizes. One bore a sign that proclaimed, "OFFICE". Carefully picking their way through the hectic activity, the couple had almost reached their destination when a familiar voice yelled at them from a open Jeep.

"Mr. Larson! Ms. Sullivan! I'm over here!" As expected, the Professor was keeping tabs on the park's progress.

It was a different Professor than the one who had visited Hap at his cabin. The impeccable dark gray suit and light blue dress shirt, topped off with a bow tie and Scottish tweed hat, had been replaced with a checkered cotton shirt, washed out blue jeans and cowboy boots. And atop his head of distinguished gray hair rested a red fez.

"I was about to drive over to your residence and see how you two were making out living in what YOU probably consider an urban setting. We who live in the suburbs of Quebec consider this area as being rural, although I'm sure you wouldn't agree, with all this noise and all." The Professor was a man of many words. "Myron called me yesterday afternoon and told me you two had arrived. We've all been waiting patiently. The technicians who dismantled your cabin wanted to begin putting it back together again without your expert assistance, but I vetoed the idea." And then, completely leaving his normal character, the Professor added, "'Cause you da man!" Although he chuckled at his own attempt at humor, Hap and Edna simply looked at each other and shrugged.

"Come, come! Follow me!", the Professor continued as he headed for the Jeep. "I've been dying to show you two around. I realize our park doesn't look like much at the moment, but you should have seen this area a month ago. You wouldn't believe the changes. Actually, our contractors are moving along quite well.

For the next several hours the threesome toured the construction area in Professor LeBlanc's Jeep. Where the main entrance would be located, a large area was being prepared for visitor parking. The lot would be large enough to park up to three hundred cars, with another adjoining lot devoted to parking tour busses and R.V.'s Near the parking area, a cement foundation had been poured, and construction was in progress on a huge Visitor's Center. Within the center would be eight separate areas, complete with video booths, scale reproductions and information about the eight different major themes the park would depict.

The log building would be shaped like an octagon. The eight theme rooms would comprise the outer edge of the eight sided building. The center, or hub area, would include an information desk, ticket counter, concession stand, and rest rooms. A retractable glass dome would cover the hub area and the plans also included a central fountain area with native fish and water plants. It all sounded very beautiful,.....and very expensive!

Next the tour guide drove Hap and Edna to various locations where each of the eight major exhibits would be erected. Pierre explained that visitors could choose to walk on paved paths to each of the exhibits or be transported by small, electric powered shuttle busses. Automobiles would not be permitted beyond the Visitor Parking Area.

The major exhibits were planned to be positioned around the parks' two hundred acres in order of the time periods they flourished. First would be a reproduction of a Algonquian Indian village, as it might have looked prior to the coming of the Vikings. Next would be a Viking settlement, it's design based on archeological remains of actual Viking settlements that were once found along the Atlantic Coast, and occupied by Viking settlers and explorers between 1000 and 1300 A.D. Third in line would be Voyageur Park, honoring the early French fur traders and missionaries who explored the continent's northern and central interior. This exhibit would also include a recreation of a Rendezvous, an annual event where the traders and Indians would gather to trade, play games and celebrate for days on end!

At this point in the tour, the temporary access road crossed a small stream that ran through the center of the park. Professor stopped the Jeep to give his guests a better perspective of how the park was being designed.

"The draglines and earth movers you see working over there are creating a small lake of about twenty acres in size. It's bottom will be covered with several feet of compacted clay to prevent water from seeping down into the earth." Pierre paused and took a drink of water from a plastic bottle. "This stream here, we are about to cross on a temporary bridge, will be diverted into the artificial lake. The outlet will then be re-routed back into the river's original streambed. We are trying very hard to keep the area as natural as possible."

"What da ya need a lake fer. Gonna plant some fish in it?", asked Hap.

"No", chuckled the Professor, "the lake, which will be situated almost in the middle of the park, will be the location for all the different historical boats, canoes and sailing vessels, along with several larger sixteenth and seventeenth century war ships. Cannons and all! We plan on staging sea battles between the ships, such as the one which is staged at Treasure Island in Las Vegas. The boat exhibit will be the final stop for our visitors, if they plan to view all eight major exhibits. And seeing all eight will no doubt take a full day, perhaps longer!"

"Boy, this is gonna be somethin', ain't it Edna?", smiled Hap.

"Yes, the scope of this project is unbelievable! I can't wait to spend a day or two viewing all the exhibits once they're finished. By the way Professor, when does The Society plan on having the project finished?", asked Edna.

"Good question! If the pace of construction keeps going like it has so far, we hope to be open to the public in another two or three years. Much will depend on how our financial support continues.", answered Pierre.

The touring trio continued their inspection. The fourth exhibit was scheduled to be a recreation of a typical eighteenth century fur trading post. Next in line, a site was being prepared for two wooden forts, one French and one British. The forts would be constructed to represent structures built at the time of the French and Indian War, and house artifacts of that period.

Continuing on, the road curved back to the banks of the stream once more. Here, the narrow temporary access road entered a thick stand of evergreens. The Professor once again stopped the Jeep and got out.

"Hap, this is the place I know you've been waiting to see." Pierre pointed to a pile of something covered by a large blue tarp. "Under that tarp rests the components of your cabin. It is here we are going to design our tribute to the wilderness trappers. How do you like the location?"

Hap climbed out of the Jeep, and gave Edna his hand as she too stepped down. Looking all around, Hap filled his corncob pipe with Bond Street, struck a match to the bowl, took a deep puff, exhaled, and then smiling at the Professor said, "Almost looks like home. I like it!"

"Wonderful! Just wonderful!", exclaimed Pierre. "I picked out the spot myself. Well, actually Myron, Conrad and Wayne were with me and I guess I'd better say WE picked it out. I'm delighted it meets with your approval."

"Yer committee did a right nice job. The old cabin'll look jist fine nestled in these trees with the crick runnin' by. Might jist move back in once she gets put back tagether." said a chuckling Hap.

A smiling Edna had something to add. "Hap Larson, if you move back into that old cabin,....why, you'll be living here all alone. I'm staying in the new house over there.", said Edna, pointing in the direction their residence was located.

"When ya git all them mechanical gizzmos and thing a ma jigs figgered out, let me know and I'll move back in with ya." joked Hap. Everyone had a short laugh.

"Now that you've seen the site, and approved of the location,.....well,.....when do you think you would like to begin supervising the cabins re-assembly?", asked the Professor.

Hap answered quickly. "How does seven a'clock tomorra mornin' sound?"

"Splendid! Just splendid!", exclaimed an excited Professor Pierre LeBlanc. "But why don't you make it eight o'clock? I'll have your crew here on the site ready to go at eight sharp!"

The area where the final exhibit would be constructed was likewise bustling with construction workers. Much of the building that would showcase the history and highlights of the Royal Canadian Mounted Police display was already completed. The exterior was constructed of enormous horizontal white pine logs, and the roof was covered with forest green tile. Again, it was apparent the Society was sparing no cost to make their exhibits esthetically appealing.

Professor LeBlanc drove Hap and Edna to the edge of the woods that separated the park from the land on which their new residence was located.

After once again thanking their friend for the tour, Edna had one additional question. "I was wondering,.....how were you able to secure such a large and beautiful tract of land for your project? I mean,..... it must have been terribly expensive."

"Oh yes, we were quite lucky to obtain this parcel.", began the Professor. "A real estate firm purchased this property from a mining company about eight years ago. For reasons unknown to me, the mining company was going bankrupt. The realtor had plans to subdivide the area and build a considerable number of expensive homes, like the one you're living in now. But he ran into a cement wall with the government's zoning rules. They wouldn't grant him permits to turn the parcel into a residential development. So, the real estate firm sold the Society this property for about what they had invested in it. Then the realtor purchased a large tract of land somewhere north of here and is presently planning to build a state of the art fishing and hunting resort."

Edna's eyes narrowed as she asked one additional question. "This realtor,.....by chance would he be a slick operator by the name of Blair Blakely?"

The Professor's eyes widened in surprise. "Why yes, he's the one! But how did you know that, Ms. Sullivan?"

Edna smiled and quietly replied, "Woman's intuition."

Part Five: "Problems"

Mr. Blair Blakely was having a string of bad luck. At least Mr. Blakely blamed his present list of problems on "bad luck". And bad luck was something that Mr. Blakely was not used to experiencing.

"Tiffany, come in here, NOW!", huffed Blair through his office intercom. The door to his office opened and a bored looking secretary entered carrying a yellow legal pad and a number two pencil tucked in her bleached blond curls.

"Am I here to take some dictation, or am I here to give you a mid day nooner?" flirted Tiffany.

""Don't talk smart Tiff.", snarled Blair. "Have you heard anything from Pesman about those permits we need to get started on that damn resort project up on Lac Nichicun? We applied almost three weeks ago."

"I called him this morning, like you asked, but he was out of his office and that dumb bitch secretary of his didn't know anything about your permits.", drolled Tiffany.

"Damn! The summer's slipping by and we need to get going on that project. I shouldn't have listened to that mole, Herman, who works for the government's Bureau of Land Management. No sweat Blair buddy. No problem buddy. You'll have the permits in a matter of days,....buddy. I'll BUDDY old Herman. All the money I've slipped under the table to that creep to push things through for me and now when I really need his help, he tells me his new boss plays strictly by the rules! DAMN!"

Tiffany, her slender shapely legs crossed, bounced her free foot up and down and loudly inhaled a small quantity of white powder she had placed on the tip of one of her long red fingernails.

"HOW MANY TIMES HAVE I TOLD YOU TO STOP SNORTING THAT CRAP DURING WORKING HOURS?, bellowed a red faced Blair. "And that reminds me of another problem........"

But before Blair could finish his sentence Tiffany was behind his desk, stroking his hair and blowing kisses in his ear. "Don't yell at your little Tiffany, honey. I just needed a little lift. Maybe you could take time to give me a little.......lift?, teased Tiffany.

"Jeeze, woman, you're going to drive me nuts yet.", said a softening Blair, as he slid his hand under Tiffany's short skirt.

Tiffany settled into her bosses lap and was just beginning to give him a long passionate kiss when the phone rang. The romantic moment was ruined.

Blair shoved his secretary off his lap and reached for the phone as Tiffany wiggled to straighten her skirt and panty hose. "Hello, Blair Blakely speaking. Oh, it's you. What the hell is going on?"

Tiffany returned to her chair, took out a piece of Double Bubble gum, and sat blowing bubbles and snapping them, while Blair spent ten minutes ranting and raving on the telephone.

Slamming the receiver down, his ranting and raving continued. "That was Bruno. Bruno the dumb ass! I should put Herman and Bruno in a bag and sink both of 'um in the St. Lawrence!", fumed Blair.

"What's the matter now, sweetie?", inquired Tiffany.

"Bruno, and his limp wrist buddy Bruce, were supposed to pick up my shipment of stuff from Mexico at that little abandoned airstrip north of St. Adolphe. As usual, they both had hangovers and were running late. Bruno was doing over a hundred, and the cops pulled them over and wrote out a nice fat ticket. That put them way behind schedule, and when the plane landed and nobody was there, IT LEFT! Damn, I can't believe it! Nothing's going right!

Blowing bubbles and filing her nails, Tiffany cooed, "But you still have me honey pie."

"Oh wonderful! That makes me feel just wonderful!" growled Blair sarcastically. "Get back to your desk and see if you can locate Pesman. Did you try his car phone number?"

"No I didn't think to try his mobile number." sighed Tiffany as she closed the door to Blair's office.

The President of Blakely Enterprises stared at the closed door for several seconds, shook his head and mumbled to himself, "The whole world is full of idiots and I've got the four dumbest ones working for me." Blair then opened a desk drawer and extracted a bottle of Black Label Scotch. It was his fourth drink of the day and it was only eleven fifteen.

Part Six: "The List"

For the next two days, after Edna and Hap toured the construction site at The Society's Historical and Cultural Park, Hap supervised the project to re-assemble his old trapper's cabin. The task of putting the old building back in its original form was much slower and painstaking than had been the task of dismantling it. However, by the end of the second day, two walls were nearly complete. The following day was Saturday, and the construction crews would be taking the week end off. Edna had plans of her own for the week end.

"Hap darling!" Edna began. Hap had already learned if a conversation began with "Hap darling", or "Hap sweetheart", or some other mushy adjective, there would be something Edna wanted him to do, or agree to. "We really need to call Tim and have him drive us somewhere so we can shop. I've started a list of what we need. Also, you and I need to sit down and discuss the purchase of several major items we really should buy, now that we have committed ourselves to stay here until the trapper's exhibit is completed at the park. And we'll be here all winter,.....or at least until they get film of you doing your trapping. Sweetheart."

"Ya, you're right. The frig is starting to look empty, and I'm down to my last pouch of Bond Street. And oh ya, the dogs need sum more dog food." Hap had covered all three of his major concerns.

"I already have food, tobacco and dog chow on my list. But that's only the beginning.", replied a sweetly smiling Edna. "Here, sit down with me and have some fresh coffee and we'll go over my shopping list."

And so the couple sat at the kitchen table with a fresh cup of coffee while Hap listened to Edna pour on the sweet talk and vocally twisted his arm..

"Hap, it just wouldn't be fair to rely on Tim to come and pick us up to go shopping, or whatever, whenever we need to go someplace or do something. So I've been thinking that you and I should buy a car."

"A CAR!", declared Hap, his eyes widening. "Holdie smokes, they ain't cheap! And who'd drive it. I ain't drove a car since I was a teenager in Newberry. And that was an old 1946 Chevy. These new fangled buggies got move levers and switches and buttons than a space ship! Bet you ain't drove one fer quite a bit neither!"

"No, I haven't. But we can learn. I mean we're not that senile yet. At least I'm not. And I even kept my old drivers license, although it expired years ago. But we MUST buy our own car. Or a truck if you'd rather have a truck. We NEED our own vehicle. I mean,....what if one of us got hurt, or....sick or something. And I needed to drive you to the hospital or the doctor's office. Or something." Edna paused to reload, but Hap already knew they were going to buy a car or truck, or.....something. And besides, he realized his Irish Lass was right, they really did need and deserve the independence a vehicle would provide.

"What's it cost ta buy a car these days?" asked a defeated Hap. "Last time my dad bought one back in '46, the old Chevy cost about eight hundred bucks. Bet they've gone up a few hundred since then." Hap had lived in the wilderness a long time.

"Tim stopped by yesterday when you were working over at the park. He dropped in to check on us and see if we needed anything. He happened to have a copy of the Quebec Daily Independent, which he gave me to read. I was looking through it, not for anything in particular you understand, and I happened to see several pages of automobile dealers advertising cars and trucks for sale." Edna paused and looked at Hap, who was stirring his coffee with his finger. "Are you listening to me Hap?"

"Ya, I'm taking it all in." Hap looked up at Edna and grinned. "Jist HAPPENED to drop by with a paper! Jist

HAPPENED ta see the ads about cars and trucks, huh? I'll bet ya called Tim and told him to bring ya a paper!"

"Well,......I,......ah,......yes,.......ah,......perhaps I did mention I'd like to see a paper. Oh, Hap sweetie pie, I should have known you'd have me all figured out. Yes, I did ask Tim to bring out a paper. But Honey! We REALLY do need to buy a car, and I knew you'd be against it!", confessed Edna with a pout and a frown.

"Naw, I ain't against it. We do need somethin' to get us around. Tim can't be our go-fer every time we need ta go ta town. Let's do it. But what does one of them fancy buggies go fer these days. I ain't got the slightest.", Hap conceded.

"Oh Hap, you're so sweet and understanding! I'm such a lucky woman to have you." smooth talked Edna, trying to avoid answering Hap's question.

"How much Edna?", asked Hap for a third time.

"For something really nice,.....I mean,.....we can afford it. Look at how much money we have between us. And you're still making money, working for the Society. I,....I mean we, owe it to ourselves to have a really nice car,.....or truck if you rather have a............." Hap interrupted before Edna could finish.

"Will ya stop with the editorializin'. I don't need no lecture. I already agreed we'd buy a car, or truck, or whatever. Jist tell me how much dough we're talkin' about!", begged Hap, getting a little testy.

Edna hesitated. "Hap sugarplum, hang on to your chair,..... tightly." Edna swallowed and looked a bit pale. "Thirty thousand dollars."

"THIRTY THOUSAND BUCKS?" The log walls of the house shifted slightly. "Ya gotta be kiddin'! What's they made outta, GOLD?" Edna cringed.

"No honey, I'm not kidding. But we can afford it. Let's do it. Here, let me show you the ads in the paper, and then we'll go over the rest of the items on my list."

Hap got up from the table and gave his head a negative shake. "No, no, no! I ain't gonna listen to the rest of your list. Jist buy what's on it and don't tell me what it's gonna cost. Why don't you get ready to go shoppin' and I'll call Tim."

Edna knew she had won. But then again, didn't she always?

Part Seven: "Shopping"

"So, you two want to spend a few hours shopping for a car? That's great. Super idea. Most of the dealers have mid-summer sales going on right now. Plus, some manufacturers are even offering a rebate on certain models." chimed Tim. Edna looked like someone who just won the lottery. Hap chewed on the stem of his pipe and looked out the side window of the limo. "Do either of you presently own a vehicle?", asked Tim, turning his head to look into the back seat.

"Oh heavens no!", began Edna. "My husband, ah,…former husband,…..he died many years ago in a logging accident…."

"I'm so sorry", interrupted Tim.

"Well, my former husband, Michael was his name, he sold our car in 1958 when we moved from Montreal to Nitchequon. I haven't driven one since. And Old Grumpy and Gloomy, sitting back here hasn't driven one since he was in high school. When was that Hap? Right after the Civil War?", needled Edna.

"Very funny Edna, very funny. Why ain't I laughin' my head off?", grumbled Hap. He already didn't like shopping, and they hadn't even started.

"Then I'll assume neither of you have a valid drivers license?", asked a more serious Tim.

"Nope.", smirked Hap. "Didn't need one ta drive a dog team."

"Very funny Hap darling. Why am I not laughing MY head off? I still have my old expired license. Don't know why I kept it. But I've got it here somewhere in my purse.", replied Edna.

"Well, tell you folks what I'd suggest. The Vehicle Operators Licensing Bureau is open until noon on Saturdays. Let's stop there first and see what problems there might be in getting you two licensed before we go car shopping.", suggested Tim.

"That would probably be a good idea.", answered Edna. "What do you think Hap?"

"Yer in charge of this shoppin' venture, Edna, so you kin call the shots. I'm jist comin' along fer the ride.", replied Hap, with a touch of sarcasm.

"OK Tim, let's go to the license place. I'll go in and Mr. Sarcastic can stay in the car if he wants.", chided Edna.

The waiting room of the Licensing Bureau was fairly crowed, which forced Hap and Edna to sit and wait for their turn for nearly a half hour. A Mr. Robert Higley ushered the couple into a small office.

"Now what can I do for you folks?" asked a stressed looking Mr. Higley.

Edna took control of the situation and for the next several minutes she filled the licensing agent in on who they were, where they had moved from, and the fact that neither of them had a drivers license that was valid anywhere in the world. And hadn't had one for many, many years.

Mr. Higley listened quietly, then looked at both of his customers and said, "Oh my. Oh dear. I don't believe I've ever run into anything quite like this before, and I've worked for the Bureau for twenty two years! This should be quite a challenge! I don't suppose either of you still have one of your expired licenses."

"Oh yes, I do!" exclaimed an excited Edna. "See Hap darling. I knew there was a reason I kept my old drivers license. I bet you didn't keep yours!" Edna knew damn well he hadn't.

Mr. Higley looked at Edna's faded and dog eared license, shook his head, and turned to his computer. Pushing buttons and staring at the screen, he finally straightened up and said, "Ah ha! Believe it or not but the Bureau still has your license number and name it its files. Got it right here on my screen. Says here you never had any violations nor accidents. Perfect record! That's good. We can waive making you take a drivers test and issue you a license today! Ms Sullivan, you just received a very lucky break. Now,......I suspect, Mr. Larson is it?, yes, Mr. Larson here may not be so lucky."

"The last time I got lucky was three nights ago.", mumbled Hap. Edna jabbed him in the ribs and glared. Hap chuckled. Mr. Higley looked back at his computer screen.

Hap reluctantly supplied Mr. Higley with a long list of personal information, which Mr. Higley recorded on a large note pad. Edna was still glaring. Then Mr. Higley went back to his computer.

The office was very quiet for nearly ten minutes. The only sound was the clicking of computer keys and an occasional "Hummm" from Mr. Higley. But his search was finally successful.

"Well, well, well! The State of Michigan still has your record on file also, Mr. Larson. However, your record is not as lily white as that of Ms Sullivan." began the licensing official.

Hap squirmed in his seat.

"Looks like you had a fender bender back in 1948 and totaled one out in 1949.", smirked Mr. Higley. "I suppose you swerved off the road to avoid hitting a deer or some other type of large mammal.", offered Mr. Higley, still smirking.

"Hap darling, you never told me you had any accidents while driving!" smirked Edna. "Could you tell me and the nice man here how you totaled a car?"

Hap was still squirming in his chair. "Well, ya know,....that was a long time ago. Don't really remember the details." He looked at Edna and Mr. Higley and knew they didn't believe him. "OK, OK, I went out with my buddies, had a little too much beer and skidded off highway 28 and rolled my old man's car. Now, are ya happy Edna?"

"It's good to confess your sins, Hap darling." teased Edna.

"Here's what we'll have to do to get Mr. Larson licensed. I'll give him a booklet containing all the driving rules and regulations. Then he'll need to study it for a few days and then come in and take a written test. If he passes the written test, well, then Mr. Larson can take a drivers test with one of our patrol officers. And if that goes well, and you,......ha, ha, ha,......doesn't roll the officer's car, we'll issue you a valid operators license."

Hap took the booklet, shoved it in his hip pocket, and he and Edna were on their way a few minutes after she received her valid operators license. Hap's day was not getting any more enjoyable.

Back in the limo, and being noon time, Tim took the couple through a fast food drive up so they could order lunch. Neither Hap nor Edna had seen golden arches in Nitchequon. And then, for the next three and a half hours they looked at cars and SUV's and trucks!

Hap and Edna had experienced many frustrating situations in their lives, but never one like shopping for a vehicle! The more they looked at vehicles and talked to salespersons, the more confused they became. And the prices! According to Hap, rare jewels were cheaper!

Finally, after considering all the options, they settled on a full sized Dodge Ram, V-8, automatic transmission, power everything, four wheel drive, extended cab, pickup truck. With a topper. And parted company with thirty one thousand, seven hundred, ninety nine dollars and ninety nine cents. The dealer threw in a wash job and a tank of gasoline.

With Tim acting as an instructor, Edna chugged around the dealer's used car lot for nearly an hour. She practiced parking, getting used to the brakes, signals, and Hap's grumbling about her driving.

Satisfied with Edna's rapid grasp of re-learning to drive, Tim led the way to a large grocery store so his two new friends could complete their primary shopping trip. After making sure Edna and Hap knew how to find their way out of the city, and back to their residence, he bid them good night and wished them a safe trip. Hap and Edna watched the limo drive out of sight and then looked at each other and wondered. "What have we just done?"

Part Eight: "Dinner At DelMonico's"

Another hour evaporated as Hap pushed a shopping cart following Edna up and down the aisles of Quebec's largest "Super Saver Food Store" Hap griped that the store was larger than the entire village of Nitchequon! And added, "Why the hell don't they give a guy a map so he kin find his was around?" Edna ignored his whining.

It was nearly seven pm by the time the groceries were stashed in the rear of their new pick up truck and Edna was cautiously heading towards home. But Edna had another good idea.

"Hap darling," asked Edna, her voice dripping in sweetness, "Why don't we stop at a nice fancy restaurant and have a nice dinner. We should splurge on something really nice. Maybe a nice thick steak or even lobster, or whatever moves our fancy."

"Hell's Bells! Why not? We bought a NICE fancy thirty thousand dollar truck. You got yerself a NICE new fancy divers license. We bought out the entire stock in that NICE fancy grocery store. Why not spend all our money in one day on a NICE 'spensive dinner? Might as well spend her all and go live in a NICE poor house." Hap made his point that he was not having a good day, and he knew they'd be eating out at a NICE expensive restaurant.

"Oh Hap, I'm so glad you agree. Look over there. That looks like a nice place.", added Edna as she turned on her left turn signal and pointed to a blinking neon sign which proclaiming "DelMonico's, Excellent Cuisine and Cocktails"

As Hap got our of their new truck and began walking towards the restaurant, he looked at the neon sign and asked Edna, "Hey Edna, I wonder what that cuisine tastes like." All he received in return was another jab in the ribs.

Blair Blakely's day had not gone well. Tiffany finally located Leonard Pesman and transferred the call to her boss's office. Attorney Pesman, as of yet, had not been successful in securing the necessary building permits to allow Blakely Enterprises, Inc. to begin construction on it's swanky new resort at Lac Nichicun. But Mr. Pesman has assured Mr. Blakely that the permits would be forthcoming as soon as the Environmental Impact Study was completed in another two or three weeks. Blair Blakely was livid!

Next, Blair spent more than an hour on the phone calling several long distant numbers trying to determine the whereabouts of the plane which Bruno and Bruce had missed. None of his informants could answer his question.

The final blow of the day came when Mr. Blakely added up his overdue bills and determined his liquid assets were insufficient to meet the demands of his creditors. And his bottle of Scotch was empty.

The hour was well past the normal time Blair and Tiffany usually closed up the office for another day. And this, a Saturday, was normally a very good business day for selling real estate. But this Saturday had yielded nothing. Not one of his three salespersons had sold anything! Blair Blakely felt his world was beginning to crumble.

Tiffany took the wheel of Blair's Mercedes and made a left turn onto the main boulevard that ran past the office of Blakely Enterprises. Blair asked grumbling, "Well Tiff, where are we going to eat dinner tonight?"

"I made reservations at our favorite restaurant. I've got an urge to have broiled shrimp at DelMonico's", chirped Tiffany.

Edna and Hap entered DelMonico's and were coolly welcomed by a stuffy looking maitre d dressed in an impeccable Kelly green sport coat, ruffled white dress shirt, black bow tie, and tailored black dress pants, with a crease so sharp you could whittle a stick with them. He also carried a white linen towel draped over his left arm.

"Good evening madam,..... and sir." greeted the maitre d stiffly, as he looked over the top of his John Lennon glasses that rested on the end of a long, pointed nose. He took several seconds to scan Hap top to bottom, taking in his shaggy beard, checkered cotton shirt, faded blue jeans and scuffed work boots. Glancing at Edna, the gentlemanly maitre d must have wondered how these two individuals ever paired up. Here was a gracious, distinguished attractive looking redhead, dressed in causal light blue slacks, neatly pressed white blouse, and matching light blue evening jacket. The maitre d judged her companion must be her father or an uncle who lived in a senior housing complex.

"And how are you two this fine evening?", but not waiting for an answer, continued, "Do we have reservations?"

Hap took the led. "No, da we need one ta git in ta eat?" He was hoping the answer was "yes", so they could leave.

The maitre d ignored Hap's question, looked all around the dimly lit dining room, picked up two huge menus, and crisply said, "Follow me."

Edna and Hap were escorted to a darkened corner booth, several tables removed from where other groups and couples were dining. The table was covered with an expensive Irish Linen table cloth, and matching napkins. A large selection of knives, forks and spoons rested beside a genuine, gleaming white china hors d'oeuvre plate. And a tiny candle flickered ever so slightly in an ornate glass candle cup. Their escort left the menus and boringly informed them, "Your waiter, D'Gorio, will be right with you. Enjoy your meal." He spun quickly on his heals, turned his head briefly once more and looked at Hap, and returned to his podium at the front door.

"Wonder why that dude kept lookin' at me?", pondered Hap. "Maybe he thought he knew me or somethin'. Maybe he saw me on TV. Sure was a strange actin' feller. Kinda funny lookin' too. Wonder why he's got that towel hangin' over his arm. Musta fergot ta leaved it in the wash room when he cleaned up." Edna looked over the top of her menu at her lover, shook her head and just smiled.

Within a few minutes D'Gorio arrived and took their drink order. Edna did the ordering. "Two glasses of merlot, in chilled long stemmed wine goblets, please." D'Gorio vanished through a swinging door.

"Wonder why it's so dark in here?" asked Hap, looking around the room. "Ain't enough light fer somebody ta see what they're eatin. Maybe I'll ask fer a bigger candle."

"But Hap, honey, isn't this romantic?, Edna bubbled enthusiastically. "Here we are all by our selves in a nice comfortable corner booth,........candlelight flickering in our eyes,.......the delightful aroma of delicious entrees drifting from the kitchen,......soft violin music floating to our ears. Don't you think it's just wonderful?"

"Probably put me ta sleep if we don't git somethin' ta eat soon.", drolled Hap.

D'Gorio arrived with the wine, asked if the couple were ready to order, and left when Edna told him, "Oh give us a few minutes longer. I haven't made up my mind yet."

D'Gorio politely nodded, and returned to the kitchen.

"What da ya mean, ya ain't made up yer mind yet. Ya told me on the way in this place ya was gonna get a big 'SPENSIVE lobster!", whispered Hap.

"I'd like to have some time to enjoy my wine before the food arrives.", whispered Edna in return, but a tad louder than Hap's whisper.

"Well, sip away darlin', I gotta take a leak. I think I saw the sign fer the men's privy around the corner. But it's so dark in here, maybe I didn't." Hap eased himself out of the corner booth and disappeared down a hallway towards the rest rooms. Edna took a deep breath, shook her head and sipped her merlot. Glancing up, Edna saw another couple enter DelMonico's.

Why good evening Mr. Blakely and Miss Torkelson. And how are you this fine evening? You're a little late, aren't your?. Must have been working overtime.", cheerfully greeted the maitre d. "Your table is waiting."

Blair and Tiffany were ushered into a corner booth, directly across the room from Edna and Hap's table. They chatted briefly with the maitre d, and he once again returned to his station at the front door.

A waiter quickly appeared, welcomed the couple, and took their drink order. Within minutes the waiter returned with a double Black Label on the rocks and a vodka martini straight up, with an olive.

Blair consumed his drink in several gulps and then announced, "Tiff, baby, when the waiter comes back, order me another double Black Label on the rocks. I need to hit the head and wash up a bit. Some cold water on my face might wake me up. Haven't been sleeping well lately.", explained Blair.

"Sure Blair, honey. All taken care of. You know your little Tiffany takes care of ALL your whims and needs." winked Tiffany, with a seductive look on her painted face.

Blair got to his feet, bent slightly and gave Tiffany's exposed thigh a small tweak as he left, then staggered through the dining room towards the rest rooms. As he passed the next corner booth, Blair suddenly stopped, backed up a step and focused his eyes on a red headed woman, who was sipping a glass of wine and looking at a menu.

"Well, I'll be damned! If it isn't the old lady who screwed me on the price of her run down boarding house in Nitchequon!", growled Mr. Blakely as his alcohol clouded mind recognized Edna's face. But what Mr. Blakely did not see was Hap Larson, who was returning from the rest room and heard Blair's opening remark to Edna.

Edna, quite surprised, looked up and immediately recognized her unwelcome visitor. "Why Mr. Blakely, how nice to see you again. And how is Tiffany? She wouldn't be your daughter, would she?"

"You're a real smart assed old bitch, ain't ya woman? And a god damned liar I might add. Told me that oil company was interested in your piece of shit boarding house. All a bunch of crap!", continued Blair, his anger rising.

"Oh, I suppose it was ok for you to lie to me about being married. And telling me your NON EXISTENT WIFE wanted to continue to run my business as a boarding house. And trying to beat down the asking price on my property JUST BECAUSE I WAS A WIDOW! I suppose that was ok for you to do, but it's not ok for me to fight fire with fire to protect MY interests. Mr. Blakely, don't be a stupid hypocrite ", huffed Edna not backing down an inch.

The President of Blakely Enterprises, Inc. totally lost control of his temper. No one ever talked back to Mr. Blair A. Blakely. Especially a woman! His anger boiled over and he raised his arm, intending to give Edna a back handed slap across her face. But his arm became immobilized by the vice like grip of someone's hand! Twisting his head to the right, Blair Blakely saw a bearded weather beaten face, highlighted by a pair of dark brown eyes that radiated rage!

"Who the hell are you?", snarled Blair. "And take your dirty filthy hand off my arm!"

"It don't matter who I am,", hissed Hap, "And I ain't takin' my hand anywhere til you apologize to the beautiful lady you jist insulted!"

Blair, his mind still foggy from his day of nipping Scotch, hesitated and backed off briefly, sensing his unknown adversary had the upper hand, at least for the moment. "Listen you unkempt hayseed, let go of my arm. Obviously you don't know who I am!"

"No I don't, and damned if I care who you are. But I got this awful feelin' in my gut that yer gonna tell me!", sneered Hap.

"I'm Mr. Blair A. Blakely, President of Blakely Enterprises. I own and control the largest land development and real estate company in Quebec!", boasted Mr. B.A. Blakely.

"Big deal! What does the "A" stand for? Asshole?" Hap just couldn't resist!

Blair Blakely's rage returned in an instant. Clenching his fist on his free arm he attempted a round house swing at Hap's head. Hap, still retaining his grip on Blair's other arm, simply ducked under Blair's wild swing, and with his free fist, belted Mr. Blakely just below the rib cage as hard as he could.

M.A. Blakely let out a "ooouuuuuuffff" and doubled over in pain. Hap's lighting quick reflexes struck again. This time Hap's fist swung in an arching upper cut and caught Blair smack on the point of his chin. Now Blakely's body straightened up and Hap popped him with number three, this time a straight, powerful jab square on the end of The President's nose. Hap then released his arm and watched Mr. Blakely sprawl flat on his back, blood gushing from his nose and trickling from the corners of his mouth. Had a referee been present, he could have counted to a thousand. For Mr. Blair A. Blakely, more than his world was crumbling.

The brief altercation in DelMonico's dining room touched off quite a bit of excitement in the usually quiet, swanky supper club. Not necessarily in order, the following events took place.

Edna jumped to her feet and cheered!

Tiffany spilled her martini in her lap, dropped her small container of white powder on the table, and screamed.

The maitre d fainted.

An elderly couple at the nearest table clapped and yelled, "Way to go stranger, the jerk had it coming!"

D'Gorio dropped the tray of food he was delivering to table number eleven and fled into the manager's office.

The manager rushed into the dining room, took one look at the bedlam, and ducked back into his office and called the police.

Hap rubbed the knuckles on his right hand, asked Edna if she was "OK", and chug-a-lugged his goblet of merlot.

Five minutes later the police arrived!

Part Nine: "All's Well That Ends Well"

Patrolman David Mullens and his rookie partner, Jeanie Brassard arrived at DelMonico's to find a paunchy, middle aged male sitting on the floor, his back resting against the wall. Two bloody pieces of Kleenex protruded from each nostril, making him look like an old walrus, who had lost a fight to the dominant bull. A nearly hysterical dizzy blond was wiping blood from the corners of the man's mouth.

DelMonico's manager was trying to get the maitre d to drink a glass of water.

A small knot of men and women were clustered around a bearded man dressed in a checkered shirt, faded blue jeans and scuffed work boots. Everyone seemed to be congratulating him about something.

A waiter was peeking at the entire scene through the glass window of the door that led to the kitchen.

Patrolman Mullens began the investigation as to why the dispatcher had sent he and his partner to "A disturbance at DelMonico's".

"Alright, who called the police about a fight?", asked Officer Mullens.

"Oh, I did.", answered the manager. Pointing towards Hap and Blair, he continued. "That one with the beard knocked that other poor gentleman out and got blood all over our new carpet!", lisped the manager. "I insist you arrest the ruffian immediately!"

Officer Mullens turned to his junior partner and asked, "Are you writing this down?"

Officer Brassard nodded in the affirmative as she scribbled notes in a small spiral notebook.

Officer Mullens, a veteran of seventeen years on the force, calmly continued. "OK, who started the ruckus?"

For a moment or two, no one spoke. Then Blair took center stage. "He did officer! That bearded weirdo.", growled Blair, pointing at Hap. Hap glared back.

"And who might you be?", asked the officer.

Hap took the cue and answered quickly, before Blair could react. "He's Mr. Blair A. Blakely, President of Blakely Enterprises, the largest land development and real estate company in Quebec. He's also an insulting jerk who tries to hit women. And oh ya, another thing. The "A." stands for Asshole."

Blair was instantly livid and struggled to his feet, making a half hearted lunge towards Hap. Officer Mullens stepped in his path and put his hand out saying, "Cool down Mister! By the looks of your face, one fight a day is enough!" Blair cooled instantly.

Next, Tiffany decided to be the spokesperson. "I saw the whole thing, officer. My poor, ah.... boyfriend, Mr. Blakely", Tiffany pointed to Blair, whose sad, battered face reflected that of a victim, "was on his way to the wash room, when for nor reason at all, this bearded goon," Tiffany now pointed at Hap, "grabbed poor Mr. Blakely and began hitting him with all his might." Tiffany closed her performance by taking a clean Kleenex out of her small purse and dabbing away at non existent tears. And she gave a horrible rendition of "boo, hoo, hoo."

Officer Mullens looked at his partner, lifted one eyebrow, and continued. "Could you give us your name and address Ms."

Tiffany gave her name and address and also added she worked for "poor Mr. Blakely".

"And where were you when the fight started?", continued the officer.

"I was sitting in that corner booth, on the other side of the room.", sobbed Tiffany, still lacking any visible tears.

"On which side of the booth, left or right?" probed Officer Mullens.

Tiffany looked at each of her hands, then glanced towards the booth and said, "Right".

"You must have remarkable eye sight Ms Torkelson. If you were seated on the right, your back would have been facing the direction where the fight took place.", explained the veteran officer. "Anybody else see what happened?"

Edna quietly spoke up. "Yes sir,....I did."

"Could you give us your name and address mam.", continued the investigator.

"Edna Sullivan. I currently live at 26754 Meadow Brook Road." For the next several minutes Edna gave the officers a detailed account of the events leading up to the so called fight. She began with the circumstances surrounding how she first met Mr. Blakely and Tiffany. Edna added how Mr. Blakely had lied about being married, and then related the details concerning the sale of her boarding house. Leaving nothing out, including Blair's vulgar language, she explained how he had insulted and threatened her at the table. And finally, how fortunate she had been that Hap Larson, the man she loved and lived with, had heroically come to her defense in just the nick of time.

"SHE'S A LYING SON OF A BITCH!", roared Mr. Blakely, his battered and swelling face taking on a deep red.

"SIR!" commanded Officer Mullens, "Either you calm down RIGHT NOW, or I'm going to cuff you and haul you down to the station. DO YOU UNDERSTAND?" Blair backed off and nodded "yes".

"Thank you Ms Sullivan." continued Officer Mullens. "Anybody else have anything to add about this situation before I question the two,.....ah,.....combatants?"

The elderly gentleman who, with his wife, had been sitting at the table nearest the squabble, stepped forward. "Yes officer. I'd like to tell you what my wife and I witnessed."

After identifying themselves, the couple took turns confirming Edna's version of what had transpired. Both witnesses emphasized Blair's apparent drunken state, and his vile comments to Edna, who had been sitting quietly at her booth minding her own business, and Blair's attempt to strike Edna with the back of his hand. The gentleman couldn't hide a small smile when he re-enacted the brief and decisive one sided fight.

Officer Mullens thanked the couple for their cooperation and testimony. He then turned to his rookie assistant and gave a order. "Officer Brassard, would you go out to our cruiser and call the station. Ask them to run a routine check on these two who had the,....ah,....disagreement. See if either one has a record. The name Blakely somehow sounds vaguely familiar."

Officer Brassard closed her note book and was starting to walk towards the door when Blair decided he had something more to say. "Ah,...don't bother officer. I might as well fess up. Mullens, you busted me two years ago on a drunk driving charge. And I've also had several speeding tickets over the past few years."

"Oh yes, now I remember you. Yes, yes, yes!", Began Officer Mullens. "As I recall the arrest took place after a rather high speed chase for several kilometers. Seems to me I remember you ran a number of red lights, sideswiped a couple of other vehicles, and then took a swing at my partner, Officer Thorneberry. You were more than drunk, you were plastered!"

Blair remained silent. Tiffany stopped feigning sorrow and distress. Hap's face contained just a hint of a grin and Edna was laughing hysterically.

But Officer Mullens was just getting warmed up. He began to recall other facts about President Blair A. Blakely. "Blakely Enterprises, hummmm. Your office is on St. Lawrence Avenue isn't it?" Blair nodded weakly. "Over the past eight or ten years our headquarters has received quite a number of calls, and personal visits from very irate citizens, concerning some highly questionable marketing methods used by your firm. But we haven't been able to pin anything illegal on you,.....yet. Oh yea! We've got quite a file on you! And it looks like we're going to add a bit more after this episode." Blair looked pale. So did Tiffany. "Officer Brassard, put the cuffs on Mr. Blakely and we'll haul him down to booking."

"What am I going to be charged with?", asked Blair, meekly.

"Well, let's see", began Officer Mullens. "drunk and disorderly, swearing in public, threatening great bodily harm, attempting to do great bodily harm, and inciting a disturbance,....that should do it for starters. Maybe I can think of something to add by the time we get downtown. GET ON YOUR FEET!"

An hour later Edna and Hap finished their dinner, paid the bill and bid farewell to D'Gorio, the maitre d and DelMonico's manager. All three looked happy to see the couple leave.

Several weeks passed. The old trapping cabin was fully restored. Work continued on building a smoke house and root cellar. Hap's Old Town canoe was receiving a face lift. Wood was being cut and split and piled next to the cabin. In general, the "trapping cabin exhibit" was nearly complete.

Hap continued to work with his now nearly full grown sled dogs. And Sadie's training to retrieve, plus learning commands such as "sit", "stay", "fetch", "heel", and "drop", which were commands a hunting dog needed to know, was also going well.

Hap took the written drivers test, and passed with flying colors. And the driving instructor likewise gave him a passing grade.

Edna kept busy enlarging and adding more flower gardens, and tending the lawn. Life was good! The couple were happy, and in love!

Blair A. Blakely received a stiff fine. He was also placed on three years probation and was forced to pay for cleaning the carpet at DelMonico's. His face eventually returned to near normal, except for the fact his nose needed some minor surgery to repair some broken cartilage. And the cut in his tongue, where two of his teeth had nearly been punched through it from the force of Hap's upper cut, still hurt a bit. Especially when a swallow of Black Label washed over it. The incident at DelMonico's, and it's aftermath, was over. But not forgotten!

(Chapter Six)

"Mission Accomplished"

Part One: "Phase Two"

By the mid August the Society's work crew finished "The Wilderness Trappers Exhibit". Hap, Edna and Sadie spent more than an hour at the site, inspecting the final product. Hap was ecstatic! The landscaping specialists had even transplanted several varieties of wild flowers at the edge of the forest and around Hap's old cabin. No detail had been overlooked.

Hap knelt down at the side of his old canoe, and with a far away look in his eye, whispered, "I wonder how many miles you and me traveled? I'd jist like ta let ya know, they was all good miles!" Edna understood Hap's emotional moment.

The work on the seven other exhibits in The Park was proceeding ahead of schedule. Spring and summer had remained fairly dry, and very little work time had been lost due to rainy or stormy weather. Some of the crews even consented to work on Saturday, with overtime pay. The Professor was also ecstatic!

Early September drifted in, along with it's subtle suggestions that summer was rapidly waning. Splotches of yellow, orange and red began to dot the hardwood groves, as the hours of sunlight began to diminish. Once the sun dipped below the horizon, the evening air cooled rapidly, chasing summer sun worshippers inside to sit by a crackling fireplace. A few small flocks of Canadian Geese, heading south, began to appear in the dark blue skies of late summer, their honks reminding homo sapiens of what lay ahead. The whitetail deer grew more cautious of humans, and their reddish summer coats were slowly changing to deep brown. And the atmosphere contained the fragrances of drying leaves, fresh mushrooms and wood smoke. Hap Larson was getting an "urge".

"Will ya look at how big these dang dogs are gittin', Edna. Seems like every mornin' I harness um up they've put on another inch and another pound." Bragged a smiling Hap. "In fact, Wolf, my lead dog looks like he's growin' two inches a day! I'm sure glad I decided ta buy that one from old Clarence. I took a real chance, not knowin' who his daddy was. And I'm beginnin' ta think Clarence was right. Maybe his pa was a wolf. He sure looks like one!"

"It's unbelievable how much those dogs enjoy getting harnessed up to pull something! I know you told me that a thousand times, but now that I watch you getting them ready for their morning training session,.....well, it's just unbelievable!", added Edna.

Hap used his ingenuity to create a new training devise to speed up the development of his teams cooperation. Each dog, individually, had mastered the art of pulling something heavy, such as a log. But getting all five dogs to work together as a team, well that was "a horse of another color", as Hap explained to Edna.

So, the old master of survival had engineered two sets of small wheels that were secured to the runners of his sled. Now he could work with his team daily on the paved surface of the driveway. By running his team from the house to Meadow Brook Road and back, the dogs could be conditioned to work together as a team by the time the snows came. Plus, riding on the back of the sled was lots of fun! Even Edna occasionally took a turn or two. And had Hap and Edna had any neighbors, they possibly might have wondered who "Wolf", "Rusty", "Star", "Bubba", and "Meathead" were.

Mr. Blair A. Blakely, on the other hand, was not having fun. His mood, which never could have been classed as "jolly", was becoming increasingly sullen and vindictive with each passing personal setback, socially and financially. The permits to begin work on his resort project at Lac Nichicum had finally been granted in late August. But by then it was already too late to begin any serious construction at the site. And even if The President of Blakely Enterprises had decided to begin construction, the necessary funds were not immediately available. And so, The President called a meeting to discuss his problems with his trusted henchmen.

Mr. Blakely's office was crowded with members of his staff. There was of course, Ms Tiffany Torkelson, seated beside her boss behind his massive desk. Leonard Pesman, brief case resting on his lap, occupied one of the two oversized stuffed chairs. Bruno, all three hundred pounds of him, occupied the second. Bruce, Herman and several of the corporations top real estate salespersons had to settle for uncomfortable folding chairs. Blair poured a stiff shot of Black Label in his morning coffee and the meeting began.

"I've called this meeting in order to give each and every one of you the same message at the same time. That way there will be no second hand versions passed around as to what I have to tell you. And I'm going to be blunt. First off, the real estate and development aspects of my diversified financial activities suck! You sales people have to get off your dead asses and start pushing harder. To begin with, I want you three so called salesmen to work up some new ads for the newspapers and radio stations. Get the graphics department to design a couple of innovative TV ads. We also need more new listings. And if sales don't start picking up SOON, the three of you will be looking for new jobs." Blakely paused, drained his cup of coffee and Black Label and asked Tiffany to get a refill. Every set of male eyes in the room, except Bruce's, zeroed in on Tiffany's long legs and tight buns as she jiggled to the coffee pot.

Blair continued. "Do you three have any questions?" The three salesmen looked at the floor and shook their heads negatively. "OK, you guys get your fat asses out of here and get started on what I told you to do, NOW!" The three scrambled for the door.

The President poured a tad more Black Label into his coffee, leaned back in his padded swivel chair, and continued. "Now it's your turn!", began Mr. Blakely, looking at Attorney Pesman and Herman. "I don't know what in hell has happened to you two, but for some reason you aren't pushing the right buttons anymore. Christ sake, took over two months to get those damn permits. There's got to be somebody in high places that will still take some money under the table to get things done faster than that!" Blair paused and took a long swig from his coffee cup, but his piercing eyes never left the faces of Pesman and Herman, who were starting to squirm in their chairs.

"Seeing that we didn't get started on my resort project up north this summer, it damn well better be ready to go next spring as soon as the weather breaks. By that time I should have enough cash to make one hell of a dent in getting that money maker off the ground. Bruno and Bruce are going to see to that, aren't you boys?" Now it was Bruno and Bruce's turn to start squirming.

Looking back at his attorney and Herman, Blair continued. "I need you two to line up somebody in Parliament or in some other god damn position of power to have that logging road that's being built north of our resort project to swing another road bed south to Nitchequon. That way we can haul our equipment and supplies closer to the resort property and save a bundle on having to fly everything in. And when we open the joint, our vacationers can drive up in their fancy cars if they want. I need all those ducks in line before the logging road is finished and all the road building equipment is moved out. Do you think you two overpaid lazy asses can handle that?" Both quickly nodded in the affirmative."

Blakely cleared his throat and continued. "I don't care how you do it, but it's GOT TO BE DONE! Offer them money, or a life time vacation package at my resort when it's done, get them some whores, or whatever they want. NOW GET ON IT!" Herman beat Leonard to the door, as the attorney almost forgot to take his briefcase with him.

"Now I have to deal with my two biggest screw ups.", began Mr. Blakely, nearly staring holes through Bruno and Bruce. Bruno was comfortably slumped in his chair, his enormous bare beer gut bulging between the bottom of his dirty t-shirt and the belt of his too tight blue jeans. "SIT UP AND PAY ATTENTION, you stupid slob!", commanded his boss. Bruno snapped upright in his chair. Bruce nervously smoothed his stringy blond hair, which was parted in the middle, and hung shoulder length. With his other hand he adjusted the gold ear ring in his right ear lobe, which made the little gold cross that hung from a tiny gold chain swing left and right. He uncrossed his skinny legs and braced himself for the onslaught.

Blair had saved the best for last. "I'm still pissed off at you two idiots for missing that shipment last July. That screw up cost me tens of thousands of dollars. And if that ever happens again, YOUR BODIES WILL NEVER BE FOUND! DO YOU JERKS UNDERSTAND?" Both nodded "yes", Bruno farted and Bruce looked like he was going to cry. "I've convinced my, ah......business associates in Mexico to begin doubling my shipments of, ah......., merchandise next month. So, you two will have to meet the plane twice a month instead of only once. So, remember, NO SCREW UPS!"

The President paused to remove an expensive Havana cigar from a humidor on his desk. Tiffany produced a lighter and held it to the end of the cigar. Blakely puffed until the end glowed red, took a deep drag, and continued. "Part of my present trouble started back in July when that Neanderthal big shot trapper jumped me from behind at DelMonico's. The moron thought I was making a pass at that old bag he squeezes once a month." Bruce and Bruno glanced at one another, knowing their boss was changing the story from what had actually taken place. "All that bullshit in the paper and on TV about ME being the bad guy really hurt my business. Nearly makes me puke the way the media coddles that illiterate bastard. Hero of the Wilderness! What a crock. A one armed Girl Scout could have taken care of those two crazy inmates, Stillwell and what's his name. After all the media crap, several of my important social contacts dropped me like a hot potato, and that's when the real estate sales dropped off. But all that will change, eventually. People got short memories.

Mr. Blakely added more Black Label to his coffee for a third time, smiled and continued. "Now comes the good part! That bearded old bum got in the first lick, but I ain't forgot about it. What goes around, comes around. He who laughs last,....and all that crap." Blair laughed out loud.

I've got a special little job for you two. Something I know you'll enjoy. I'd like to do it personally, but I can't risk it." Bruno and Bruce looked nervously at each other. "I want you guys to find the time and the place to beat the shit out of that old fart. Bust a couple of ribs. Maybe an arm or a leg. A smashed knee cap would be nice. Bust his nose too. Make a real mess out of him. Just don't go too far and kill him. That would spell real trouble. Make it look like a robbery or something. Even you two retards should be able to come up with something original." Blair tapped the ashes off the end of his cigar.

Bruce became the spokesman for the dynamic duo. "But......, but......, we don't even know where he lives! I mean......., how we going to find him? What if he's carrying a gun?" Beads of sweat were popping out on Bruce's forehead. Violence was not Bruce's cup of tea.

Blair scowled. "I know where he lives. You know where I used to live out on Meadow Brook Road? He lives there. In MY old house! It's a real quiet area. No neighbors. All you two have to do is sneak around, watch the place for a couple of days to figure out his routine, and then pick a time and a place to work him over. And if that old red headed smart assed bitch he lives with happens to get in the way, give her a couple of good raps too! Just make sure neither of them can recognize you. Wear ski masks or whatever. Maybe Bruce has a pair of old panty hose you can slip over your head.", finished the boss with an evil laugh. Bruce blushed and adjusted his ear ring again.

Bruno flashed a sly grin and replied, "You can count on us boss! I ain't beat anybody up for a month or two. We'll mess him up real good!" Bruce swallowed hard and didn't even blink. And he was getting sick to his stomach.

Part Two: "The Hit"

October! Fall was at it's finest! The hardwood hills and hollows radiated brilliant fall colors of gold, scarlet and orange, which decorated the oak, maple, ash, and aspen . The air was crisp and sweet, the pollen and dust of summer having been washed away by the cool rains of autumn. Hap's dog team was nearing perfection, as their daily training sessions continued. And the old trapper was busy boiling his traps in water saturated with hemlock bark. This procedure removed all human scent and stained them a woodsy dark brown color.

The Professor was successful in locating an isolated area in which Hap could trap, once the snows came. Located forty kilomters northeast of Quebec, near the community of St.Adolphe, lay a sprawling national forest named "Res Faunique Des Laurentides". The Bureau of Fish and Game Management agreed to cooperate with The Society to Preserve Quebec's Culture and Heritage and allow a minimal number of fur bearing animals to be harvested. Some would be sent to a taxidermist to be mounted for display at the Historical and Cultural Park's Visitor Center. Other hides would be tanned and displayed in the wilderness trapping exhibit. The Society, with the assistance of WQEB, would film Hap as he tended his trap line, and after editing, produce a video tape which would be shown at The Park, and of course, as another hour long special on television. And of course, copies of the tape would also be sold to the public.

But there was more. Located at the southwestern border of the national forest was an abandoned airfield. The Royal Canadian Air Force had built the complex to house and train pilots during World War II. The base had been abandoned as a training site since 1969, but the buildings had been maintained. Occasionally, special events would be held there and non profit organizations were permitted to rent time and space after being granted permission by the Ministry of Defense. The Society had qualified as a legitimate non profit organization and was granted permission to rent one of the hangers and a dormitory for a period of a month while the trapping sequence was being filmed. Now all that was needed was some snow.

Bruno eased his truck off Meadow Brook Road about a quarter of a kilometer from the driveway that led to Hap and Edna's residence, and parked in a thick grove of evergreens. For several mornings previous, the duo of Bruno and Bruce had watched Hap with binoculars from a small hilltop as he put his dog team through their morning practice sessions. A perfect ambush point had been selected where Hap always turned his team around for the return run back to the mansion. A thick hedge row of manicured cedar, which bordered the driveway, would hide the hit men from view, allowing their planned attack on Hap to take place suddenly. And the sharp curve in the driveway would prevent Edna, or anyone else, from seeing the attack from the house. A full half hour before Hap normally made his first training run of the morning, the pair of attackers, with panty hose stretched over their heads, were in place!

"Boy", whispered Bruno, "he ain't gonna know what hit him! When he gets off that sled to turn it around, I'll jump out and whack him over the head with this piece of pipe. Once he's down, we'll just wail the shit out of him. Boy, is this gonna be fun!" Bruce felt sick to his stomach again.

Hap had allowed his traps to soak overnight in the kettle where he had boiled them the day before. An overnight soaking would allow the hemlock's tannic acid to thoroughly stain his steel traps the desired dark brown color. He was just beginning to remove them from the kettle when Edna came up beside him. Edna had a suggestion.

"Honey, why don't I take the dogs on their run this morning and you can finish doing whatever you are doing with those traps. I haven't had a sled ride for several days and I'm getting bored."

"Fine with me Edna. I need ta twist some new wire on the trap chains so I kin fasten 'um ta my trappin' stakes. I'll help ya get the harnesses on the dogs and hook up the sled. Then ya kin take as many rides as yer little heart desires!"

Within ten minutes the team was harnessed and eager to go. Just before Edna took control of the reins, she playfully grabbed Hap's Kromer from his head, and teasingly said, "Look Hap darling. If I push my hair up and pull your hat down tightly, I look almost like you, except for the beard. I'm Hap Larson, Hero of the Wilderness!" And with a girlish giggle she yelled "mush", and headed the team down the driveway, with Sadie racing ahead!

Securely hidden behind the thick cedar hedge, the two hit men waited. The barking of the dogs alerted them to the fact that the first run of the morning would soon take place. Bruno whispered, "Too bad the old fart ain't gonna finish his training session this morning." Bruce closed his eyes and wished he was someplace else. "Here he comes! Get down and don't move until he gets off the sled and turns his back.", hissed Bruno.

As the dogs neared the gate at the end of the driveway, they slowed their pace and then stopped, right where they always turned around for the return run. Wolf, leading the pack, began making a slow turn to the left, as Edna dismounted to turn the bulky sled one hundred and eighty degrees.

Bruno and Bruce, squinting through the mesh of their panty hose masks, plus peering through the thick cedar branches, could not detect the driver of the sled was not their intended target. And when Edna's back was turned, they attacked!

Bruno was in the lead, a two foot section of iron well pipe raised to strike his unsuspecting victim. Bruce, trying to stay close to Bruno, caught his toe on a tree root and fell sprawling on the ground, letting loose a audible, "oooouuuuffff!"

Edna spun around at the sound, the twisting of her neck allowing some of her long red hair to flow from beneath Hap's Kromer. At the sight of Bruno closing the gap between them, with an obvious motive in mind, Edna SCREAMED!

Bruno, suddenly realizing the person standing before him was not Hap Larson, but a woman, lowered his weapon and skidded to a stop. Sadie, who had been in the woods investigating some animal's scent, came charging out of the trees at the sound of Edna's terrified screaming. With hair standing on end, and a deep throated growl, Sadie sank her fangs into Bruno's leg. As Sadie's teeth clamped down on Bruno's leg, Wolf completed his turn and lunged ahead grabbing Bruce by the shoulder, as he was attempting to regain his feet. The four remaining sled dogs, although harnessed together, managed to get in on the action. One was able to grab Bruno's other leg, and the three others joined Wolf in ganging up on Bruce. The air was filled with barking, screaming, swearing and snarling.

Hap easily heard the distant din and realized in an instant that something was terribly wrong. He dropped the trap he was working on, jumped in his pickup truck and sped down the driveway. Rounding the sharp curve in the driveway, an incredible sight greeted his astonished eyes. Edna was standing by the side of the driveway, holding her head in both hands and screaming. An extremely large, overweight man was swinging something at Sadie and Meathead, and trying to kick both dogs at the same time. A second individual was on the ground, with Wolf, Star, Rusty, and Bubba chewing the hell out of,..... whoever it was. Hap floored the truck, causing the wheels to shriek, and headed for the melee.

Bruno, now realizing the "fun" he had been anticipating was not materializing, saw a pickup truck bearing down on the ruckus. He somehow managed to break free from the attacking dogs, and quickly disappeared into the woods running at full speed towards his truck. Sadie, having been struck with Bruno's weapon, declined to pursue the departing would be hit man. Meathead, still harnessed to her companions, joined her team mates and began chewing on a now hysterical and bleeding Bruce.

Hap's truck skidded to a halt, as he leaped from the drivers seat. "EDNA, EDNA, ARE YOU OK? WHAT THE HELL IS GOIN' ON?"

Edna, not knowing what was going on, hugged Hap around his neck and replied, "Thank God you're here! Who are these men?"

Hap, not knowing who they were, or why his dogs were trying to rearrange somebody's anatomy, answered, "How the hell do I know?"

Bruce however, decided it was his turn to scream! "HELP, HELP! GET THESE WILD BEASTS OFF ME!"

With a good deal of yelling, yanking and kicking his own dogs, Hap finally ended the vicious attack. It was Bruce, not Hap who had been badly beaten. Perhaps "chewed" would be a better word.

Bruce's pant legs were shredded , as were the lower portions of his legs and his right thigh. Both of his arms were badly bitten and Wolf had succeeded in nearly tearing off his panty hose mask, along with creating several long gashes in his face. Large bleeding bites had also been inflicted to his neck, plus the lobe of his right ear was torn where an ear ring once hung.

Edna regained enough of her composure to begin attempting to explain to Hap what had happened. "Oh my God, it all happened so suddenly. As I was turning the sled around, I heard a noise behind me,.....I turned around and saw a big, fat, ugly man charging at me with a iron pipe in his hand. He looked like he wanted to kill me. When he saw my face, he suddenly stopped and looked very surprised. Then Sadie grabbed one of his legs,....and somehow Meathead grabbed the other one." Edna was nearly out of breath and paused to reload.

"What was this here dude doing while all that was going on?", asked a still puzzled looking Hap, pointing to Bruce.

"I'm not sure.", answered Edna. When I turned around, he was sprawled on the ground and Wolf was on him before he could get up. Then the other three dogs jumped on him too. It was awful!"

By now, Bruce had stopped screaming and had pulled himself into a sitting position, leaning heavily against the cedar hedge. Hap began the interrogation.

Picking up the iron pipe that Bruno had dropped, Hap loomed over the wounded would be attacker. "Who the hell are ya, mister? And why'd ya try to attack my woman?" Hap's voice cut like a knife.

Bruce remained silent. His eyes were closed and he was groaning, "Get me to a doctor, take me to the hospital! I'm bleeding to death! PLEASE!"

Hap bent down, grabbed the bleeding man by what was left of his shirt and shook him, hard! "I ain't takin' ya nowhere until ya answer my question. Then we'll think about taking ya to a doctor."

"I'm Bruce. Bruce Snedley. My partner made me come here. I didn't want to do it. I don't like violence."

"Why'd ya want to beat up Edna? She ain't done nobody no harm.", quizzed Hap.

"We weren't after her,........we were after you.", blubbered Bruce.

"What the hell were ya after me fer? Ya better fess up and be honest or I'm gonna cut off the part of yer body that 'posed to make ya a man!" Snarled Hap, taking a long hunting knife out of a sheath.

Bruce's eyes jumped open to saucer size. He blinked once, let out a small moan, and fainted. A yellow colored stain spread quickly around the crotch of his blue jeans.

Part Three: "Partial Confessions"

The squad car arrived at 26754 Meadow Brook Road twenty five minutes later. An ambulance was close behind. The squad contain two officers who were not strangers to Hap and Edna.

"Well, well, if it ain't Officer Mullens and Officer Brassard. We meet again!", greeted Hap as the two familiar police officers got out of their squad. "We gotta stop meetin' like this." Hap's humor was not received as well as he had hoped.

"Now who did you beat up this time, Larson?", asked Officer Mullens dryly.

"Ain't laid a finger on anybody this time. But whoever this joker is,....well, he looks a lot worse than that Blakely dude did."

Bruce was stretched out in the back of Hap's truck, and with his body covered in blood, the scene reminded Officer Mullens of a deer hunter who had just hauled his trophy out of the woods. "What in the name of God happened to him?", asked a serious looking Officer Brassard, just as the ambulance pulled up.

"Well", began Hap, as he pulled out his corncob pipe and tobacco pouch. "This here creep,....says his name is Bruce Snedley,...and some other great big fat fella,....well, they snuck over here and hid in the bushes up the road a piece with the idea of ambushin' me. Fer what reason I have no clue. My woman, Edna, jist happened to be takin' my sled dogs fer a run up the driveway and they jumped her,...thinkin' it was me, I guess."

"Were you injured?", asked Officer Mullens, looking at Edna.

"Naw", Hap answered for Edna, "before they knew what was happenin' my six dogs jumped 'um. The big guy got away jist as I was a comin' ta the rescue in my truck. But poor ole Bruce here,....well, he got chewed up pretty bad before I could get my dogs offa him. But ya know,....I'm havein' a hell of a time feelin' sorry for the creep.", said Hap, pointing the stem of his pipe at Bruce.

The ambulance crew quickly appeared with a gurney and began moving Bruce to the emergency vehicle in order to temporarily attend to his wounds.

Officer Mullens instructed the EMTs to take the injured man to the hospital. He and his partner would visit the accused attacker at the hospital later and question him. Within minutes the ambulance was headed towards the hospital, sirens blaring and lights flashing. Bruce's ordeal was far from over.

For the next half hour, Hap and Edna continued to give testimony as to what had taken place. The big question still remained. Why? Officer Mullens had a hunch as to why.

"Now you say the one who got away was really big. How big, and what did he look like? His face I mean.", continued Officer Mullens.

"He was really fat and ugly", remembered Edna. "He was about two meters tall, and very overweight. He had a real noticeable,....what I would call a beer gut. I couldn't get a good look at his face as both he and his partner here had their faces covered with panty hose. The fat one was wearing a dark blue baseball jacket and dirty levis, and it looked like he was wearing combat boots. Let's see, what else? Oh yes, he wasn't wearing a cap, and......his hair looked to be very dark, almost black. And what I could see of it hanging out below the panty hose looked very greasy. UK! Just the thought of him gives me the shivers." Edna was an excellent witness.

Officer Mullens had another question for the couple. "Have you had any run ins, any trouble, anything at all with anyone besides Blakely?"

"Nope. Gittin' along with everybody else we've met. And there ain't been too many others. We've kinda stayed close to our humble home here.", smiled Hap, gesturing at their residence.

"Oh, I'm no stranger to this house, Mr. Larson. I was called to this address several times when Blakely and his ex-wife lived here. He'd get drunk and beat her up. She'd call the police and we'd haul him in. She'd never press charges and next day he'd be out again. I guess she finally got sick of the abuse and gave him the heave ho.", recalled Officer Mullens.

"My", sneered Edna, "he certainly is a wonderful human being."

"I'm sure I know who the other attacker is.", continued Officer Mullens. It was probably Bruno Gambino. He and this Bruce Snedley have been hanging around together for several years. Rumor has it there're also lovers."

Edna's face twisted into a gruesome knot as she exclaimed, "Oh My God, just the thought and mental image of that makes me sick to my stomach!"

Officer Brassard giggled. "Yes, that wouldn't be a pretty sight. A porno movie of those two between the sheets might make one give up sex for good."

Officer Mullens gave his rookie partner a stern glance. Officer Brassard stopped giggling.

"I don't want to overly alarm you Mr. Larson and Ms Sullivan, but I know for a fact that Bruno and Bruce work for Blakely. At least part time. What exactly they do, I don't know. But they have been seen hanging around his office now and then.", warned Officer Mullens.

"Well, looks like one thing they might be tryin' ta do is beat people up.", offered Hap. "Guess Edna and me are lucky they ain't honed their technique too good.", added Hap, trying to make light out of a bad situation.

"Well, Officer Brassard and I are very happy the two of you came out of this situation without injury. It could have ended quite differently, if it hadn't been for the protective instincts of your dogs. You two watch your backs. Rest assured the police will look much further into this incident. If anything else of a suspicious nature occurs, call 911 immediately.", suggested Officer Mullens. "We have to be going. We've got to question

Bruce Snedley at the hospital and see if we can pry anything out of him as why they were after you. But if I were a betting man, Blair Blakely is behind this entire episode. But don't quote me. Take care."

Hap and Edna watched the police cruiser disappear down the driveway. They looked at each other and hugged. "I ain't gonna let ya out of my sight till this mystery is solved.", said a concerned Hap. "Maybe I autta start totin' my .44 again."

"No Hap, don't do that.", replied Edna. "We'll just lock our doors and let the police handle this."

"Hap looked at his watch and exclaimed, "Where'd the time go? It's noon already. Let's go have some lunch."

As the ambulance sped towards the hospital's emergency room, Bruce lay in agony as the EMTs worked to clean the numerous wounds and punctures that had been inflicted by Hap's dogs. And as he fought the throbbing pain that seemed to be radiating throughout his entire body, he began to think. And plan.

Bruce knew all too well that Blair Blakely would go ballistic with rage when he discovered the planned attack on Hap Larson had failed. It had more than failed, it had turned into a major disaster! Even now, as he lay bleeding and hurting, the police were probably already beginning a full scale investigation into the affair. And if somehow the trail led to the door of Mr. Blair A. Blakely, he'd undoubtedly go to prison. After all, it was he who ordered the assault on Hap Larson.

Bruce also knew that Blair Blakely, with his sudden mood swings and violent temper, was a dangerous man. If he were to be implicated in this failed attack, he would waste no time in extracting retribution from those who "ratted" on him. And the only persons who knew of the planned beating were Tiffany, Bruno and himself.

By the time Bruce was being wheeled into the emergency room, he had formulated a story. He would tell the police investigators that he and Bruno had planned to rob Hap Larson and his girl friend. He would tell them that they, and they alone, had hatched the plot and attempted to carry it out. That would be his simple confession. As in the words of a country western song he was familiar with, "That's my story and I'm stickin' to it!"

An hour later, after the doctors and nurses had bandaged Bruce's wounds and given him a substantial dose of antibiotics, Officers Mullens and Brassard arrived to question the injured would be attacker. They questioned him for nearly a half hour, and his simple confession never varied. And although the officers knew he was not telling the truth, there was nothing more they could do. At least for the moment.

Bruno moved more quickly than he had in years. His headlong dash to the thicket where his truck was hidden was not without incident. Several times he stumbled and fell. Blackberry briars and tree branches tore at his face, hand and portions of his legs which were exposed through the tears in his jeans from Sadie and Meathead's fangs. By the time he reached the sanctuary of his truck, his lungs were nearly bursting and his body was soaked with sweat and blood. The blackberry briars had scratched his face, making him look like he had been attacked by an enraged tom cat. Bruno was a mess!

Not knowing exactly what to do next, he made the mistake of driving directly to the office of Blakely Enterprises, Inc.

Bruce was correct. Blair Blakely went ballistic upon hearing Bruno's oral report concerning the botched attack on Hap Larson. But Mr. Blakely was able to keep his anger bottled up inside while Bruno related his tale of woe.

When Bruno finished his confession, Blair calmly rose from his desk and began pacing his office floor. His mind raced, rapidly considering all the possible scenarios and options open to him. He knew all too well that the police would probably make a connection between himself and his two henchmen. After all, both had been part time employees for several years, and numerous persons, probably including the police, most likely had witnessed Bruno and Bruce coming and going from his office.

Blair Blakely knew he was in trouble, Very deep trouble. But possibly there was a way out!

Bruno was very thankful his boss had been so understanding and helpful. Bruno was also very surprised. He had expected a severe tongue lashing, or worse! But Mr. Blakely had quickly come up with a plan to shield his employee from the police, and make arrangements to get him out of Quebec and moved to some secure place where he would be safe. Bruno's fear of arrest and being sentenced to prison had been put to rest. After cleaning himself up a bit in Mr. Blakely's washroom, he quickly drove to the location his boss had directed him. With a hard rock tape blaring in his truck Bruno reached his destination in fifteen minutes. His spirits were once again on the rise.

Bruno used a key Blair had given him and gained entrance into a building. He drove his truck inside the large equipment storage buildings owned by Blakely Enterprises, Inc. Getting out of his truck, he pushed a button and lowered the overhead door. Within this large complex were housed the construction equipment the corporation owned which was used to develop new residential and commercial building sites. Bruno had been ordered to hide out here for a day or two until his boss arranged for him to be transported to safe location. Bruno was very happy that he worked for a boss who was so supportive and understanding.

Shortly before visiting hours ended, Bruce Snedley received a visitor. A visitor he had expected. "Hello Mr. Blakely.", greeted Bruce weakly.

Blair Blakely got to the main reason for his visit very quickly. "What did you tell the cops? I know they must have questioned you already.", commanded Blair, very gruffly.

"I didn't say nothing about you being involved, boss. Honest! I,....I,...told them that Bruno and me planned the whole thing. I told them we thought that Larson guy had lots of money and we were going to rob him. Did Bruno talk to you?" answered Bruce.

"Ya, he came stumbling in my office and spilled his guts. That's how I knew you'd be here, after he told me how he left you at the scene. Looks like those mutts chewed hell out of you. You're sure that's all you told the cops? You better not be lying to me Bruce!", threatened Blair.

"No, no, I didn't say anything more. Just about Bruno and me. I wouldn't think of getting you in trouble Mr. Blakely. I'm a loyal employee!", pleaded Bruce.

"Well, the cops will be back. They probably didn't believe your story. BUT YOU BETTER KEEP YOUR TRAP SHUT,.......OR ELSE!" I don't want to go to jail because you two fucked up. Damn, I should have known you two would screw something up." Blair's anger was on the rise.

"Mr. Blakely, I'll keep quiet,....swear to God I will! You can trust me. Really you can! Where is Bruno? How's he doing?, asked Bruce.

Blair Blakely's eyes narrowed into evil slits as he answered, "Don't worry about your boyfriend Bruno. I'm going to take care of him. Real good care of him!" Blair took one more piercing look at Bruce and hurried out of the hospital room.

Part Four: "The Cover Up"

A relaxed Bruno was reclining on a small cot in one of the storage rooms. He munched on some chips and slurped a soda he had extracted from the vending machines in the construction complex office, while thinking how lucky he was to have a boss like Blair Blakely.

The time was nearing ten pm when Bruno heard a car drive up and stop. A few seconds later Mr. Blakely entered the equipment shed. The light coming from the open door of a storage room told him where Bruno was hiding out.

"Hi boss.", greeted Bruno cheerfully. "This hide out ain't so bad after all. Have you figured out where you're going to send me, and when?" , asked Bruno.

"Oh yes, I've got it all planned out. And it's all going to happen real soon.", replied Blair soothingly.

"ALRIGHT!", exclaimed Bruno. When do I leave?"

"Well, not just this moment. I've got a little more planning to do. Come out in the equipment storage area, There's something I'd like to show you.", continued Mr. Blakely.

Blair flipped a switch and the overhead lights illuminated the inside of the large metal building, making all the various pieces of construction equipment visible. "Follow me Bruno, I'd like to show you one of my company's new purchases."

Near the center of the huge building was a shiny new rock crusher. Large rocks could be fed onto a conveyor belt, which would move the stones upward and into an opening where they would slide down a metal trough into a massive grinder. The stone would be reduced to small bits and pieces, then mixed with cement to form a more substantial mixture for the foundations of large buildings. The rock would also reduce the amount of cement required to complete a job, and in the long run save Mr. Blakely's company money. And he loved saving money!

"Isn't this a beauty, Bruno?" asked a smiling, friendly, Mr. Blakely.

"Ah,...ya,....I guess so. But why did you want to show me this?", asked a puzzled Bruno.

"Because, this machine is going to help you reach your new home.", continued a still smiling Blair.

Bruno, who had looking up at the monstrous machine turned his head towards his boss and said, "Huh?" But his question went unanswered, as the barrel of a 9mm semi-automatic pistol was pressed between his eyes."

Blair whispered, "Good bye Bruno, have a nice trip." And he pulled the trigger.

Blair Blakely worked quickly. He positioned one of his cement trucks to accept the discharge from rock crusher. Then he started a fork lift and hoisted Bruno's massive body onto the conveyor belt. With a push of a button, an electric motor began moving its cargo upward towards the entrance to the grinder. Another lever engaged the whirring grinding wheels . Bruno's body slid downward, striking the grinding wheels with a liquid slurping sound. The resulting mixture was deposited into the cement truck.

Next, Blair connected a long water hose to a faucet and carefully washed the inside of the grinder. The bloody residue trickled into the cement truck with the rest of Bruno's remains.

The cement truck was then loaded with fresh cement from the automated mixer, and the trucks drum shaped cement container was set in motion to thoroughly mix all the contents. While the ingredients were mixing, Blair drove Bruno's truck to an abandoned gravel pit near the back of the large complex. The pit had filled with water and was quite deep. He positioned the truck at the edge of a sharp embankment, put a rock on the accelerator, and dropped the gear shift into drive. Seconds late the truck rested on the bottom of the watery pit.

Blair then drove the loaded cement truck to a site on his property where forms had been placed to receive cement for a new storage building he was preparing to build. Fifteen minutes later nearly five tons of cement rested in the forms. And three hundred pounds were what remained of Bruno Gambino. He had reached his hiding place.

As Bruce's condition improved so did his sense of the real danger he faced. Danger much worse than being attacked by Hap Larson's dogs! Blair Blakely had much worse weapons than fangs and claws. His bosses warning rang in his brain, "YOUR BODIES WILL NEVER BE FOUND!" The realization that his friend and lover had not called nor visited him rang the final alarm bell in his head. Bruce knew what he would have to do, once he was released from the hospital. And he also knew he would have to do it quickly.

Two days after being admitted to the hospital, Bruce was released. He hastily took a cab to his apartment, packed a suitcase and then took the cab to the bus station. He purchased a ticket for Vancouver, British Columbia under a false name and boarded the bus a hour later. Bruce was on his way to a new home and a new life.

Part Five: "Res. Faunique Des Laurentides"

The first permanent snow arrived in mid November. Several back to back storms rolled up the New England coast, covering that area plus Canada's Maritime Provinces and eastern Quebec with a thick mantle of white. Hap's time had arrived!

"Gull dang it Edna, didn't think I'd miss my trappin' this much till I saw all this nice fresh snow. I guess when somethin' gets in a man's blood,......well, it jist sticks there fer good!" Hap Larson was in a great mood.

Hap and Edna were nearly packed and ready to head north to begin Hap's final assignment for The Society. The old woodsman had constructed a set of dog kennels in the cargo area of his truck and a rack on top to carry his sled. Professor LeBlanc and Harry Timmermann had put together a team of technicians, camera operators, and a moderator to add narrative to the filming of Hap's trapping sequence. The entire entourage would be heading to their temporary quarters the following morning.

By eight thirty am, five vehicles were streaming north on highway 175 towards an abandoned military airbase north of St. Adolphe Leading the procession was a one ton pickup truck, equipped with a snow plow. The truck was owned by "Canadian Petroleum, Inc." and was on loan to The Society for a month. Compliments of Myron Silverman. Next came two large vans. One bore the markings, "University of Quebec", and the other proclaimed, "WQEB NEWS, Channel 4, Quebec". Both vans were pulling flatbed trailers filled with snowmobiles and cargo sleds. The fourth vehicle contained a Conservation Officer assigned to oversee the fur harvest. In the back of his pick up truck rested another snowmobile and a pair of snowshoes. Hap, Edna, and a truck loaded with six dogs brought up the rear.

Canadian Petroleum was also providing two general handy men types who could repair most anything that might need repairing. Maintenance of the snowmobiles, which the filming crews would use to follow Hap on his trap line, was of primary importance.

In the university's van rode three staff members. Tom Moran was a biologist and a skilled taxidermist. He would be in charge of caring for the skins which would eventually be mounted for exhibits at The Historical and Cultural Park. Chuck Stiloski and Sharon Roberts were university employees who worked in the college cafeteria. They would be in charge of preparing meals for the team. The van's cargo area was piled with boxes of food, pots, pans, and kettles.

The WQEB van carried four individuals. In fact, they were the same four that had flown to Nitchequon to assist with Hap's first interview. Ed Hostad, Kevin Kirby, and Bob Benson comprised the team of lighting, camera, and sound technicians. Faith Zurstadt was the woman who had assisted Jacqueline Bower prepare her makeup for the filming. Jacqueline Bower was conspicuous by her absence.

Officer Ben "Bud" Jorgensen had worked as a Conservation Fish and Game Warden for the Province of Quebec for nearly thirty years, and had volunteered for this assignment. As the overseer of this specially allowed fur harvest, approved by The Bureau of Fish and Game Management, The Society had been given permission to harvest two specimens of ten different fur bearing species. Warden Jorgensen was present to see that the harvest was carried out fairly and within the legal limits of Quebec's trapping regulations.

Within an hour the troupe reached the gates of Montcalm Field, the military base that once was used to train Canada's World War II pilots. Curiously, the road through the air base had recently been plowed. And although a few inches of new snow had fallen, the road and the landing strip bore faint signs of having been used.

At the far end of the field were the main barracks and a hanger the Ministry of Defense had agreed to allow the group to use. Several weeks earlier a maintenance crew from the university had been sent to the base to get all systems in the living quarters up and running. The heating, and water systems had been checked, repaired and upgraded. Electricity and phone service was turned on. And all the rooms, including the windows were cleaned. It wasn't the Ritz, but it would suffice.

The group spent the remainder of day one settling into their temporary quarters, checking equipment and making sure the snowmobiles were gassed and ready for use whenever Hap Larson gave them the green light. Anticipation and excitement was running high! For tomorrow the "Old Pro" was heading out to scout for signs of fur bearers in the Res. Faunique Des Laurentides.

Breakfast was served at seven thirty am. Platters of scrambled eggs, French toast and blueberry pancakes filled one end of the dining room table. Hash brown potatoes, thick slices of ham, sausage links and crisp bacon rested on more platters at the tables other end. In the center rested a gallon of milk and glasses filled with orange juice, plus insulated containers of steaming hot coffee. The team members were just sitting down to eat when a sporty red sports car rolled up to the door. Its owner announced her arrival with several toots of the horn. Seconds later Jacqueline Bower strutted through the door.

Dressed in a tight fitting ski outfit, the wolverine fur lining of her jackets hood outlined her beaming face. "Oh,", Jacqueline began, "looks like I timed my arrival just right! Is there room for me? I'm starving!" Ms Bower seemed to take control of any situation.

"Well," greeted Kevin Kirby, "You did get the job after all. I thought the brass was not going to let you get away to do the play by play for this program. How did you swing this one Jacqueline?"

"I just twisted Harry's arm a bit. I also begged a little. He finally gave in and let me go. He was going to send that new announcer, Jake Gamble, but I reminded Harry that I have much more experience in this type of setting.", explained Jacqueline.

"I'll bet you have lots of experience in many different types of settings, Ms Bower." Edna couldn't resist a little jealous dig. And then under her breath Edna mumbled, "I bet she twisted more than Harry's arm."

Hap and Warden Jorgensen headed out into the Res. Faunique Des Laurentides on snowmobiles shortly after nine am. The region where Hap would be setting out his traps had not been open for trapping for over thirty years. Detailed maps of the area indicated the landscape was dotted with small lakes, ponds, streams and marshlands. Hap expected to find the location would be an excellent fur producing area. Returning to base seven hours later, the smile on his face indicated he had not been disappointed.

Blair Blakely's plan for moving Bruce Snedley to a safe location had not been completed. And although Mr. Blakely moved heaven and earth to locate his missing henchman, his search had been unsuccessful. And so, two new thugs were hired.

It hadn't been easy to find the type of personnel Blakely Enterprises was looking for, but after making his job description known in the seedier parts of Quebec, Blair was successful. Melvin Murvis had served time for breaking and entering, plus a second stint in the coop for attempting to deliver a controlled substance. Chester Morgan was an x-heavy weight boxer, who had recently been released from prison. He had served four and a half years for nearly killing a prostitute who had refused to perform a particular disgusting sex act. Both were drug addicts. Both were exactly what Mr. Blakely was looking for.

Hap and Bud's preliminary venture into the national forest indicated that a wide variety of fur bearing animals inhabited the region. Both of the veteran woodsmen were amazed at the number and variety of tracks and animal sign they had witnessed during their circuit of the planned trapping area. By the following morning all systems were "go".

"OK, now that we all got our bellies full of breakfast, and a big cooler full of stuff fer lunch, I guess it's time we git this show on the road." The team leader was obviously ready. Less than thirty minutes later the procession was lined up and ready to rumble.

In the lead would be Hap, with his team of dogs pulling his sled on the now packed snowmobile trail that he and Bud Jorgensen had created the day before. The pulling would be fairly easy for Hap's young, and inexperienced team.

Next in line were six snowmobiles, two of which were pulling small sleds filled with filming equipment, the lunch cooler, and various other miscellaneous emergency items. Kevin Kirby would drive the first snowmobile and pull a specially designed sled which contained Ed Hostad, who would operate the video recording equipment. Jacqueline and Faith would ride double, and follow Kevin. Next came Warden Jorgensen, then Bob Benson pulling one of the equipment sleds. Following next would be Tom Moran's snowmobile pulling the second sled, then Edna, simply an observer, brought up the rear.

Hap climbed up on the small platform on the rear of his sled, grabbed the reins and the sled's handles. He looked back at the line of colorfully dressed individuals, snowmobiles and equipment behind him, smiled, pulled down the bill of his Kromer, and yelled, "Mush!"

It was a very tired, but happy looking group that returned to base just as a pale, early winter sun was slipping from sight beneath the southwestern horizon. The Old Master had given his followers an enlightening seminar on the fine art of setting traps. Sets had been made for fox, wild cat, coyote, mink, otter, muskrat, beaver, pine marten, ermine, and fisher.

The conversation that took place around the dinner table focused mostly on how much everyone was awestruck as to what a true science trapping really was. Warden Jorgensen and Tom Moran were the exceptions. Being a complete woodsman himself, Bud was well aware of how difficult it was to master the art of trapping such a wide range of fur bearers. And having watched Hap Larson select the locations for his various sets, Bud Jorgensen was convinced "The Hero of the Wilderness", had indeed mastered his profession.

"Oh I've lived such a sheltered life!", chirped Jacqueline. "I thought all there was to trapping was setting some traps under a tree or something and then a dumb animal would just stumble into it. It looks to me that finding just the right place to create a set is much like shopping. One must do a lot of looking to find just the right item!", giggled Jacqueline as she sipped a third glass of wine.

From Kevin came, "I trapped a couple of skunks when I was a kid, but all I had to do was set a trap in my old man's garbage can. Ha, ha, ha."

Faith's turn resulted in, "From what I've heard and read about trappers,.......well, it leads one to believe that people who trap are some sort of sub human species. A Neanderthal type if you will. But after what I saw today, it takes some smarts to know where and how to set and bait a trap. I'm impressed."

Similar comments were generated by Ed, and Bob. Tom Moran had also done some trapping in his younger days and was well aware of the real challenges connected with being a professional trapper.

By nine p.m. everyone was yawning. By nine thirty every member of the team was sound asleep. Tomorrow would prove whether Hap Larson knew what he was doing,...... or not!

Shortly after midnight Blair Blakely received an urgent phone call. The phone rang six times before his alcohol drugged mind was able to clear sufficiently to realize the ringing sound was his phone. Tiffany pulled a pillow over her head as Blair snapped on his bedside light.

"Halow", groaned a sleep drugged Blair. Then as his eyes focused on the digital time read out on his alarm clock he added, "This better be important. Who the hell's calling at this hour?"

"It's me, Miguel. There's been a change in plans."

"A change in what plans?", asked a still groggy Mr. Blakely.

"We've got a hellava serious problem down here. The damn U.S. and Mexican Narc agents are planning a raid on our warehouse in Matamoros two days from now. One of our informants tipped us off. We gotta get all our stuff moved out of here tomorrow.", explained Miguel.

"So what's your problem got to do with me?", asked Blair, his mind still refusing to comprehend his suppliers dilemma.

"I have to ship your December order out tomorrow. The plane will be arriving at your pick up point on Thursday, the ninth. Today's the sixth. The plane's got several stops before it gets to Canada, so our pilot will be dropping off your shipment about dusk on the ninth. Also, I understand there's a lot of snow on the runway where we drop your stash, so we'll have to attach skis to the wheels of the plane during our stop near Detroit. Do you understand?", asked Miguel.

"Ya, ya, I got it. I'll have my boys there to pick it up.", replied Blair.

"One more thing.", concluded Miguel. "I don't know where we'll be setting up after we leave Matamoros. So you'll only be getting one shipment this month. I'll let you know later when to expect another. However, the method of payment remains unchanged."

"OK, thanks for the warning.", mumbled Blair.

Fifteen minutes later Mr. Blakely was once again snoring soundly.

Part Six: "Delivering The Goods"

For the next two days, the successfulness of Hap's trapping played out like a perfectly scripted movie. Six animals were harvested on the first day. Two adult beaver, two muskrats, one mink, and a red fox. Having reached the quota of beaver and muskrats, those sets were picked up. Day two produced three additional specimens. One mink, one otter, and one coyote.

Already Ed had over three hours of video tape recorded. The camera man, as well as the others, were highly impressed by the quick and professional manner in which their trapper friend completed his tasks. Ed, of course, had filmed Hap making his sets on the first day out. On the second and third days he recorded Hap's technique of skinning the animals in the woods. The carcasses were then used as bait to attract other predators. Once back at the base, Hap demonstrated how to scrape the pelts to remove all the flesh and fat. And the final chore was placing the green skins on the stretching boards to dry. In the case of the beaver hide, the skin was tacked to a wall in the shape of a circle. When dried, the beaver pelts were referred to as "blankets". After the demonstrations were complete, the team members spent a half hour complimenting the old trapper on his obvious skills. Hap strutted around the dining room like a conquering Roman General.

"Well", Hap drawled as he addressed his team mates, who were clustered around the dining room table awaiting dinner, "looks like we ain't gonna haftta stay here a whole month like I figgured we might. Got nine of the twenty critters we need in the first two days. And I only got sixteen sets out. Not a bad average if I do say so myself!"

"I've seen a lot of different trappers in my day," began Warden Jorgensen, "but you, Mr. Larson, are definitely in the top five. Maybe even the top three. Congratulations are in order for your early success. But trapping two wild cats may be a challenge. They're real smart cookies! We may be here for the entire month."

"We'll see.", countered Hap. "But I got this good feelin' in my gut that we're gonna be autta here in a week,…. or ten days at the most." Hap was feeling mighty cocky.

After a gourmet dinner of prime rib, double baked potatoes, creamed asparagus and toasted garlic bread, all washed down with several different aged red wines, the team gathered around the television set to watch the news and the weather. As usual, the news was all negative. The weather report was worse.

Tomorrow afternoon, December 9th, a very messy storm was scheduled to move into the area. The leading edge of the front would produce rain, then freezing rain changing to snow by nightfall. Hap gloated with glee. "Ya man, with a low pressure front like that one comin' in tomorrow, the whole woods full of critters will be on the move tonight chowin' down ahead of the storm. Mark my words, we'll have fur in my traps tomorra!"

Hap's prediction proved to be quite correct. So was the weatherman's. By late afternoon the veteran trapper had harvested another seven animals. Two ermine, one pine martin, one otter, one fisher, one coyote and a wild cat. Sixteen down and four to go! Hap Larson was indeed delivering the goods! And it looked more and more like his prediction of being finished with the trapping video in a week might also come to pass.

The early morning had begun sunny and balmy, with high cirrus clouds. But a highly visible "sundog" circled the sun accurately predicting a rapidly deteriorating weather condition. By noon heavy dark clouds rolled in, temperatures began to skid, and by two thirty light rain had begun to fall.

The team members arrived back at the base about three thirty. They drove all the vehicles inside the hanger to prevent them from being covered with ice and snow by morning. Hap, with Bud assisting, completed the task of fleshing the fresh skins and placing them on stretching boards to dry. By the time they had finished, the rain had turned to sleet, and the landscape was being blanketed with a frozen crust. It was then the sound of a low flying plane reached their ears.

The twin engine Beachcraft had taken off from a small airstrip east of Detroit shortly after noon, Quebec time. Then it landed near Ottawa to refuel. Fifty miles west of Montcalm Field, the plane encountered rain. Then the rain began to freeze on the plane's wings and fuselage.

With no other place to land safely, the pilot and co-pilot had no other choice but to continue towards their destination,....... to deliver the goods.

Part Seven: "Justice Prevails"

Upon reaching his office Thursday morning, Mr. Blair A. Blakely was reminded by his secretary, Tiffany Torkelson, that his "Mexican Delivery" would be arriving late this afternoon.

As usual, Blair had neglected to contact his two new henchmen about the change in delivery dates. And also as usual, he had a good excuse.

"Christ sakes Tiff, I got so damn much on my mind these days, dealing with all the stupid assholes that work for me. Get in touch with the two M & M's, Murvis and Morgan. Transfer the call to my office when you get a hold of them. I'll explain the details and pick up time to make sure they are at the strip when Miguel's plane arrives." Boss Blakely had a bunch of calls to make himself. He was still trying to locate Bruce.

Tiffany's efforts to locate the M & M's were in vain. Both were shacked up with a couple of hookers they had picked up at a local dive the evening before. And all four were sleeping off major hangovers in a cheap motel.

By three thirty, Blair was frantic. Every effort to locate his pick up men had failed. Red faced and steaming mad he slammed the door to his office shut and barked at Tiffany. "Grab your coat, I'll bring one of the vans around front. Lock up the office on your way out. . We'll have to pick up the damn shipment ourselves. If someone ain't there to meet the plane, it'll leave and Miguel will really be pissed off at me. I can't afford to loose that contact. The stuff he delivers is what's keeping my business afloat."

Five minutes later Blair and Tiffany were heading north on highway 175, towards Montcalm Field.

As the ice thickened on the Beachcraft's wings, the additional weight began to cause the powerful twin engine aircraft to lose altitude. The controls became sluggish making the craft increasingly difficult to control. The pilot knew he was in trouble, but Montcalm Field was now only minutes away. He increased the throttle to full power and grabbed the wheel with both hands, fighting to keep the plane airborne.

Although driving conditions were terrible, Blair and Tiffany reached their destination in just a little over an hour. Blair pulled the van close to the base of the flight control tower, which offered some protection from the freezing rain, now mixed with snow. Even with the vehicle's heater running full blast, only half of the windshield was being kept free of ice.

"Damn the weather," snorted Blair. He poured another half cup of Black Label in his travel mug and tried to see out the side window. "The damn plane probably won't even show up. If that pilot is flying in this shit, he's nuts." Tiffany snorted a dab of white powder and then lit a cigarette.

"I'm going outside for a couple of minutes and listen for the plane. If he ain't here in another fifteen minutes, it'll be too damn dark to land. Bet he ain't gonna show." Blair opened the van's door and stepped outside to look and listen. The plane, struggling to maintain air speed was just bearing down on Montcalm Field.

Hap and Warden Jorgensen, who were the only team members still in the hanger, rushed outside to see the low flying airplane. It zoomed over the runway at tree top level, banked sluggishly, and appeared to be attempting a landing. Bud was the first to realize the plane was in trouble. It was heading right for the flight control tower!

Blair pounded his fist on top of the van and yelled at Tiffany. "Hey Tiff! He's here! The plane just buzzed the field and is swinging back to land." Tiffany had the radio cranked and didn't hear her boss or the plane. Actually, in her condition, she didn't care one way or another.

For a few seconds after the pilot completed his turn, he thought they had made it safely. But looking through a icy, fogged up cockpit window, he misjudged his position. And then a sudden gust of wind caused the overweight plane to bank slightly to the left,......and one wing smashed into the flight control tower!

Hap and Bud, mouths hanging open in shock and disbelief, looked with unbelieving eyes as the plane struck the tower. One wing sheared off, causing the fuselage and the remaining wing to rotate sharply towards the tower,..... and then the plane exploded! There was an enormous ball of flame as burning debris plunged to earth at the base of the damaged tower! Both men started running towards the scene of the accident, which was nearly a quarter kilometer distance. And as they ran they faintly heard what sounded like a woman screaming.

Blair, shielding his eyes from the wind driven ice and snow, was watching the plane make its final approach. "Why," he thought, "is that damned idiot going to land so close to the tower?" It was the last question Blair A. Blakely would ever ask.

As the plane's wing struck the tower, the engine's propeller separated from the drive shaft and spun crazily earthward. Blair saw something spinning towards him, but it was moving so fast he had no chance to get out of its way. As Blair's lifeless body slumped to the ground, what was left of his head rolled twenty six meters before it came to rest.

The President of Blakely Enterprises and Tiffany Torkleson had met their maker.

Within hour and a half Montcalm Field was crawling with activity. Jacqueline's phone call to 911 created quite a stir among the powers that govern. Six highway patrol officers, two ambulances, four Royal Canadian Mounted

Police officers, a Canadian Air Force General with his staff of twelve, three undercover drug agents, the medical examiner and his staff of four, a tow truck, Professor LeBlanc, Harry Timmermann, Myron Silverman, and possibly a partridge in a pear tree.

It was well past midnight before the assembled officials pieced together the pieces of the puzzle, recorded their findings, hauled away what was left of four corpses, towed the charred remains of Blair's van away, and disappeared into the snowy night. Hap and his team mates sat around the dining room table discussing the incredible incident until nearly two am. And even after retiring to their bunks, no one slept well.

Three more days passed before Hap's trap line produced the additions specimens which completed his assignment. Bud Jorgensen had been somewhat correct. A wild cat was the final animal to be harvested. And Hap's prediction that the twenty specimens would be secured in a week turned out to be totally correct.

By noon of the eighth day five vehicles were headed south on highway 175 towards Quebec.

Part Eight: "New Plans "

"Ya know, I really had a great time last week.", reminisced Hap. "And I think all them people who came along for the ride enjoyed it too. That accident kinda messed up our fun fer a while, but seein' who it happened too, well, maybe they all had it comin' to um."

"Now Hap honey, that's no way to talk about someone who died a horrible death.", scolded Edna.

"Whatda mean, it ain't no way ta talk. Ya know dang well it was that jerk, Blakely, who sent them two idiots over here ta try and knock my brains out. The guy was a real creep and he got his just reward. I do kinda feel sorry for his dizzy blond girlfriend though. Under all that makeup she might have been a decent person. And them two pilots. Ain't got any idea what kinda people they was, but anybody who flies drugs around the country ta sell ta kids and folks who don't know no better about usin' that crap, well, I'd guess they got what was comin' ta them too. But then again, I always said, Birds of a feather flock together." The old trapper was finished with his sermon.

"After spending time with you in the forest, watching you trap, realizing what a beautiful and peaceful place a winter woods can be,......well,....I've got a much better understanding why a life style like that could get into someone's blood.", admitted Edna.

"Ya, it sure beats livin' in some rat race city. Even livin' out here on the fringe of city life is startin' ta git ta me. I still hear cars drivin' by durin' the night, planes flyin' over every few minutes, the air ain't clean and sweet. Now that I'm done workin' fer the Society, I'm ready to git autta here. What about you Edna?" , asked Hap.

"Well, we've talked several times about our future plans after you finished your work for the Society. I've truly enjoyed living in this beautiful log mansion. And I've

251

enjoyed watching you complete the jobs you promised Pierre you'd do. But you're right. I too am ready to move on. We have our own lives to live and I know I wouldn't be happy continuing to live here. I'm ready."

"Before we pack up and leave, I think we autta throw a little party fer all the nice people we've met and worked with. I think we owe 'um that much. Whatda ya think honey?" inquired Hap.

"Good idea. Let's make a list and I'll give them a call. We can have a cook out on the deck. Sounds like fun. We really have made some wonderful friends. And I do have to admit,.....I even learned to like Jacqueline, after I got a chance to really know her. She's really a nice person. Did you know she's married and has three children?" confessed Edna.

"Ya, I knew that.", grinned Hap.

"Then why didn't you tell me?", inquired Edna

"Cause ya didn't ask me.", replied Hap.

Edna shook her head, smiled, and kissed Hap's cheek.

Two days later Hap and Edna hosted a "farewell party" at their residence. The guest list wasn't overly long.

Professor Pierre LeBlanc, Harry Timmerman, Myron Silverman, Officers Mullens and Brassard, Tim McKinley, Kevin Kirby, Faith Zurstadt, Ed Hodstad, Bob Benson, Tom Moran, Bud Jorgensen, and Jacqueline Bower.

Hap grilled steaks on the gas grille on the deck. The old woodsman had finally mastered cooking on something besides a wood stove or an open fire. Edna made a tossed salad, baked potatoes, and garlic bread. The bar in the living room was stocked with several varieties of wine, beer, liquor and soft drinks. And had a social reporter been present, a written report would have noted, "And a good time was had by all."

After dinner, the group sat in the spacious living room and chatted. Everyone seemed to have some memorable memory pertaining to the events of the last few months. The atmosphere was one of total relaxation.

Professor LeBlanc convinced Hap and Edna that they MUST return to Quebec for the Grand Opening of the Historical and Cultural Park. They agreed to do so.

The party began to break up shortly before ten. As the guests were putting on their coats, Hap asked for everyone's attention.

"Ah,....I got one more thing ta say. Somethin' that jist might interest ya all." There was a pause as Hap cleared his throat. "Me and Edna is gittin' married."

The announcement required one more round of hugs and handshakes, plus the normal words of congratulations.

As the guests departed, Hap called after them, "We'll let ya know when and where the weddin's gonna be. And you're all invited!"

"Epilog"

Lights throughout the Larson homestead were still burning brightly, although the hour was well past the time Hap and Edna would normally be sound asleep. A brilliant yellow full moon illuminated the early winter landscape as the mercury in the thermometer, which was nailed to an ancient oak tree, nudged minus thirty degrees. Countless millions of snowflakes sparkled and danced in the dazzling moonlight, and equal numbers of stars twinkled overhead.

The outside world was locked in muted silence. But from the Larson's home came the sounds of many people enjoying a double celebration. Strings of lights adorned the eves and deck railings, and a decorated balsam fir radiated it's colorful Christmas colors through the window panes, which were outlined with frost.

It was December twenty fourth, and Mr. & Mrs. Eric Sever Larson had been united in Holy Matrimony several hours earlier. It was the seventeenth wedding to be celebrated in Newberry, Michigan this year.

It had been a simple wedding, the ceremony taking place in the Larson's living room. Reverend William Cooper had read the vows and pronounced the couple "Man and Wife". Charles Baldwin was the Best Man and Jacqueline Bower served as Maid of Honor.

Also in attendance were Shirley Baldwin, Bill Osborne, Jacque LePage, Mr. & Mrs. Clarence Johnson, Gino Vernetti, Professor LeBlanc, and Myron Silverman, Edna's daughter, Colleen and her husband plus their three children, Edna's son, Shawn,.......and six dogs.

Below the Larson home, a narrow sliver of ice free water in the mighty Tahquamenon River mirrored the nighttime sky, as it silently meandered east, towards the Great Lake the Indians called "Gitch Gumee".